Modern real estate practice

An introduction to a career in real estate brokerage

Modern real estate practice

An introduction to a career in real estate brokerage

HARRY GRANT ATKINSON
and
PERCY E. WAGNER

 1974

DOW JONES-IRWIN, INC.   Homewood, Illinois   60430

HD
1375
.A82
1974

©DOW JONES-IRWIN, INC., 1969, 1974

All rights reserved. No part of this publication may be reproduced, stored in a retrieval system, or transmitted, in any form or by any means, electronic, mechanical, photocopying, recording, or otherwise, without the prior written permission of the publisher.

This publication is designed to provide accurate and authoritative information in regard to the subject matter covered. It is sold with the understanding that the publisher is not engaged in rendering legal, accounting, or other professional service. If legal advice or other expert assistance is required, the services of a competent professional person should be sought.

From a Declaration of Principles jointly adopted by a Committee of the American Bar Association and a Committee of Publishers.

First Printing, February 1974

ISBN 0-87094-074-0
Library of Congress Catalog Card No. 73-20550
Printed in the United States of America

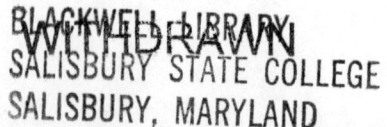

Preface

This book is a revised and expanded edition of *Management and Policies of Real Estate Brokerage,* which was first published in 1969. We have changed the title because we feel this new title more accurately reflects the book's broad coverage of today's real estate activities. We have added two new chapters to this edition— one on condominiums and one on the management of real property.

This book is intended to prepare you for a career in real estate. It will complement and supplement courses in appraisal, mortgage finance, management, land development, building construction, and property insurance. It will broaden your understanding of the real estate vocation in general.

It was also designed for any property owner (or aspiring property owner) who wants to understand more about how property is bought, sold, or rented.

February 1974   H. G. A.
                                                                                                                      P. E. W.

Contents

1. **The nature and functions of real estate brokerage** 1

   The broker is needed by the seller. The buyer needs the broker. The community needs the broker.

2. **Qualifications of the real estate broker** 11

   Sincerity of purpose. Integrity. Knowledge. Social trends. Economic trends. Regulations: *Building codes. Safeguarding of health. Other local government functions that affect real estate. Federal regulations.*

3. **Principles of land utilization** 25

   The principle of change. The principle of scarcity. Highest and best use. The principle of anticipation. The principle of contribution. The principle of increasing and decreasing returns. The principle of substitution. The principle of balance. The principle of proportionality. The factors in production.

4. **Real estate markets** 43

   Relation of real estate markets to policies and planning of activities. The nature of markets. Analysis of real estate markets.

5. Appraisal principles and methods 51

Bracketing. Cost as evidence of value. Site valuation. Reproduction cost. Depreciation. The income approach. Market data approach. Correlation.

6. Basic policies 63

The broker's territory. Specialization. Legal counsel. Tax counsel. Type of organization. Location of the office. Membership in associations and other organizations. The broker's reference library.

7. Organization and equipment of the broker's office 75

The reception area. Conference and closing room. Private offices. Files. Maps. Recording machines. Duplicating equipment. Typewriters. Adding machines and comptometers. Cameras and photographs. Signs. Library. Forms. The office manual.

8. Office personnel 89

Sources of new employees. Selection of new employees. Training and supervision. Employee records. Office rules. Incentives and morale: *Salaries. Health and hospital insurance. Retirement insurance. Other morale-building devices.*

9. Selection of salesmen 101

Importance of selection. Sources of new salesmen. The first step in selection. The written application. The personal interview. The applicant's background. His attitude.

10. Training and the sales force 111

Basic policies. Office procedures. Real estate fundamentals. Territorial analysis. Training in getting listings. Training the salesman to get prospects. Kibitzing actual sales. Coaching through actual deals. Training of experienced salesmen. Functions of supervision. Technique of supervision.

Contents ix

11. Compensation of the sales force **127**

The dual character of the broker. The three basic income requirements of the salesman. Variations in compensation policies. The salary plan. Drawing accounts. Splitting of commissions. Listing commissions. Commissions on prospects. Conditions under which salesmen earn commissions.

12. Types and sources of listings **137**

Elements of the listing contract. Standard listing contracts. The open listing. The exclusive listing. The exclusive right to sell. The multiple listing. Sources of listings.

13. Condominiums **147**

A concept of ownership. Eligible property. Procedures. Condominium management. Financing: *Analysis of the proposal. The appraisal report. Mortgages. Payout precautions. Insurance.* Profit opportunities in conversions. Prospects of success. Construction lending procedure for condominium projects. Checklist for developing a condominium project.

14. Executive control of listings **169**

The first step in executive control. Inspection of prospective listings. Listing files. The net listing. Assignment of listings to salesmen. Checking up on unsold listings. Periodic reports to the broker.

15. Executive control of prospects................... **181**

Sources of prospects: *The man next door. Friends and acquaintances. Persons who have listed properties for sale. Persons who have recently sold property. The columns of local newspapers. Arrivals and moves in the city. Directories and rosters. Apartment dwellers. Former customers and clients. Lists of payers of high income taxes. Lists of owners of large properties. Investors. Other real estate brokers.* Analysis of prospects.

x   Contents

16.   The management of real property **193**

Owners' objectives and interests. Tenants' rights and interests. Managers' rights and duties: *Leasing program requirements. Budgeting.* The brokerage office.

17.   Financial control **205**

The twofold problem of executive control. Budgeting. Consultation with a CPA and tax expert. Syndicates. Relation of type of organization to financial control. Sources of income. Classification of expenses.

18.   Government aid and restrictions **215**

Importance of real estate causes government to take interest in its activities. Broker must be familiar with local, state, and federal regulations. Zoning, buildings, and rent control. Financial assistance by government. License to practice, state laws. Government agencies.

Bibliography **227**

Appendix A **235**

Code of ethics of the National Association of Real Estate Boards

Appendix B **243**

Code of ethics of the American Institute of Real Estate Appraisers

Appendix C **245**

Real estate license law, and supplementary rules and regulations

Index **269**

CHAPTER ONE

The nature and functions of real estate brokerage

Real estate brokerage is one of the most essential and constructive vocations in America. It has exerted a profound influence in the development of all parts of the country. It is indispensable to the further development and maintenance of the distinctive economy that has made the United States the greatest nation in history. It is a service vocation. It has nothing to sell except personal services. Its existence is due solely to the fact that people need and must have expert assistance in acquiring and in disposing of real property interests. It affords opportunities for vitally important personal services to one's fellow men which are unexcelled by any profession. It is challenged by moral and ethical responsibilities to communities and to the nation which are not imposed on any other vocational group. It combines the satisfaction of making important personal contributions to the welfare and happiness of one's fellow man with the pride of meriting public respect and the assurance of substantial financial reward for faithful and efficient workmanship. Because of the moral and ethical responsibility which the real estate broker has to the public, he must be an educated man and have specialized knowledge in the performance of his responsibilities.

The real estate broker, in his business activities, must strive for and attain professional status. He must possess the attributes of honesty, reliability, education, and experience. He must use these in the performance of his duties before he can attain professional recognition.

Professions are made up of professional men. There must be professional men before there can be professions. No group can be recognized as being genuinely professional unless the majority of its members are truly professional in character. Although the basic functions of a vocation may be purely professional in character, the individual in the vocation cannot be recognized as a professional man unless he meets certain high standards of ability, superiority of workmanship, and ethical conduct.

To understand the nature, the functions, and the place which real estate brokerage has in the business life of the nation, it is necessary to realize it has a dual character. It is both a business and a profession.

To understand this dual capacity it might be well to define a profession and then relate the brokerage business to its professional character. An accepted definition of a profession is that its members: (1) have adopted an organized body of knowledge, (2) have pursued a course of study and continue to study, (3) provide training for those who contemplate entering the profession, (4) have established and accepted a code of ethics, (5) have standards for admission and disqualification, and (6) recognize that their interest and service to others comes before self-interest.[1]

Many colleges and universities have organized courses of study which are basic in presenting an organized body of knowledge for those who desire to study and equip themselves for the real estate profession. Text books have been written by eminent professors who have studied the requirements necessary to prepare a person for entry into the profession. These same colleges and universities offer courses which give specialized training and continuing training thru seminars and advanced study. The National Association of Real Estate Boards has adopted a code of ethics to which its members must adhere. State license law officials have set up written examinations and require preparatory training which must be passed by applicants for brokers and salesmen real estate licenses. State laws for brokers and salesmen contain grounds for disqualification and revocation of licenses.

1/ Carlton A. Pederson and Milburn D. Wright, *Salesmanship: Principles and Methods* (4th ed.; Homewood, Ill.: Richard D. Irwin, Inc., 1966), p. 46.

The real estate broker is a businessman and his compensation is dependent upon performance. He is not paid for a service unless it is successfully completed. In this respect his position is different from the learned professional man who is compensated regardless of the success of the undertaking. However, this distinction in compensation does not relieve the businessman from his responsibility to the public. He still renders the same high quality of service as rendered by the professional man who receives a fee for his services.

The businessman conducting a real estate business is engaged in a vocation which renders expert and ethically reliable personal services to persons who are not expert in the field but are vitally in need of such services. The real estate profession renders such personal services to sellers and buyers by undertaking and faithfully endeavoring to effect the sale or purchase of rights in real property.

Every profession has a vital significance to society as a whole as well as to the individual who is in actual or potential need of its services. This fact is recognized, for example, in the maintenance of publicly supported medical schools and the public health services, in publicly supported law schools and the court system of the country. Similar evidences of national significance are found in connection with every other profession.

Recognition of the place that real estate has in the national economy is leading to the establishment of chairs of real estate in universities throughout the country and the creation of numerous govermental agencies to deal with real estate problems.

Few persons realize the importance of real property to the individual citizens of the United States, to the economic and social structures of our country, and to our government. The value of real property is in excess of two thirds of our national wealth. Everyone uses real property. Everyone pays for it, whether owner or tenant. About one fourth of the typical family income is required to pay rent or to acquire and maintain home ownership. An enormous sum is required in addition to create and maintain industrial, commercial, and other types of nonresidential real property, all of which is and must be fully supported indirectly by the income of the people through prices paid for commodities and for personal services. Under the private property system (which is still enjoyed to a large extent in the United States), real estate

4 *Modern real estate practice*

interests may be bought and sold by the individual citizen. The annual volume of such transactions is enormous. The actual number of annual sales in the country as a whole is not recorded, but it is reasonable to assume that the sale of fee and lease interests is yearly far in excess of several million transactions.

At least 500,000 persons are engaged in real estate activities in one way or another. The significance of this number lies in the fact that it indicates the need which people in general have for expert services to handle their real estate problems—a need so great that a half million specialists are required to serve it. It is estimated that the normal attrition by deaths and retirement requires the annual entry of about 20,000 new men into this field as replacements.

The broker is needed by the seller

One of the three major functions of the real estate broker is to furnish a specialized and expert service to the individual who for any reason wants to sell his real property. Year in and year out, throughout the country, tens upon tens of thousands of owners find it desirable or necessary to sell their properties. These occasions arise because of basic changes which take place in the needs, fortunes, and desires of the people. Among such changes, the following are most common:

1. A home owner may lose his job and find employment in a different and remote section of the city, or he may find a better position in a location far removed from his home, or his employer may want him to transfer to a branch or to a headquarters in a different city, or for some other reason employment conditions may make it expedient or necessary for him to change his place of residence. Under such circumstances he wants to sell his home and buy another closer to his place of employment.
2. In many cases the death of a property owner is closely followed by the necessity of dividing his estate among his heirs. Or the surviving spouse may want to change place of residence or convert the property into cash to meet some urgent personal need or to acquire a different type of investment.

3. An owner may believe that real estate prices are about to fall drastically and remain low for a long period of time. In that belief he may consider it to his advantage to convert his real estate into cash or other liquid assets quickly to avoid the necessity of having to take a lower price later. Or he may feel that he is facing a period of uncertainty in which he might at some point need to have substantial liquid assets immediately available. Or he may be a business man in need of funds for inventories or for some other business use which promises high returns.
4. A homeowner may have an increase in the size of his family, making it desirable to have a house with an additional bedroom. Or the size of his family may be reduced by marriage of sons or daughters, leading to a desire for a smaller house or for quarters in an apartment building.
5. A homeowner may prosper in his business or profession and desire a home more in keeping with the social standing and activities that his increased earnings enable him to afford.
6. A homeowner may suffer a serious reduction in business or professional income and face the necessity of establishing his residence in less expensive property.
7. In all sizable urban communities there are men who make a business of buying and selling real estate in order to make profits. Such owners are always ready to buy or sell quickly when a substantial profit can be made. They are known as "real estate operators." They frequently need to use the services of alert brokers.
8. Sometimes a man over a period of years has acquired ownership of a number of scattered pieces of real estate. Eventually he may find it burden ome to give his attention to his scattered holdings and decide to sell some or all of them in order to consolidate the wealth they represent into a few or one property. The alert broker may be able to show him that it is to his advantage to do this.
9. An owner of a larger high-value property may come to the conclusion that it is unwise to "keep all of his eggs in one basket" and decide to sell the property and buy several smaller well-located properties of diversified type in scattered locations.

There are many other reasons why owners may desire to sell and need the services of the broker.

The real estate involved may constitute a substantial amount of wealth. It may be a dwelling that represents the lifetime savings of the owner and his family. It may be a dwelling that he inherited or that was given to him. Regardless of how the ownership was acquired, it is accumulated wealth. Someone had to labor and save to bring it into being. For example, its value may be equal to the entire five-year gross income of the owner. It is indeed a precious asset. Yet conditions have arisen which make it desirable or necessary for him to sell the property. The dwelling has been a sort of savings bank into which he, or someone, has, by dint of thrift and savings, accumulated a substantial amount of wealth. Now he needs money for another purpose and is obliged to convert his savings accumulated in the real estate into cash.

Or, to consider another example, the property may be an apartment building, a retail store, or some other type of income or investment property. Whatever the type, it represents the self-denial and thrift of someone who saved to amass enough money to create or acquire it. Its value may be hundreds or thousands of times greater than the dwelling. It provides essential accommodations for the tenants who occupy it, and it affords at least two important functions for the owner. It serves as a depository for his wealth and it provides an income for him. The net income from the rents may be the only income the owner has. It may, therefore, be of really vital importance to him. Yet conditions arise which may make it necessary or desirable to convert the property into cash, and the property must be sold.

The sale of real property is seldom merely a routine business transaction. There is no well-defined established market for real estate such as is true in other commodities. No two real properties are ever exactly alike. Each one has its own distinctive characteristics. The total value of each runs into thousands of dollars. Prospective buyers are generally relatively few in number and are usually difficult to find. The making of the sale may require a knowledge of economic, social, and political trends. It may require a knowledge of legal requirements and limitations, financing, and other complex matters. In addition, it may require skillful salesmanship.

Few owners have the knowledge, skill, or time to handle all of the necessary details connected with a real estate sale. They need the services of experts to make sure of getting maximum prices for their properties. This, then, is one of the major functions of the real estate broker—to make sales for owners who for any reason want to convert their property into cash. He performs the function of the professional specialist on whom the owner-client relies to have the knowledge and the skill to analyze the property and its environs, to find someone who needs the property, to handle or to arrange for the handling of the complex financial and legal matters involved, and to obtain the highest price possible.

When the broker accepts an assignment to undertake the selling of a property, he places himself under certain professional and ethical obligations to his client. These include (1) prompt, continuous, and faithful efforts to find a buyer and make the sale and (2) the securing, if possible, of the selling price set by the client.

The buyer needs the broker

The second major function of the broker is to furnish professional services to individuals who want to buy real property. We live in a changing world. The needs, desires, and capabilities of individuals change with the passage of time. These changing conditions are constantly creating new prospective purchasers of real property. Each of these prospects has a definite real property need, and he may have the financial ability to buy and the desire. But he usually does not know just where to find the property or how to negotiate the deal to his best advantage if he does find it. He needs the services of a specialist, of a professional broker, to do these things for him. The broker's opportunity to act as the representative of the buyer is just as great as that of representing the seller. There must be a buyer as well as a seller in every transaction. The broker may choose to develop his practice by finding owners who want to sell and then finding a buyer, or he may seek individuals who desire to buy and then search for property matching their needs; he may use both methods.

Never, however, can he be the agent of both buyer and seller without the consent of each—or collect compensation from both without the full knowledge and consent of each. If he undertakes to be the agent of the seller, he must get the highest price obtainable for the property and the seller pays him for this service. If he is the agent of the buyer, he must purchase the property at the lowest possible price for which the owner will agree to sell, and the buyer pays him for this service. In an exchange of one property for another, however, it is customary for each of the parties served in the transaction to pay a full commission on the property the broker transfers. In transactions of this type the broker is the agent of each of the parties since each of them acts in the capacity of a seller as well as a buyer.

The community needs the broker

The broker who makes a thorough and continuing study of the trends and potentialities in his territory can find many opportunities to create transactions. For example, he may find a property that could economically be converted to another use. The owner may not be in a position to undertake the conversion or be interested in the project anyway, but he may be willing to sell. Then a prospective buyer may be found who has the required financial resources and who could be benefited by investing in the project. Or there may be a real need in the community for a certain type of store or shop, for a hotel, a garage, or some other improvement. The broker discovers the need, finds a suitable location that can be secured by purchase or lease at a figure which the contemplated occupant can afford to pay, and then works to find a purchaser or tenant.

In any sizable urban community there always exists a great variety of potential transactions which can be created by the able broker. This activity benefits the community as well as buyers and sellers. The broker's basic function in this connection can best be understood when one realizes that any urban community is a network of human activities, all of which are interrelated and interdependent. People have certain basic needs for food, shelter, clothing, jobs, recreation, religion, and education. There is a definite balance or equilibrium in all these things. They all require the use of real property. There must be residential property, factories, stores and shops, offices, studios, churches, schools, amusement and recreational facilities, cemeteries, and improvements dedicated to other uses. The type, class, and amount of land and improvements allocated to these various uses must be in balance to insure a smooth and efficient functioning of the community as a whole in serving the basic needs of the people. Too much or too little of any one class or type of use throws the community structure out of balance. It is this imbalance and the foresighted prevention or correction of it which creates opportunities for creative brokerage. It is here that the broker can function as a community builder and as a conservator of community values.

In a very real sense the real estate broker is the only one who can function on a professional level in this capacity. It is he who has the proper background, understanding, incentive, and time to do it. He is the expert in this field. It's his job. That is his function in the social and economic life of the community. This function imposes obligations upon him which go far beyond those of ordinary commerce. He has patriotic as well as ethical duties to the community. Failure to perform these duties faithfully and efficiently adversely affects not only his clients and others closely connected with his transactions but also the basic welfare of the community. Misplaced improvements, underimprovements, functionally deficient developments, and the like, cause neighboring properties to lose value to some degree and may constitute a blight in the area. It is the broker's job to know what type and class of use is needed for each site and to be skillful enough in preparing development plans and in negotiating with owners, purchasers, lessees, representatives of financial institutions, and government officials to make certain that the proper use is made of the site. It is his ability to do these things which makes him a "community builder," and the community needs him for this purpose.

CHAPTER TWO

Qualifications of the real estate broker

To achieve success in any vocation you must possess the knowledge, personal aptitudes, and talents which prolonged activities in that vocation require for maximum achievement and personal satisfaction. If you contemplate a lifetime career in real estate brokerage you will do well to consider whether you have, or can acquire, the personal character, the knowledge, and the skills that are requisite for success in this field.

You should realize, at the outset, that real estate brokerage is a service vocation. The broker is not a manufacturer or a merchant. He has nothing but personal services to sell. Knowledge, talent, and time constitute his stock in trade. As a professional man the real estate broker has these two major functions: (1) To render expert and ethical personal services to individuals who are concerned with real property, and (2) to know thoroughly his community and furnish leadership and support in the development and maintenance of the community which constitutes the scene of his activities. Unless you enter the land-development field as a real estate broker, you are not required to invest in raw materials or in manufactured products as the industrialist and the merchant must do. But you do have to invest heavily in the acquisition of knowledge and training and in the development of certain personal attributes if you expect to merit and secure the respect, the confidence, and the patronage of people who need real estate brokerage services.

The making of a satisfactory livelihood and the hope of attaining economic security are primary motivations for entering the field of real estate brokerage. However, to succeed in this field these objectives must be kept secondary to the professional character of the services that you, as a real estate broker, render. The successful broker does make money and achieve a secure financial footing in his community. But this accomplishment is the reward for his competence and skill. His success is due to the fact that he renders a continuing personal professional service to people in the community who need his help—a service which develops respect and confidence and enduring friendships in an ever-widening circle. In addition, of course, he must have the ability to plan and manage his activities in accordance with sound business principles.

Sincerity of purpose

This means that, as a real estate broker, you must really want to help people solve their real estate problems. You must find a fascination in helping people acquire the type of real property they need. You must enjoy finding locations best suited to your clients. You must sense and respond to the challenge of locating property not only which your client needs and wants but also which he can afford to own or to rent. You must obtain personal pleasure in being able to help a client secure a property in which he takes pride and from which he derives satisfaction. Guided by such motivation, you are already on the road to success. Such service to a client, where his interests are kept paramount, results in creating enduring business and often personal friendships without which it is impossible to develop a clientele. Such service is professional service. Purely aside from the monetary rewards, it brings to you the vocational satisfaction that comes to the teacher, the minister, the physician, the lawyer, and others whose professions are dedicated to the well-being of their fellow man.

Of equal importance to the professional attitudes in rendering personal services to a client is your service to your community, your first-hand knowledge of it, and your help in building and maintaining it as a highly desirable place in which to live.

Personal and community services are fused in the professional functions of the real estate broker and impose upon him obligations beyond those of ordinary commerce. The well-being of the individuals cannot be separated from the welfare of the community. They are interrelated and interdependent. A community in which there are healthy real estate conditions is one in which the utilization of the land is in reasonably proper balance. Often the improvement of land in urban areas tends to get out of balance.

Changes are constantly taking place in the area. Some buildings are destroyed by fire. Some are converted to new uses. Owners of vacant lots, in an endeavor to make profits or to recapture capital invested in the vacant sites, construct buildings of one kind or another which may or may not attract purchasers or tenants. People come into the area seeking housing for residential, commercial, or other purposes. Owners or tenants of retail store property fail in business and move out. New families are created. Other families increase or decrease in size, making it desirable or necessary to secure larger or smaller quarters. Other families are broken up by death or divorce. Streets are widened to make room for increasing automobile traffic, and other changes occur in the makeup of population, creating economic and civic characteristics of the area which disturb the real estate equilibrium of the community. Those engaged in the real estate vocation have the professional responsibility of watching changing trends in real estate utilization and of knowing what to do about making adjustments to safeguard community values.

You must work with human beings who need or want your expert services in solving important personal problems involving decisions about real estate. You do not deal with real estate directly—only indirectly, for the land and buildings are merely accessories to human life. They are inert and in themselves have no value. Value resides in the rights which human beings may have to own, occupy, use, or control the land and buildings. So, the broker deals with people. He cannot deal with them successfully from either their or his own point of view unless he is interested in them, unless he really enjoys being of service to them. He cannot confine his contacts to only a few persons. He must have a wide circle of contacts. He must be constantly on the alert to meet and get to know more and more people. Equally important, he must have pride in his community and be restlessly eager to help develop and improve it. Without the ambition to do these things, he lacks sincerity of purpose and had better go into some other vocation where he can respond more fully to some personal interest that is more challenging to him.

Integrity

The most important of all requirements for success in real estate brokerage is personal integrity and ethical conduct. Integrity is reliability. It is that uprightness of character which justifiably inspires implicit confidence. The man of integrity tries always to do the right thing. He conforms to fine ideals of manhood and professional ethics. He is honest. He is fair. He is trustworthy. He is loyal to any confidence placed in him. He never indulges in "sharp" practices. He urges transactions only when he believes that they will be beneficial to those concerned. No man who regulates his conduct according to what the law permits rather than according to what conscience, honor, and decency require is worthy of membership in a profession. Being ethical, purely and solely for the sake of being so, is an inherent characteristic of the professional man. Moreover, there is abundant evidence in every profession which proves that it pays to acquire and merit a reputation of being ethical. People avoid transactions with persons who are said to be unreliable. This applies with especial force to the real estate broker.

Unfortunately there are real estate brokers who lack personal integrity. That is an important reason why many have failed and have had to leave the vocation. It is one reason why there are some brokers, even today, who barely make a living in the vocation. The unscrupulous or the incompetent broker may negotiate a few transactions to make a "fast buck," but sooner or later prospective clients, hearing rumors or knowing positively about his unreliability, lose confidence in him and avoid him. Lack of integrity on the part of some real estate brokers is one of the major reasons why states have enacted license laws. These laws are designed, among other things, eventually to screen out the dishonest men who seek to practice real estate brokerage. They provide means for canceling the licenses and of imposing other penalties upon brokers found guilty of dishonest practices. It was to aid the public in identifying reliable brokers that the National Association of Real Estate Boards created the term "Realtor" and adopted its Code of Ethics. One reason why many prospective sellers and buyers of real estate advertise direct and avoid real estate brokers is that they do not have confidence in them. The unethical conduct of some unscrupulous brokers has destroyed the confidence of many prospective buyers and sellers in all real estate brokers. This unfortunate condition is not as widespread today as it was years ago, but it is still a matter of concern to all who realize the importance of the vocation to the millions of people who need professional service in the solution of their real estate problems.

Integrity must be lived day after day. There can be no exceptions, no lapses, if you want to establish acceptance of your reliability. Just one shady transaction will live in the memories of your clients, of their friends, and of their acquaintances. A reputation for integrity is worth more than tens of thousands of dollars spent in advertising to attract new clients and to develop transactions with old clients. Advertising is necessary, of course. Real estate brokerage cannot be conducted without it. But no amount of advertising will bring a man to your door if he believes that he cannot trust you. If he doubts your integrity, he will disregard your advertising and may make damaging remarks about you to others.

You cannot build your reputation for integrity overnight. It takes time. It develops out of satisfactory services rendered to many clients. It grows out of promises kept and out of contracts that are promptly and faithfully fulfilled. It is engendered, equally as importantly, by your refusal to commit yourself to undertakings which you cannot or do not carry out. Disappointment breeds distrust. For this reason, if for no other, you should not list a property exclusively unless you believe it can be sold at a price which the owner is likely to take. Moreover, you should not list a property exclusively unless the owner will give you adequate time in which to find a buyer. To fail to make a sale in the allotted time, at a price which the owner feels justified in taking, is to disappoint him. When you fail to satisfy him, you lose his confidence. Make no promises you cannot fulfill.

The broker whose reputation for integrity has been established often finds that one transaction leads to another. Satisfied clients come to his office or telephone him to tell about properties they want to sell or to buy. Satisfied clients not only return to him for any additional real estate services, but they recommend him to their friends and acquaintances. Thus, as the years go by, his reputation for trustworthiness creates an ever-widening circle of clients and friends.

Knowledge

There are few, if any, vocations which require as great a diversity and range of knowledge as does real estate brokerage.

The decision to sell or to buy any real property usually, if not always, grows out of consideration of its cost, its price, or its value. These are decisive matters with which the broker must deal in effecting a purchase or a sale. He must understand and know how to interpret the various factors which determine the level of costs, prices, and values. These are legion, but they are bound up in the three basic dynamic forces: (1) social standards, (2) economic trends, and (3) political regulations.

These three forces create or destroy the value of real estate. The levels of costs and prices are the resultant of their movements. The interplay of these dynamic basic forces—costs, prices, and values—is changing, sometimes only slightly but sometimes very widely in a given period of time. Comprehension of the nature and behavior of these forces is dependent upon an understanding of the various factors which motivate them. Each trend is a complex of a great many different interdependent and closely related factors of cause and effect.

Social trends

The most important of the many factors which combine to give character and force to social trends is the factor of population. The need for real estate in a given area is in approximate proportion to the number and character of persons and the number of families living in that area. An oversimplified example will partially illustrate this statement. Assume two different urban areas in each of which there are 50,000 persons. Let us call one of these cities "A-Ville" and the other "B-Ville." Assume further that there are four persons per family in A-Ville and only two persons per family in B-Ville. It follows that A-Ville requires 12,500 residential family dwelling units and that B-Ville requires 25,000 residential family units. The need for dwelling units in B-Ville is twice the need which exists in A-Ville. But neither population in these urban areas is static. Each of them is either growing or declining, both in numbers of persons and in numbers of families.

Although B-Ville needs twice as many dwelling units as A-Ville, it does not need twice as many retail stores, amusement and recreational facilities, or other types of real estate. The volume of shopping facilities, offices, schools, and other nonresidential types of real estate will depend upon age groups, cultural levels, customs, and economic status of the respective populations.

The real estate broker, to be expert in his field, must know a great deal about the population and its characteristics in his territory. How many persons? How many families? Are the numbers increasing or decreasing? How rapidly? Why? Is there a shortage or a surplus of housing and other real estate facilities? How much? Where? Why? Approximately how many persons are there in each age group? What does this portend in reference to future housing needs? If expansion of housing facilities is indicated, what type and class of housing will be needed? Where can such expansion take place? Who now owns the properties that will be needed for housing expansion? Are they available for purchase? At what prices? How can they best be acquired and improved to meet the developing needs? What properties are likely to come onto the market because of deaths, family breakups, marriages, business failures, or other reasons? What are the conditions of these properties? Can they be used as they are or will it be necessary to develop, remodel, modernize, or rehabilitate them? To what extent will they take care of the changing population needs?

If the population trend is downward, it follows that there will be an increase in vacancies attended by shifts in tenancies to take advantage of falling rents or to secure more desirable facilities. As these shifts take place, older buildings in the least desirable locations may stand vacant. What can be done with them?

These are only a few of the bits of knowledge about population which the broker must have in order to be prepared to function well in the rendering of expert professional service to clients and in order to do his part in developing and maintaining community values in his territory.

There are other factors which exert pressures in generating and shaping the direction and force of social trends affecting real estate markets. Among them are the changing preferences of people for building material, architectural design, building layout, and innovations which provide greater comforts and conveniences. A swing in preference to ranch-style, one-story dwellings, for example, creates obsolescence in two-story buildings and makes them more difficult to sell. Marketability of dwellings may be affected by such matters as whether or not the living area and dining areas are separate or combined; whether the house is constructed on one, two, or three levels; whether the heat is gas, electric, or coal; whether there is an alley or not; the garage facilities furnished; the number, size, and location of closets; the style of electric lighting fixtures; and any one of many other preferences of prospective buyers and tenants reflecting purely social ideals as to amenities and conveniences.

The broker must know the people in his area well enough to know what their current preferences are. He must remember that preferences change as new generations come into the market—as improvements are developed in building material, building design and layout, and building equipment. Preferences of people change as they grow older. Increased or decreased family incomes, unless on a temporary basis, force or stimulate changes in preferences.

Other social factors which have significance to the real estate broker include:

1. The desire of people in the area for certain amusement and recreational facilities
2. Composition and distribution of racial groups
3. Provision for the education of children
4. Composition and distribution of religious groups
5. Fraternal organizations
6. The strength and activities of civic and service groups
7. Other activities designed to serve various social aspirations of the people who live in the area.

The broker cannot afford to be uninformed about any of these social forces in his territory. After all, land and the improvements upon it are merely accessories to human living. Real estate is a means to an end. It is a natural resource which must be used, and used wisely, to sustain human life and attain community security and individual happiness. It is the function of the broker to guide people to the wise and the proper use of real estate so as to achieve maximum social benefits.

Economic trends

Social instincts and social standards are basic to all human activities. Preservation of life; intimate association with fellow humans; attainment and enjoyment of economic security, comforts and conveniences; satisfaction of intellectual, emotional, and religious yearnings—these, separately and collectively, are the elements upon which human progress either flourishes or diminishes. To exist, every human being is dependent upon the use of land.

In order to approach the attainment of these subjective values—intellectual, emotional, and spiritual in character—it is necessary to provide appropriate physical instrumentalities.

Mankind requires food, clothing, shelter, and suitable tools. Man's need for and dependence upon land use leads him into the complex realm of economics. Economics embraces all of mankind's efforts to make a living.

As a real estate broker, it is essential that you continuously study and thoroughly understand the character and the relationships of the many factors influencing real estate which make up the economic structure of your territory and its environs. They are many. Among the more important, to mention a few, are:

1. Population and its growth patterns
2. Employment sources and opportunities
3. Industrial production and commercial activities
4. Money—its purchasing power and family income levels
5. Credit availability and interest rates
6. Tax levels and trends
7. Supply and rate of depletion of natural resources such as gas, oil, coal, forests, water, topsoil, and other vital materials
8. Community facilities, utilities, transportation, etc.

The effective demand for real estate is circumscribed by economic conditions prevailing at any given time. They limit the capacity of people to buy or rent real estate. They influence the availability and cost of long-term mortgage credit and thus effectively set ceilings upon the scope and quality of new developments. They are real, although often indirect, pressures affecting each individual seller, buyer, lessor, and lessee who enters the real estate market.

Regulations

Another force which determines the level of real estate costs, prices, and values is political regulation.

In a heterogeneous society embracing diverse racial and religious groups, containing various educational and cultural levels, encompassing various degrees of comprehension of moral and ethical conduct, including people at all economic levels from the very poor to the very rich and including, also, varying degrees of ambition for economic and political power, there are bound to be many clashes of personal interest. Efforts to gratify conflicting personal interests often lead not only to personal injustices but also to public detriment. This is why it is necessary to have laws and law enforcement agencies.

Because real estate constitutes the bulk of the wealth in any community and there is always keen competition to secure the benefits to be derived from the ownership and control of real estate, a multitude of political regulations have been developed affecting the transfer and use of real property. Such regulations are designed to protect the owners and users of real property and also to safeguard community values arising out of land utilization. The broker must know what these regulations are, why they were imposed, how they are enforced, what protections they afford, and what limitations they place upon owners and tenants of real estate.

It is not feasible to attempt here a detailed discussion of any one of these regulations, but a few comments about some of them should serve to show their importance and why the real estate broker must have a working knowledge of them in order to function as an expert.

Building codes

Many municipalities have enacted building codes which lay down specific rules governing selection of building material, the percentage of lot area that can be occupied by a building, overhanging projections, building heights, and other building characteristics believed to constitute hazards to nearby properties or to public safety.

Most municipalities have zoning laws. These laws map the urban area into zones and prescribe what type of occupancy will be permitted in each zone. Thus certain areas are restricted to single-family dwellings, certain areas to apartment buildings, certain areas to commercial property, and certain areas to industrial use, etc.

The real estate broker must be thoroughly familiar with the zoning laws in his territory. He should have up-to-date zoning maps. He should study the maps from time to time, not only to be prepared to advise clients but also to discover opportunities for creative brokerage at points where land utilization is out of balance with the needs of the community.

Safeguarding of health

When people are crowded together as they must be to live in urban centers, special precautions must be taken to safeguard their health. These safeguards include, among other measures, the providing of an adequate supply of pure water for drinking, industry, and other purposes. Provision must be made also for the disposal of sewage, rubbish, and waste. Such health measures are formulated and regulated by the enactment of suitable laws and are supported by taxes levied upon real estate. Health measures properly administered stabilize real estate values. Lack of such measures, or failure to enforce them, subjects real estate in the area to economic obsolescence.

The broker should be aware of the health regulations that apply in his territory. In addition, he has a professional obligation to aid in securing legislation that may be necessary to protect the health of the people, and to lend support to any civic movements to enforce proper administration of public health provisions.

Other local government functions that affect real estate

There are many other local governmental functions and regulations which influence the marketability and price levels of real estate. They include, to name only a few, police and fire protection, street maintenance, regulation of automobile traffic, automobile parking, licenses to engage in retail business or other commercial enterprises, schools, municipally owned and operated streetcar and bus lines, and air-pollution control. Any one of these may affect ownership or tenancy of real property either favorably or adversely, depending upon the need for the regulation, the wisdom with which the law has been drawn, and the honesty and efficiency with which the law is administered. The broker cannot afford to be ignorant of any of these regulations. Not only must he be fully informed about existing regulations, he must also be alert to pending changes and to new ordinances that are under consideration.

Federal regulations

There are also many federal regulations that influence real estate markets either directly or indirectly. Governmental guarantees of loans on real property are accompanied by architectural standards, controlled interest rates, and various mortgage provision requirements. These regulations are intended to encourage new construction, rehabilitation and maintenance of properties, and place real estate ownership within the reach of greater numbers of people. They are intended also to insure the use of proper building material and sound construction methods. They are not an unmixed blessing, however, for all people. Their strong and weak points should be carefully studied by the broker.

Federal regulations have, and may again, include rent control, allocations, and priorities. Income and other federal taxes often exert profound effects upon the prices at which properties are sold. Since these regulations are revised from time to time, it is imperative that the broker continuously review them to be sure that his knowledge of them is up to date.

The real estate broker must have a thorough working knowledge in the fields of land use, community growth, real estate law, and business administration. In addition, he should have some knowledge in the closely related fields of property management, accounting, appraising, construction and planning, engineering, architecture, and financing.

CHAPTER THREE

Principles of land utilization

Success in the real estate brokerage vocation to a large extent depends upon having a practical grasp of the basic economics of land utilization. Ignorance of economic laws, or a failure to be guided by them, makes the decision to spend one's life in real estate brokerage a hazardous commitment. Human experience under basic economic laws has resulted in the discovery of principles and the formulation of certain rules which apply to the utilization of land.

Remember, however, that these principles and rules are not immutable laws which operate at all times in exactly the same way. They do operate, but the results of their operation cannot be forecast with precision. This is because land economics is a social science and, like all social sciences, deals with human behavior and trends. The rules of land utilization are subject to numerous exceptions, but they do furnish valuable and practical guides to the broker in making decisions about real estate and in giving professional advice to buyers and sellers of real property.

Economics is an inexact science. It is a science of tendencies. Nonetheless, it is based upon principles derived from experience with human behaviors, which tend to be the same in all places and at all times. Land economics deals with principles of land utilization. The principles of land use are interrelated one with another to such an extent that it is difficult to separate them for independent study. But each and every one of them, in one way or another, exerts an influence upon real estate value and real estate markets.

Land in an economic sense is man-made. Real property is socially created wealth. The quality of real property anywhere is the product of human choice. Therefore, the problems of making the best use of urban land must be approached with a knowledge of the human components within a community.

It is a generally accepted truism among real estate men that the value of an urban property is not an intrinsic attribute of the land and the improvements upon the land but the resultant of the possible intensity of its use and the favorable and unfavorable features of the surrounding environment. This concept may be expressed in many different ways, but the meaning is the same: The value of an urban property is contingent upon the use to which it is put, the relationship of such use on the site in question to the uses of other sites in the area, and the intensity of the effective demand for control of a particular site.

Failure to use land properly becomes an economic waste. Numerous sites in our urban areas are not properly improved. Some are underimproved, some are overimproved, and some are encumbered by misplaced improvements. Each such improper improvement is a violation of one or more principles of land utilization. Improper improvement of a site impairs its value and depreciates the value of surrounding properties. To know what type and class of improvement to put on a given site, we must understand the principles of land utilization and know how to apply them. To be able to analyze an improved site and ascertain whether it has been properly improved, we must have this same knowledge and the skill to apply it in many different situations.

More than 5,000 years ago the economics of rural land was being studied. This study resulted in the long-since established and very practical science of agriculture. In recent times, with the ever-increasing shift of population into urban areas, there commenced the study of the economics of urban land use. Principles have been discovered and rules formulated which are gradually giving rise to the science of urbiculture. The urban real estate broker must understand the principles of land utilization and apply them. Otherwise he is likely to miss many golden opportunities to develop and consummate creative brokerage transactions.

There is a certain parallelism between the attributes of a community and those of a human body. Both grow, not only externally but also internally. Both progress from very simple structures to very complex integrated structures. In the progress of growth, not only are the number of units increased but the units themselves expand and become diversified. A city is not an agglomeration of buildings, but a living organism so interrelated and bound together that no part of it can be separated or destroyed without affecting the whole. There is constant change, both growth and decay, both life and death. Decaying tissues must be cast off and replaced with vigorous live tissue or else creeping death will eventually destroy the entire organism.

Complexity rests not only on the likeness of the parts but also upon the character and the strength of the bonds between the parts. Transportation and communication are as essential to the city as nerves and blood vessels are to the human body. The simple urban community of former times had little need for transportation and community facilities, for they were small and self-sustaining. But a modern urban community cannot exist without them.

In addition to transportation and communication tissues, the modern city has industrial, commercial, recreational, residential, and other tissues of various kinds. Like the structure of the human body, the city has a physical structure—the land and the buildings that improve the land. This parallelism between the living community and the living human body is, of course, not perfect, but it emphasizes the dependence of both upon a sound framework and upon proper coordination of functions. Each part must perform its functions for the life of the whole in order to be efficient. Each is essential for a balanced and healthy existence.

There are cities which are overwhelmingly industrial and in which other functions are dwarfed. Yet an industrial community cannot exist without a resident labor supply, without residents, without wholesale and retail distribution, without transportation, without certain specialized personal services, and without civic protection and control. Each of these elements exists somewhere in the area or region as an integral part of the community. The same may be said of communities that are predominantly recreational (such as Miami Beach, Florida) or governmental (such as Washington, D.C.).

Geographically, certain elements may be rather far removed from the main part of the community, but actually each element is closely bound to the living organism by lines of transportation and communication; there is loss of efficiency, but the essential functioning of each part does go on.

Land is related to every human activity. In an economic sense, value is attributed to land only as a result of the intensity of the use which is or may be made of it by people. Land is the basic element in production. Land requires the application of human activity to become productive and have value in a market sense.

The principle of change

Perhaps the most important of all the forces that affect real estate value is the principle of change. We live in a universe of cause and effect. Everything is at all times undergoing a process of change, or evolution. Nothing remains static. All life is characterized by birth, growth, maturity, decline, and death. All inanimate things are characterized by disintegration. The forces of nature, such as wind, moisture, and temperature, are working constantly to change the face of the earth. In the cosmos, heavenly bodies are believed to be changing through combustion and other forces.

Buildings, street paving, trees and landscaping, and other physical characteristics of the city deteriorate and are damaged or destroyed by fires, earthquakes, winds, freezing and thawing, insects, and other agents of destruction. The desirability of building is lessened not only by these physical agencies but also by the changing needs and demands of people. The same is true of neighborhoods and of entire urban areas. There is constant change, and as change takes place in the factors that give rise to value, value also changes.

It is important for the broker to realize at all times that every physical property and every neighborhood is constantly in a state of flux. Population, families, economic conditions, social conditions, political forces—all are in a state of continuous transition. He should keep in mind that what he sees today is a result of yesterday's conditions. He should understand that tomorrow's conditions will be the result of today's conditions which resulted from yesterday's human activities. Causes and effects are linked together in an endless chain; each effect in turn becomes a cause to produce other effects. This series of changes constitutes a trend. The broker who watches the nature of trends, their force, their direction, and their rate is in a strong position to advise sellers and buyers and to spot opportunities to create transactions that will help to develop or to maintain community values and at the same time produce substantial commissions.

The principle of scarcity

Land, in the sense of standing room or support, is apparently a free good. But in an economic sense, land is far from free. This is because land has different qualities. Some land is more favorably located for certain kinds of use than is other land. Some is fertile, some is sandy, some is rocky, some is marshy, the surface of some is steeply sloped. Even as standing room, the utilization of a given site is dependent to some extent upon the ability of the land to carry the weight of the building erected upon it.

Engineering can solve many of these problems. An example is the famous Imperial Hotel in Tokyo, which was built by Frank Lloyd Wright upon a cheeselike top soil over a lake of mud that is subject to frequent earthquakes. Engineers in Chicago have erected giant skyscrapers on land that was once a swamp. Support, in the sense of standing room, is a factor in economic utilization, but it is less significant than other considerations.

The supply of land suitable for a particular purpose is limited, in amount or in accessibility, and is often insufficient to meet the competition of demand for its use. This is the reason we find high value attaching to centrally located business property. Such value is the result both of limited area—scarcity—and of the fact that no two pieces of land are ever exactly alike. Each site is individual in quality.

The Chicago Loop district, approximately a square mile within the artificial boundary of the elevated railway structure, has high unit value because the area within this transportation rectangle is limited and because the economic forces of the entire Middle West find managerial concentration in one form or another within this area, with the result that it has become an extremely active center of commercial life. At the same time, some locations within the area are more advantageous than others for certain purposes and therefore have value corresponding to their separate locations.

On the New York City waterfront, the land available for docks and warehouses is extensive, but there is still not enough to serve the need. There is not enough land for all of the waterfront interests that seek its control. Many interests, therefore, must share dock facilities. Interests that are unable to pay the high costs controlling water frontage must yield to those whose services to society can command a higher price. Similarly, the available sites for apartments adjacent to city parks, riverfronts, and lakefronts are limited and hence command higher value because of their scarcity.

The principle of scarcity applies not only to sites but also to all real estate rental markets. In a given apartment area, for example, there may be a severe shortage of four-room apartments at the same time that there is a surplus of eight-room apartments. The size of, and the rent that must be paid for, the larger apartments effectively limits the demand for them. The market for single-family dwellings is diversified into low-cost, medium-cost, and high-cost properties. At any one time there may be a shortage in one of these three different markets and a surplus in another. Scarcity in relationship to effective demand determines the character of the market.

Anything to have value must have utility and be in scarce supply. The greater the utility, the greater the necessity or desire to possess it. The greater the degree of scarcity, the greater the competition to secure it and the greater its value. Land has value in proportion to the benefits it will yield to mankind and in inverse proportion to the total amount of land available and capable of producing the same benefits.

The real estate broker needs to know what lands in his territory are available for expansion for various types of use. He needs to know what improved properties of various types and classes are currently and potentially available. In this connection, he needs to know whether the population is increasing or decreasing and at what approximate rate. If the community has a population of

100,000 and is increasing at the rate of 2 percent a year, he can assume that within the next five years housing will have to be provided for an additional 10,000 persons. Where in the city, with choice locations already in short supply, can this additional housing be provided? What type and class of housing? In what price range? Who now owns the land that will be needed? Who can develop it? How can financing be secured? These and related questions must and will be answered by someone in the course of time. The alert and competent broker, constantly studying his territory, develops sound answers to all of these questions before the problems really become acute.

Highest and best use

Another basic principle of land utilization is the principle of highest and best use. Highest and best use may be defined as that use which will be most likely to produce the greatest net return over a given period of time.

Generally speaking, each urban site is better suited for some one kind of use than for any other kind of use. Some locations are ideal for industrial use, some for low-cost single-family dwellings, some for luxury dwellings, some for unfurnished apartments, some for furnished kitchenette apartments, some for retail stores and shops, and some for still other uses. The most important factor determining the proper use of any site is the maximum net income it can produce—either monetary or amenities or both.

Ideally, if all of the sites in an urban area were properly used, i.e., devoted to their highest and best use, the area would be in perfect economic balance. When some sites are not in proper use, imbalance exists and property values in the entire area are affected. Perfect economic balance in the use of land is actually never attained in any urban area. There are at least two reasons for this:

1. The constant changes taking place in all phases of urban life.
2. Variations in the objectives and economic capabilities of the owners and tenants of real property. There are always forces at work which tend to prevent the attainment of balance, and always there are other forces which tend to encourage such

attainment. It is in this scene of changing conditions and resultant real estate market flux, with every property owner and tenant earnestly seeking maximum yields of money income and amenities, that the real estate broker finds his opportunities for service.

With all this in mind, the broker will do well to make a continuing study of the uses to which sites in his territory are put and are capable of being put. Through systematic study of ownership and use maps, through personal inspection of properties, and through periodic interviews with owners and tenants, he will develop numerous opportunities for constructive brokerage which he would otherwise miss entirely.

The principle of anticipation

The principle of anticipation is another factor that affects the market value of urban land. In the price paid for an improved site or for the development of an unimproved site, there is usually some element of anticipation. Belief that land will inevitably increase in value is so universal in this country that almost any offer to buy real estate includes some degree of anticipation.

One reason for this is the durability of land. Improvements eventually wear out, but land does not alter materially over a long period of time. Land is limited in supply. It cannot be multiplied to meet the competition of the people who want to use it. Therefore the price paid in a real estate transaction usually is a compromise between present and anticipated future demand for use of the property.

The high cost of most improvements upon land prohibits ready adaptation to sudden shifts in utilization or rapid fluctuations of value. The permanent nature of the investment in a costly improvement on a site tends to hold the site to its original use even though the character of the district changes. The inertia of large capital investments anchors and tends to stabilize land use. This gives assurance of continuing earning power, and this earning capacity is reflected by the price a particular property will command.

Every sound real estate development results from a long-term forecast—a forecast made much more difficult by the dynamic character of urban growth and decline. The assumption of the risk in real estate development is made in the belief and with the hope that the compensating rewards will prove to be adequate for the risks assumed. The rapid, often unforeseen, changes in urban developments may make a building obsolete long before it is torn down. But scarcity and the growth of population tend to maintain or increase the site value until a demand is developed for a use profitable enough to justify the expense of wrecking the existing structure and erecting a new one.

Another reason why the price of real estate so often includes the element of anticipation is the human tendency to discount the future in favor of the present. A discounted future value in the present is more desired than a remote return which is subject to all the risks of a dynamic society. This is true even though the remote return, if waited for, might be much larger than the present estimate. Every present estimate, then, has in it some element of faith in an increasing return in the future.

Building in advance of demand is a universal characteristic of urban real estate. This is done because land and structure become one in use and cannot easily be enlarged piecemeal to keep pace with a growing demand. A building that is adequate for a 20-year period may be wholly inadequate for a 50-year period. Such a building, therefore, may not reflect or yield the full capacity of its site during the life of the building.

It is not feasible to build a foundation and a substructure on which a 20-story building can be erected a story or two at a time throughout the years as demand warrants. Such a procedure would necessitate initial investments so large that it would be impossible to secure an adequate return on them. Furthermore, the inconvenience of building additions to the structure must be considered together with the probability that construction costs will vary through the years.

A building may be inadequate and yield a low income but still be the highest and best use of the site because of the cost involved in wrecking it and constructing another. The earning power of the site is limited by the structure until such time as the potential earning power of the site will cover the cost of demolishing the old structure and erecting a new one in its place. Buildings must be planned in anticipation of potential demand even though it is expected that demand will not fully develop for several years.

The principle of contribution

From an economic standpoint it is not prudent to invest more capital in a property than the income from the property will support. The income from an investment must be sufficient to (1) cover all costs of operation, (2) return all of the invested capital during the useful life of the improvement, and (3) pay interest on the total investment commensurate with the risk involved.

Any investment that meets these three tests satisfactorily is sound.

This basic principle must be kept in mind when considering whether or not to improve vacant land or to put additional capital into improvements already on the land. The point to consider is whether or not the contemplated addition of capital will *contribute additional value* to the property.

Practical applications of this principle are legion. A few examples will be sufficient to illustrate it and make it clear. Mr. A owns a vacant lot. It is, or can be, leased as a parking lot for a certain annual rental, or it can be improved with a retail store building which can be leased for a certain annual sum. If the net income from the retail store is greater than from the parking lot and is sufficiently large to return to the owner the entire cost of the improvement during its useful life and pay an adequate interest on the capital invested in the improvement plus adequate interest on the value of the vacant lot, the erection of the retail store building would be justified from an economic and investment point of view.

Mr. B owns an apartment building property consisting of eight-room family units. He is getting a certain annual net income from the property. It is suggested that the eight-room units be divided into smaller kitchenette apartments. This raises the question of whether such addition of capital would *contribute additional value* to the property. No such contribution will be made unless the net income is increased in an amount sufficient to return all of the added capital plus a proper interest on it during the life of the structure plus a proper interest on the capital value of the property as is.

Mr. C owns an apartment building property where the kitchen and bath facilities are obsolete. The suggestion is made that the

Principles of land utilization 35

obsolete equipment be replaced by new, modern fixtures. Such a project will be economically sound if the modern equipment will make it possible to increase the rents in an amount sufficient to return all of the costs plus a proper interest on the added capital during the economic life of the new fixtures. Then the replacement of the equipment would *contribute to the value* of the property.

It should be noted that addition of capital to a real estate holding is economically sound, even if it does not increase the property value, provided such addition is necessary to maintain current value. Of course, the added capital must be recaptured with proper interest during the remaining useful life of the improvement. In this case the added capital contributes to the maintenance of value and forestalls pending economic loss.

The principle of contribution may be defined as follows: Capital should be added to an investment in real estate only if such action will produce increased revenue sufficient to amortize the added capital and pay a proper interest on it, or if the failure to make such addition of capital will result in a loss of net income greater in amount than the capital and the interest on it necessary to maintain the current value of the property.

An understanding of this principle plus the ability to demonstrate and illustrate it to clients will often enable a broker to create transactions in certain instances and to lead prospective buyers to sound decisions in others.

The principle of increasing and decreasing returns

The principle of contribution and the principle of increasing and decreasing returns are closely related. The principle of contribution governs the amount of labor, services, and capital that can be added to a property to increase its value. The principle of increasing and decreasing returns serves the same purpose but is more specifically concerned with successive application of equal amounts of labor, services, or capital to ascertain at what point maximum yield is achieved.

The theory of the principle is that, up to a certain point, each successive application of either labor, services, or capital contributes to the value of the property by increasing its yield. When an addition, in a series of equal applications, produces an increased yield greater in amount than the increased yield produced by the immediately preceding application, the principle of *increasing returns* is operative. If the series of additional equal applications is continued long enough, a point is reached, eventually, at which another addition will not produce an increased yield greater than was produced by the preceding application. This point is known as the point of *diminishing returns*. When this point has been reached, each succeeding addition produces a slightly less return than was produced by the preceding addition. Under this condition, the principle of decreasing returns is operative.

A knowledge of the principle of increasing and decreasing returns is valuable for use in planning farmland crop programs to decide how much fertilizer to use, how much machinery to buy, and how much labor to employ. It is valuable in the planning of a new building—such as an office building, a hotel, or a multifamily apartment—to aid in deciding how tall the structure should be, floor area, what kind and what quality of equipment to install, etc., what personal services to provide for tenants, and many other planning problems which can only be solved by viewing them in the light of the principle of increasing and decreasing returns.

In all studies to estimate highest and best use, it is essential that thinking be guided by the principle of increasing and decreasing returns as well as by other basic principles of land utilization. The problem in such a study is to ascertain, by careful consideration of alternate uses and by the hypothetical application of varying degrees of capital and labor, which use will produce the greatest net return and at what point it is no longer profitable to continue the addition of capital and labor to the improvement.

A real estate broker is not fully equipped to advise clients unless he has a working knowledge of this principle. The professional broker, from a moral and ethical standpoint, is more than a mere agent for the seller or the buyer. He has obligations to both buyer and seller and also to the community, and his knowledge will assist him to better serve his client.

The principle of substitution

One of the basic principles regulating human action with reference to the buying and selling of real estate is the principle of substitution. The principle of substitution is based on the economic fact that, when utility is not lessened, the cheaper product or service tends to prevail over all other similar products or services. Stated in other terms: A prudent man will not pay more for a real property than it would cost him to secure a substitute property of equal utility and desirability, assuming no unusual or costly delay in obtaining possession. The real estate broker must keep this principle in mind when showing available properties to a prospective purchaser. Otherwise, he is likely to lose the sale. If a prospective purchaser of a single-family dwelling inspects and considers two or more available properties that are equally desirable from the standpoint of location, building material, design, size, layout, etc., he will buy the one offered at the lowest price. Similarly, the prospective purchaser of an investment property, when considering two or more available properties of approximately equal quality and net earning capacity, will buy the one which is offered at the lowest price.

The broker can make effective use of this principle not only in showing properties to a prospect but, more importantly, in planning the sale before he ever takes the prospect to see the properties. The use of this principle is valuable also in the listing of properties. The owner who wants to sell quite naturally wants to get the highest possible price for his property. Usually he wants a higher price than the broker will ever be able to get in a sale. In order to get the owner to be willing to accept an offer that is in line with the market, it is necessary to convince him that substitute properties are available at lower prices. For this reason it is desirable for the broker to have authentic information at hand about the prices at which comparable properties in the area have been sold recently and also about the asking prices of comparable substitute properties currently available when he is negotiating with the owner to list his property.

The principle of substitution has broad applications in the real estate field. It is a guide to the broker in listing and selling property. It is helpful to the manager in developing rent schedules. It is vitally important to the land developer and builder in planning and selling building projects. It must be kept in mind by the mortgage man when considering the lending of funds on real property as security. And it is, of course, an indispensable guide to the real estate appraiser in estimating market value. No property is worth more than it would cost to acquire a substitute property of equal utility and desirability, assuming no unusual or costly delay in obtaining possession.

The principle of substitution also is significant from a different point of view. There is a well-recognized principle in finance which has taught us that when two kinds of money circulate together, the poorer money will drive the better money out of circulation. This principle is known in economics as Gresham's law. This law is controlling in many other fields. Of two commodities or services of unequal quality but fulfilling the same need, the lower priced commodity or service tends to drive the higher priced commodity or service off the market. Of two apartments, equally desirable but differently priced, the lower priced one will be rented first. Or of two single-family dwellings, equally desirable but differently priced, the lower priced property usually will sell first.

The principle of balance

Land as an economic entity is not unlimited. It is scarce. Since its availability is limited at any one time or place, it is important to apportion the land among its uses in such a way that all demands can be adequately satisfied. The essential elements of the physical properties of a city should be so proportioned with respect to each other that the life of the city can proceed with minimum friction and without sacrificing the future.

The various types and classes of real estate required by the people in a given area must be in proper proportion to each other to provide social, economic, and civic efficiency in land use. This is in conformity to the principle of balance or equilibrium—a natural law applying to everything in the universe. It applies to the structure of atoms. It applies to the structure of the limitless universe made up of swirling suns, comets, planets, and stars. It is observable in the interdependence of one form of life upon another in the plant and animal worlds. It is the controlling factor in the interdependence of the various parts of the human body. It is seen in the proportioning of the essential elements that compose air, water, wood, steel, milk, eggs, and everything else material to which mankind has given a name.

The people in an urban area need residences, factories, offices, stores, cemeteries, schools, churches, and many other types of real estate. Within each type, as a rule, they need two or more classes of property. Low cost and luxury residences; department stores and specialty shops; grade schools, high schools, and colleges; through streets, side streets, and classes of use must be in proper proportion to each other. Not too much of any one, nor too little.

There is a limit to the number of meat markets, drugstores, barber shops, theaters, shoe repair shops, restaurants, and laundries that the people in a given area can support. When there are too many of any one type, they all suffer because the principle of balance has been violated. Gross incomes decline, rent-paying ability wanes, building maintenance is neglected, services deteriorate, and property values depreciate. Vacancies occur, to be filled with weaker tenants. Blight spreads through the area.

When there are not enough of any one type of use, congestion results. Rents and prices soar. Inordinate profits are realized. Burdensome time and expenses are incurred by the people in traveling to distant points to work, to play, to shop, to park their cars. When such inadequacy develops, the area is out of balance. Corrective real estate brokerage of a creative character is needed. Such conditions are not uncommon, especially in rapidly growing areas. As population grows and spreads through the area, the broker will find no great difficulty in locating clients who want dwellings, stores, offices, and other real estate facilities. The problem of getting suitable locations for them may not be so easy, but to a resourceful and well-informed broker it is not an insuperable task.

One of the most important of all the functions of the real estate broker is that of keeping his territory in real estate balance. Through a systematic and periodic study of the area he is likely to find that there is a shortage of some type and class of use that the community needs. Maybe it is a barber shop, a beauty parlor, a five-and-ten-cent store, a restaurant of a certain class, a kitchenette apartment building. He may find that there are too many stores of a certain type and class. In any such case he faces an opportunity to work out a transaction that will benefit the community and that will reward him with a commission.

The principle of proportionality

Closely related to the principle of balance is the principle of proportionality. This principle lays down the rule that value is created and maintained in the improvement of urban land, other factors being favorable, by keeping the various elements of the improvement in proper proportion to each other. Disequilibrium in the relationship of essential parts tends to destroy value or to prevent the maximum development of value.

In a single-family dwelling, for example, living room, dining area, kitchen, bedrooms, closets, and other component parts of the structure must all be in proper proportion as to size and arrangement to insure maximum livability. In an office building there is a proper proportioning as between elevator facilities, public corridors, number and size of rentable units, rest and wash rooms, and other essential elements in the structure.

The principle of proportionality applies also to the relationship between the dimensions of an urban lot and the dimensions of the building it supports; between the width of streets, parkways, sidewalks, and alleys; between equity and mortgage; between gross and net income; between the cost of a lot and the cost of the building erected upon it; between the type and quality of services given to tenants of a building and the rents that they pay; and between numerous other relationships that affect the desirability and the productivity of improved real property.

To be an expert real estate man, the broker must understand the principle of proportionality as it affects the value and the marketability of improved land. He must learn, through the study of the properties and the market behavior in his area, what constitutes proper proportioning of the various elements in the types of properties with which he and his clients are concerned. Such knowledge will help in listing properties at obtainable prices. It will help, also, in honest and effective presentation of properties to intelligent prospective buyers.

The factors in production

The value of a property lies in the worth of the income which it produces or which it may be expected to produce, that is, either yields in the form of minerals, grain, fruit, vegetable or forest products, livestock, fowl, rents paid in money, or amenities.

Income is derived from a combination of four different productive factors. These factors are labor, entrepreneurship, capital, and land. Entrepreneurship may be thought of as including coordinating factors other than labor, capital, and land. None of these factors is a free agent. Each one must be utilized and each one must be paid. Operating together, they produce a gross product or gross rent. Each one has a claim on this gross rent. First priority goes to labor. It must be paid first, even though nothing is left for any of the other agents. What is left of the gross rent after labor has been paid is residual to the other three agents. The second priority goes to entrepreneurship or the coordinating agents. It must be paid next, after labor. What is left of the gross rent after labor and entrepreneurship have been paid is residual to capital and land. Capital has the third priority. What is left after labor, entrepreneurship, and capital have been paid is residual to land. If the residue to land is greater than comparable land in the area is typically earning, this residue may contain a profit as well as a return to the land.

This principle governing the priority of claim upon the gross income of improved real estate is of tremendous importance to the appraiser, the investor, and the broker. The appraiser must keep it constantly in mind as he goes through the appraisal process to estimate the value of land. The investor must consider it when deciding whether or not to hazard capital in the purchase of equities or securities attaching to real estate, and the broker, with a working knowledge of the operation of these agents in production, is well-equipped to advise prospective sellers and buyers. He can use this knowledge in getting listings at saleable prices and in convincing a prospective purchaser that he should or should not acquire ownership of a given property.

CHAPTER FOUR
Real estate markets

In order to plan and manage your real estate brokerage business efficiently and be able to advise your clients and customers, you must understand real estate markets. You must know what a real estate market is, what real estate markets exist in your territory, and the approximate current status of each one. You should be able within reasonable limits to estimate the strength and weakness of each market during future time periods. This is true especially for short-term plans, say from 1 to 5 or 10 years. It is important also when making preparations to take advantage of changes in the social and economic structure of the community that are likely to take place at more distant times in the future.

You must consider the existence and strength of local real estate markets in deciding what specialized services to offer the public, what departments to have in your organization, how many employees you will need, what equipment you will require, what gross income is probable, and what your costs of operation are likely to be. These and related matters of importance in the organization and operation of your business must be in balance with the real estate market potentials of your territory.

A good working knowledge of current and probable future market trends will help you list properties at salable prices, equip you to advise buyers for use and investors for future gains. Knowledge is essential equipment for creative brokerage activities.

You must realize that no real estate market is ever static, that every real estate market is always changing—going up or going down, sometimes fast for short periods, sometimes slowly for long periods. You ought to know why such changes are occurring. You need to develop skill in forecasting rate of change and shift in direction of movement. This requires familiarity with basic principles of land utilization, with the social and economic structure of the area, and several years of experience with market behavior.

The term "market" has various meanings, including:

1. A place where merchandise is exposed for sale
2. A private store for the sale of provisions
3. A state of trade as determined by prices, supply, and demand
4. A geographic area where a certain commodity is in demand

There are a multitude of special markets. They include markets for automobiles, radios, television sets, books, pencils, men's suits, ladies wear, and scores of other. Each of these may be subdivided into high-priced, medium-priced, and low-priced commodities or services. Broadly speaking, there is a market for the sale of legal services, another for the sale of medical services, another for barbering services, another for teaching services, and another for each of many different specialized services needed or desired by people in a specific area.

The essential features of all markets include:

1. People who need or desire a particular product or service and who have adequate purchasing power to acquire it
2. An available for-sale supply of whatever it is that people need or desire
3. A geographic area within which it is economically feasible to offer the product or service for sale.

People make values. People make markets. It is for people that commodities are produced and services are offered. The more people, the greater the potential for sale of any product or service, provided it is needed or desired and there is supporting purchasing power.

The term "real estate market" embraces many different types and classes of real property. Each type is composed, usually, of two or more different classes of property, such as high-priced or luxury property and low-cost property. Low-cost residential housing constitutes one market, luxury residential housing constitutes another market. Neighborhood retail store locations and sites for shopping centers constitute different markets. Other markets are light and heavy manufacturing plants, low-price and high-price office space, walk-up and high-rise apartment buildings, gasoline service stations and deluxe car-washing establishments. Each class is a separate market. All real estate markets have certain characteristics in common, but each one is unique and different in certain respects from all others. One or more of these markets may be active at the same time that one or more other markets are slow or dormant. In a specific geographic area there may be no market at all for luxury dwellings, for commercial hotels, for manufacturing plants, or for any one of many different kinds of land utilization. In the same area there may be an active market for single-family dwellings, for gasoline service stations, for retail stores, for resort properties, and for other kinds of land utilization. There may be a "buyers' market" for one class of real estate when at the same time there is a "sellers' market" for another class of real estate. It all depends upon the pressure of population, the needs and desires of the people, the supply of available properties, and the strength of the purchasing power of the people.

In any geographic area at any specific time there is a definite number of real estate parcels—a certain number of vacant lots; a certain number of single-family dwellings; a certain number of retail stores, office buildings, and gasoline service stations; and a certain number of every type of real property. Ideally, as a real estate broker, you should know how many properties there are in each of these categories in your territory, since their numbers indicate maximum sales potentials. You may be able to get some or all of this information from recent U.S. census studies or from the local tax assessor's office. The number of each type and class of property tends to remain the same over a long period of time. It is a fixed quantity in each category, except for an increase due to a subdivision operation or a decrease due to a mergering of ownership. Variation in the percentages of these properties offered for sale or for rent reveals the market trend. An increase in the number of offerings may indicate a weakening of demand. A decrease in the number of offerings may indicate an accelerated demand.

46   *Modern real estate practice*

It is certain that the ownership of each privately held property in the territory will change hands in course of time, by sale, gift, inheritance, or escheat. The increasing and decreasing volumes of these transactions indicate the real estate market trends in the area. From a practical point of view your greatest interest is in the volume of transactions that will take place in the future. You cannot know just what this volume will be, but you can estimate it in the light of the volume and character of recent transactions and the number of each type of property currently offered for sale.

At any time you know, or can quickly ascertain, how many listings of each type and class of property are in your office. These listings constitute the supply, or inventory, immediately available to you. Assuming that your office is equally as efficient as other brokers' offices in your territory, the number of listings that you have in comparison with previous months, quarters, and years, is a good indication of current market trends. If you find that the listings in your office are decreasing in number, you should find out whether the cause is changing social or economic conditions in the area or is a weakness of your firm in maintaining the inventory. Conversely, if you find that the number of listings in your office is increasing in volume, you should discover whether the increase is due to neighborhood factors or to more diligent work by your sales force.

The classified advertising columns of the local newspapers reflect real estate market conditions and trends. The direction and strength of the market trends of each kind of property can be estimated by keeping a daily record of the number of properties that are advertised for sale and for rent.

Other significant clues to current market conditions include noticeable increase or decrease in the number of "For Sale" and "For Rent" signs attached to properties in the area.

Supply and demand are counterbalancing forces. It is unlikely that they are ever exactly equal for long. If they were, the price level would remain stable. The price level of real estate responds to supply and demand forces just as does any other commodity, but the total physical amount of land in any area is a constant quantity. It cannot be increased or curtailed as a manufactured product can be to match a strengthening or a weakening demand. An increase in the supply of real property on the market is due to an increase in the number of dissatisfied owners or renters, to the subdivision of land, or to the construction of multistory buildings for rental housing or for cooperative ownership.

Once you have made a study of the real estate geography of your territory and have catalogued the various uses to which the land has been put, it is not an impossible task to keep reasonably well-informed about the current supply of properties available for sale or rent and to stay up to date on supply trends.

The strength of demand trend is more difficult to estimate. This is because, unlike land, the quantity of persons needing, wanting, and able to buy or to rent is not fixed. The number of potential clients and customers varies with increases, decreases, and shift of population. Willingness to buy or rent specific types and classes of property is favorably or adversely affected by architectural and technological developments in housing and in transportation. Ability to buy or to rent is linked to economic factors that set limits upon purchasing power. Nevertheless, you can form a practical estimate of potential demand by giving thoughtful attention to several different general social and economic trends in the area.

Most significant of all indicators of market conditions is population growth, decline, and shifts from one area to another. Trends revealed by U.S. census reports are important in showing 10-year swings. It is not practical, however, to rely upon them year after year between census takings. There are several local sources of information that are reasonably up to date and accurate. Among them is the registration of births. These figures can be secured monthly and charted to show trends in comparison with previous periods. A substantial increase in the number of births may in itself forecast a greater demand for houses or apartments with additional bedrooms to accommodate growing families. An increasing number of babies forecasts an accelerated demand for baby foods, infant wear, and many other products designed for consumption by babies and by their parents. This means, for example, a greater volume of business for drug stores and food stores. An increasing number of births is closely related to demand for residential property, for retail stores of certain kinds, for offices for doctors and dentists, for school facilities, and for many other utilities and services closely related to the functions of the real estate broker.

Closely related to birth statistics as an aid in long-range forecasting of demand for real estate is the record of school enrollment. Pupils enrolled in the first grade will have a strong impact on residential housing markets 15 to 20 years later. Pupils enrolled in the high schools will be in need of residential housing in 10 to 15 years. Students enrolled in first year college classes will come into the market for homes in 5 to 10 years. Students graduating from college are likely to be good prospects for dwellings in one to five years. These statistics are not difficult to secure. They can be obtained from the local school superintendent for all grades through the high school and junior college level. Local college enrollments can be obtained from the office of the college registrar.

Of more immediate value in forecasting residential market demand is the volume of local marriage licenses issued. When a young man and a young woman get married, a new family housing unit is needed. An increasing volume of marriage licenses issued foreshadows an increasing demand for dwellings.

Any and every thing that influences supply of or need for housing of any kind is of interest to some degree to the broker who seeks to keep himself well-informed on market trends. Need for new or additional housing is created by marriages. A divorce breaks up an existing family and frequently leads to the need for one or two additional family housing units. A death in a family often leads to change of residence, adding one dwelling to the market supply and creating demand for another. For these reasons you must be interested not only in noting the changing volume of deaths and divorces in your territory but also in checking on individual cases to find immediate opportunities for business deals.

The strength of the residential housing market is reflected by the increasing or decreasing number of families evicted for nonpayment of rent and the number of mortgage foreclosures on single-family dwellings. Another significant statistic is the number of unemployed persons in the territory. This information can be secured from governmental and from private employment agencies. The existence of families on relief, families evicted for nonpayment of rent, families with foreclosed mortgages, and breadwinners who are unemployed are a heavy weight upon all real estate markets. In planning creative brokerage deals and in advising clients and customers, you should give careful consideration to whether these trends are upward or downward and also the rate at which they are moving.

An increasing or a decreasing volume of building permits reflects a growing or a waning confidence in real estate ownership. You will do well not only to know whether the volume of permits is increasing or decreasing but also to find out just why more or fewer permits are being issued. The same is true of new mortgages. The major lending institutions have had many years of experience with real estate markets. They are constantly studying economic trends affecting the personal financial capabilities of borrowers and the marketability of loans on real estate. The areas in which they will make loans, the types of property they will accept as security, the percentage of loans to appraised value, the interest rates charged, the regulations imposed by governmental agencies that insure mortgages, all reflect evaluations of local real estate markets made by men who are experienced in analyzing and forecasting market trends. Since the market for the purchase and sale of real property is so closely intertwined with the market for mortgage money, you need to keep yourself well-informed at all times on the availability of mortgage loans on each type of property in your territory and on the terms that govern the availability of these loans.

Real estate markets are generally confined to local areas. This is true of residential properties with the exception of resort dwellings and luxury dwellings desired by wealthy families for seasonal occupancy. The market for industrial properties may be nationwide or even international in geographic scope. The purchasers of high-valued investment properties, such as hotels, office buildings, and shopping centers may be found in distant cities.

The marketability of real estate is closely linked, however, to general economic conditions. When the economy is on the upswing, real estate prices are firm or rising. In periods of recession or depression, real estate prices are shaky or declining. As a real estate broker, therefore, you are well advised to keep in touch with general business conditions and trends and to note or estimate to what extent they affect the marketability and prices of real estate in your territory.

There are many different sources from which you can secure

information about general business conditions and trends. They include reports issued periodically by the federal reserve bank in your area and reports issued by state universities. Some of the larger savings and loan associations issue economic reports on a periodic basis. Usually these reports can be secured gratis or at nominal cost. Some of the departments of the federal government issue reports on economic trends. In addition there are several private research organizations that issue periodic bulletins on current conditions and forecasting the direction and strength of future trends. Among these are the Kiplinger service, the Wenzlick letters from St. Louis, Missouri, and the Real Estate Research Corporation letter service from Chicago.

General business trends reflect the ability of people to buy or rent real estate. In addition they influence the attitudes of people. They may cause people to be optimistic or pessimistic about future conditions. They may encourage potential purchasers or make them reluctant to commit themselves to financial obligations. This is why you should watch general business trends, noting their apparent strength and direction of movement.

CHAPTER FIVE

Appraisal principles and methods

A real estate broker may also be a qualified professional appraiser. Many brokers are. The ability to merit and earn a professional appraisal designation gives the broker a unique and powerful advantage in competition with other brokers who are not so well equipped.

A successful career as a real estate broker, however, is not dependent upon being recognized as a professional appraiser. Many highly successful brokers have never engaged in professional appraisal work, but it is unlikely that any broker can develop and maintain a successful practice unless he has a working knowledge of valuation principles and methods.

Such knowledge is useful in listing properties for sale. Usually the owner who wants to sell will ask a higher price than can be secured. He may have the mistaken idea that real estate always appreciates in value. He may believe that his property is worth somewhat more than it cost him to acquire it and improve it. Besides, he wants to make a profit. If the broker accepts the listing at the asking price of such an owner, he may waste time and money trying to sell it at that price. He can try to beat the asking price down by securing and submitting offers at lower levels, but such a policy is uncertain and time-consuming. It tends to destroy whatever respect and confidence the owner originally had in the broker. It is far better policy for the broker to refuse to list a property at a price he knows to be far out of line with the market. If he knows current market conditions, if he knows and can explain appraisal principles and methods, he can, more often than not, sign up the listing at a realistic price.

A working knowledge of appraisal principles and methods is helpful in presenting properties to prospective purchasers. By use of the cost approach, or the income approach, or the market data approach, it may be possible to convince the prospect that the asking price is actually less than it would cost to acquire any other similar property having equal points of desirability.

Investors who have had experience with income-producing real property are already familiar, to some extent at least, with valuation principles and methods—or they think that they are. The broker should know more about appraising than they do. To deal with them he should be able to convince them, using sound valuation principles.

To build up a clientele or to develop a reputation for competent and reliable service, the broker must at all times deal fairly with both seller and buyer. He should know and remember that his reputation for competency and fair dealing is the only asset he has as a real estate broker. Since he is dealing with property values in every transaction, it is basically important that he be able to estimate values and explain them. Disgruntled sellers and defrauded buyers are liabilities that no broker can afford. Their disparaging comments to potential clients can have lingering bad effects throughout a widening circle in the broker's territory.

A detailed exposition of the many essential and optional steps in the appraisal process would constitute a complete textbook on appraisals. That is outside the scope of this book. Readers who want to acquire such detailed information are referred to the official textbook of the American Institute of Real Estate Appraisers. We are concerned here with real estate brokerage. This chapter will present only a general outline of the appraisal process, with brief comments about some of the most important steps it includes.

An appraisal of a real property is an *estimate* of its value. An estimate is not a guess nor a hunch. It is the end result of a reasoning process. It is a conclusion that can be supported with pertinent facts. A real estate appraisal is based on valuation principles. It is developed by the use of reasonable and understandable processes. Sellers, buyers, and users of real property, generally speaking, lack the knowledge and skill to make dependable appraisals. Their estimates are likely to be guesses, or hunches, or be based on local rules-of-thumb which may be inaccurate or inapplicable to the property. They often make costly mistakes. One of the most important functions of the real estate broker is to help such persons avoid these mistakes.

Bracketing

No one is wise or skillful enough to measure or weigh or otherwise determine the exact value of any real property. The best that can be done is to *estimate* the value. Value is the estimated equivalent of a thing or service. The equivalent of a thing can be estimated only by comparing it with other things having similar utilities and points of desirability. Such estimates are usually in terms of money—the standard medium of exchange.

The informed broker (even the veteran appraiser) realizes that he cannot prove that any property has a value of any definitely stated amount of money. He can prove that any given property has a value of *at least* so many dollars—$18,000, for example. He can prove that this same property does not have a value of more than another certain number of dollars—$20,000, for example. He can prove both of these figures to the satisfaction of anyone. These two figures set up brackets between which the actual value of the property lies. Precisely where and at exactly what amount he cannot say, but by the use of proven technical processes he can narrow the brackets until he *approaches* so close to the actual value that any reasonable person is willing to accept his estimate.

Cost as evidence of value

One or more of three widely used technical approaches may be used to narrow the brackets. These approaches are known as the cost approach, the income approach, and the market data approach.

The cost approach is sometimes called the "physical approach." It is also known as the "summation approach." By whatever name you may wish to call it, it is based on the principle of substitution. This principle affirms that no rational person will pay more for a property than it would cost him to acquire a similar property with equivalent utilities and factors of desirability within a reasonable period of time.

The cost approach includes the following important steps:

1. Estimation of the value of the land in the property, as if vacant.
2. Estimation of the reproduction cost (new) of the improvements in the property.
3. Estimation of accrued depreciation (if any) in the property.
4. Subtraction of total estimated depreciation from the estimated cost of reproduction new.
5. Addition of the estimated value of the land to the estimated depreciated value of the improvements.

As a general rule, it is believed that the cost approach sets the upper limit of value, but each of the several steps in this approach is an estimate and is subject to error. For this reason, the value estimate which it develops should be considered a preliminary estimate until it has been checked and correlated with preliminary estimates developed by the income and market data approaches.

Now let us consider briefly some of the important aspects of the first three steps in this approach.

Site valuation

The first step in the cost approach is to estimate the value of the land. There are two ways of doing this. One method is to assume that the land is vacant and compare it with a number of vacant sites of similar size and quality that have been sold recently. The relative desirability of the subject site balanced against each comparable site is estimated in dollars. Vacant sites, if any, in the area that are currently offered for sale are also considered in conformity with the principle of substitution.

Another method that can be used, if the subject property is an income-producing property, is the land residual technique from the income approach.

Appraisal principles and methods 55

Reproduction cost

The second step in the cost approach is the estimation of the reproduction cost new of the improvements. This may be done by any one of several different methods. One of these is the quantity survey method. This requires a detailed inventory of all material and equipment plus all labor by trades necessary to reproduce the building. The cost of each item in the inventory is then estimated in terms of current prices. The total of these costs is assumed to be the value of the building, provided it represents the highest and best use of the site.

Another way of estimating the reproduction cost new of a building is known as the unit-cost-in-place method. This is a variation of the quantity survey method, but it is not as detailed nor is it likely to be as accurate. It estimates the cost in place, including labor, of separate parts or sections of the structure, such as the foundation, the roof, the walls, the flooring, the ceiling, the wiring, etc. The unit of computation varies with the trade or the part of the building to which it applies. It may be the square foot, the square yard, the cubic foot, the cubic yard, the running foot, or some other gross unit in common use by the trade involved. The sum total of these unit cost estimates is taken to be the value of the building, provided it is believed to be the highest and best use of the site.

A third way of estimating reproduction cost new is the square foot method. There are three steps in this procedure:
1. Computation of the number of square feet in the building.
2. Selection or development of a square foot multiplier derived by dividing the known costs of comparable buildings by their respective number of square feet. The typical quotient thus secured is generally considered to be a satisfactory multiplier for use in estimating the cost of truly comparable structures.
3. Multiplication of the number of square feet in the building by the typical quotient developed as explained in step 2 above.

A fourth way of estimating reproduction cost new is the cubic foot method. This method is concerned with cubic content rather than with square foot areas. It is considered by many to be much more accurate than the square foot method. The cubic foot multiplier is derived in the same manner as the square foot multiplier.

Depreciation

The third major step in the cost approach is the estimation of accrued depreciation, if any, in the property.

For this purpose it may be assumed that cost is the value of the property if the site is properly developed in its highest and best use with new improvements. From this assumed value, deductions must be made for one or more of three different conditions that lessen the utility or the desirability of the property, if such conditions exist in it. These conditions constitute loss in value as compared with the perfect newly improved property and are included in the general term "depreciation."

There are three different kinds of depreciation, *viz.*, physical deterioration, functional obsolescence, and economic obsolescence. They are all included in the general definition: "Depreciation is loss in value from any cause."

Physical deterioration is lessening of desirability, or of the life of the part affected, caused by "wear and tear" or by weathering. It may be curable or incurable. Curable deterioration is impairment of parts of the structure that can be repaired or replaced without the incurrence of uneconomic costs—for example, roofs, floors, stair treads, paint. Incurable deterioration is impairment of concealed parts of the structure, such as steel framing, foundations, and other parts which cannot be repaired or replaced without incurring irrecoverable costs.

The amount to be deducted for curable deterioration is the estimated amount necessary to cure the defects.

There are several different ways of estimating incurable deterioration. One method that appears to have gained much favor among professional appraisers consists of the following steps:

1. Make a complete inventory of parts of the building not economically repairable or replaceable in the immediate future
2. Estimate the expected life of each part in years when new
3. Estimate what percentage of the life of each part has passed
4. Estimate the current cost new of each part
5. Multiply the current cost new of each part by the percentage of its life that has expired
6. Add the results of step 5 to arrive at the estimated amount of incurable deterioration in the structure.

Functional obsolescence is loss in value owing to functional defects. Such defects may be deficiencies, such as inadequate or obsolete kitchens, bathrooms, electric equipment, room sizes, and room layout. The defects may be functional excesses, such as inordinately heavy construction, oversize rooms, and luxurious equipment.

Inadequacies that can be overcome at nonprohibitive costs are classed as curable functional obsolescence. The estimated amount necessary to make such corrections is the measure of this type of depreciation. Inadequacies that cannot be corrected except at prohibitive costs are classed as incurable functional obsolescence. The measure of this type of depreciation is the capitalized difference between the net rental income of the property and the net rental income of similar properties not suffering from such defects.

Economic obsolescence is loss in value from causes outside the property itself. Such causes include lessening of desirability owing to infiltration into the area of inharmonious occupancies, the deterioration of civic services, protracted crime waves, sharp increases in real estate taxes, adverse population movements, and any other factor that impairs the desirability of the location.

Economic obsolescence is estimated by capitalizing the difference between the net rental income of the subject property and the net rental income of similar properties in comparable neighborhoods of the same region not affected by these adverse economic influences.

By way of summary: The cost approach to the value estimate consists of (1) estimating the value of the land, (2) estimating the reproduction cost new of the improvements, (3) estimating the total amount of depreciation, if any, that has accrued in the subject property, (4) deducting the estimated depreciation from the estimated reproduction cost new of the improvements, and (5) adding the depreciated estimation cost new of the improvements to the estimated value of the land.

The income approach

The income approach to the final value estimate is also based on the principle of substitution. In addition it conforms to the theory that the value of a property is the present worth of its future income.

58   *Modern real estate practice*

There are eight major steps in the income approach:[1]

1. Estimation of the highest and best use
2. Estimation of probable gross income
3. Estimation of costs of operation
4. Estimation of net income before making provision to recapture the capital invested in the improvements
5. Estimation of the amount of time necessary to recapture the capital invested in the improvements
6. Selection of the most appropriate method of processing the net income to estimate how much of it is imputable to the building and how to process it to recapture the capital invested in the building by the end of its economic life
7. Selection or development of a capitalization rate that best reflects the current market requirements of typical investors
8. Completion of the necessary mathematical processes.

Highest and best use is that use which can reasonably be expected to produce the greatest net income over a given period of time. The estimation of highest and best use must be made before undertaking to estimate probable gross income, since gross income will vary with different kinds of occupancy.

Estimation of probable gross income consists of four important steps:

1. Selection of the best source or type of utilization
2. Estimation of the annual amount of gross income
3. Appraisal of the quality of the gross income
4. Estimation of the durability of the gross income.

Estimation of the gross income is the first step in the development of a reasonable operating statement. The second step is the estimation of the costs of operation. The costs of operation include all costs necessary to develop and maintain maximum net income. These costs will vary with climate, type of property, and

---

[1] No attempt is made here to explain the various steps in detail. Full information about them can be found in the official textbook of the American Institute of Real Estate Appraisers. For the purpose of this book it will suffice to offer a few brief comments about the nature and importance of each of these steps.

class of occupancy. They consist of such items as decoration, painting, heating, cooling, taxes, labor, etc. As a guide in estimating the itemized costs it is important to know the typical costs in the area. Then consideration must be given as to whether or not the cost of each item in the subject property can reasonably be expected to conform to the typical and, if not, to what extent it is likely to vary and why. For one reason or another the operating statement of the subject property during the past year or so may contain irrelevant items or items that are too high or too low as compared with the standards of efficient management. For this reason it is often necessary to reconstruct its past year's operating statement to bring it more closely in line with the standards of efficient management and the capabilities of the property.

The broker will do well to develop and maintain a checklist of standard operating costs for various kinds of property in his territory. He can use these not only in the making of appraisals but also and often quite effectively in the listing and selling of properties.

The typical investor expects to get as much interest on the money he puts into a property as he could secure from any other source. He also wants to get his money back. He wants to recapture the capital invested in the improvements. The length of time required to effect this recapture depends upon the remaining economic life of the improvements. When this has been estimated, there are certain methods that can be used in the appraisal process to provide for the return of the capital. These include what are known as the straight line, the sinking fund, and the annuity methods of depreciation. The appropriate method to be used in any case depends upon the nature of the income, its expected duration, and the requirements of the investor.

The amount of interest to be expected and the most appropriate method of recapturing the capital investment must be carefully considered in the selection or the development of a capitalization rate. The best guide to a decision in this matter is the requirements of typical investors plus the capabilities of the subject property.

To be on safe ground in listing and offering income properties for sale, the broker needs to be thoroughly familiar with current market standards and be well grounded in appraisal principles and methods.

Market data approach

The most widely used and the best-known approach to the value estimate is the market data approach. It is sometimes called the comparison approach, and sometimes the sales approach. It includes cost and income concepts, and it reflects accrued depreciation. It is an extremely valuable check on the other two approaches.

The market data approach is the method used by appraisers and brokers to test the relative desirability of a subject property in comparison with similar properties recently sold or currently offered for sale. The technique used in this approach varies with the type and class of property under consideration.

The first step is to analyze the property under consideration and then locate several properties in the same neighborhood that: (1) are similar as to type and class, (2) have been sold recently or are currently offered for sale.

In the case of single family dwellings comparisons are made to many significant features, such as:

1. Architectural design
2. Layout and livability
3. Lot area and dimensions
4. Taxes; rate, and assessment
5. Number of bedrooms and bathrooms and their location
6. Number and location of closets
7. Landscaping and type of planting
8. Age and physical condition of property
9. Age and condition of plumbing, heating, wiring, and fixtures

Comparison is then made as to what extent the subject property is more or less desirable than each of the comparable properties.

The price at which each comparable property has been sold or offered for sale is then considered and they are compared pricewise with the subject property; by this comparison an estimate is made as to what a typical buyer is likely to pay for the subject property.

Others matters to be considered are: (1) the length of time required to consummate sale of comparable properties, (2) how recently the sales were made, (3) the terms of sale.

In the appraisal of commercial and industrial property the comparison may be the size by cubic or square footage and adaptability to use. The rate of return on the investment and the cash flow engendered by leverage are most important in all investment type properties.

In the market data approach it is important that the properties be similar in use, construction, and location. Similarity in location is defined as similar in the basic elements of locational factors. If the property appraised is a residence the property should be compared with property in a residential neighborhood. Also to be considered are the economic level of the people, whether the location is in an urban, suburban, or rural area, and whether the building is a misplaced improvement or in a nonconforming zone. The buildings must be similar in construction. All types of property whether residential, commercial, or industrial have specifications which are peculiar to the type of structure. Adjustments must be made for materials such as brick v. wood, steel v. concrete, forced air v. hot water heating, and a myriad of other specifications.

The appraiser seeks to compare like for like in use, construction, and location. To find exact comparisons is sometimes difficult but by diligent search they can be found. The number of adjustments is thereby reduced. An extreme example in making adjustments would be comparing and adjusting a residence valued at $75,000 with a modest residence which could be reproduced for $20,000.

In theory any one of the three standard approaches to the value estimate will result in a reasonable and acceptable final value estimate. This is true *if* all pertinent data have been considered and properly evaluated and *if* there are no errors in processing the data. But it is difficult to be sure that all pertinent data have been secured, that the assumptions have been perfectly sound, and that there have been no errors in processing the data. After all, each approach involves several basic assumptions and several estimates, each one of which may be only an approximation. For these reasons, the prudent valuator will consider the value estimate derived in each of the standard three approaches as a preliminary estimate subject to review and correlation with the estimates developed by the other two approaches. This means that, having used all three approaches, he will have three preliminary estimates, no two of which are likely to be the same.

Correlation

Which preliminary estimate should be accepted as being the value of the property? Probably none of them. At this point he is faced by the necessity of correlating these preliminary estimates to arrive at a final value estimate. This he does by reviewing each approach in detail to reconsider his assumptions, to check for errors in processing, and finally to consider which of the three preliminary estimates seems to be most in conformity with the prices being paid for similar properties in the local market. He does not add the three preliminary estimates and divide by three to get an average. He considers the brackets set by the high and the low estimates and finally decides upon a figure in between which seems to be most reasonable and can be supported by data and reasoning.

CHAPTER SIX

Basic policies

Real estate brokerage is carried on in a highly competitive field. Because of the ease with which the vocation can be entered, as compared with many other vocations, the field of real estate brokerage is crowded. As in all other fields of human endeavor, it contains many individuals who are ill-informed, who lack experience, and who do mediocre work. But it also contains many practitioners who are experienced, skilled, and truly expert—many, indeed, who are well established in public esteem. To attain the greatest measure of success, the newcomer must be able to compete effectively with brokers who know the territory thoroughly, who are experts in all phases of the development and consummation of real estate transactions, and who are already well established in public confidence.

It is unlikely that long-range success can be attained by haphazard and dilatory tactics. A successful career in any field usually follows careful preparation, planning, and efficient management of talent, resources, and time factors. This means the fixing of definite objectives and the adoption of sound basic policies. Consideration must be given to many important questions when planning to launch a career as a real estate broker.

The volume of real estate brokerage that is possible in any given area is dependent upon population factors; the size of the geographic area; and the social, economic, and political trends in the area. All of these conditions should be carefully considered by the individual who contemplates committing himself to a career as a real estate broker.

Since the broker is essentially an agent serving sellers and buyers of real property, he deals with people rather than with land and buildings. After all, land and buildings are only means for serving human needs and human wants. It is what people need and want in reference to location and shelter that is of first importance. The broker's job is to match these needs and wants with available or procurable real estate at costs consistent with the purchasing power of the individuals he serves.

The broker's territory

One of the first things that the broker should do in planning his career is to make a study of the population in the general area where he would like to do business. Such a study will help him decide whether to confine his activities to a particular neighborhood or to undertake a citywide or a regional business. Up-to-the-minute and thoroughly detailed accurate information about population may not be procurable, but reasonable approximations can be obtained from a study of reports issued by the government and by various letter services. These reports, plus personal inspection of the geographical area, will help to estimate the total number of people in the area, the total number of families, the size of families, whether the population is expanding or declining, the sources and stability of employment, the approximate income levels of the people, social standards, spending habits, and other pertinent characteristics of the social and economic structure of the area.

It should be noted that each class of property constitutes a separate real estate market. Low-cost single-family dwellings constitute one market, luxury single-family dwellings constitute another market. Other separate markets include neighborhood retail stores, shopping centers, office buildings, gasoline service stations, and many others. During the same period that one or more of these markets is active, other markets in the same area may be stagnant. It takes all types and classes of land utilization to make up a metropolitan area and to conform to the principle of balance. Before selecting the geographic area in which to concentrate his activities, the broker will do well to contemplate the relative sizes of the various real estate markets, their potentials, and whether or not they appear to be in or out of balance with the needs of the people in the area. Imbalance in land utilization in relation to population needs of any area presents a potent opportunity for the development of real estate transactions.

The broker cannot deal with people in the mass. He deals with individuals. This means that to be successful in developing business volume he must become acquainted with many different persons, learn about their respective real estate needs, make careful note of their economic capabilities, and put forth a sincere effort to be of personal help to individuals.

Specialization

The distribution and density of the population and the predominant social standards of the people are significant factors to consider before deciding whether to undertake a general real estate brokerage business or to specialize on only one or two types of property. In metropolitan areas, some brokers devote most or all of their time to the listing and selling of single-family dwellings. Others specialize on commercial property or on industrial property. Such specialization is possible and highly practical for some brokers in the larger cities, but in smaller urban areas, the broker may not be able to support himself on the income he can get through specialization. He will usually do a general business, handling all types of real estate and, possibly, at the same time acting as an insurance agent and as a property manager.

Legal counsel

The real estate broker is not, except in rare instances, an attorney. In most states he is prohibited by law from practicing law. He may be subject to a fine for an action which the court construes as legal practice. Yet, every real estate transaction, of whatever character, involves some legal instrument since it deals with property rights that are protected by law. For this reason the individual entering the real estate brokerage vocation needs not only some elementary knowledge of law but he also needs an attorney to advise him and direct him. He needs legal counsel not only for his own protection but also to safeguard the interests of his clients and customers, all of whom rely upon him for dependable service.

Legal advice is helpful, if not actually necessary, in deciding upon the type of organization under which to operate as a broker. Before making this decision, the broker will do well to consult an attorney to give him complete information about his background, his resources, and the objectives toward which he wishes to work. His attorney can advise him on being an individual operator, a member of a partnership, or a principal of a corporation. In any setup except that of an individual operator there should be and may have to be legal instruments prepared and signed. In a partnership there should be articles of agreement or contracts prepared and signed by all interested parties. In a corporation it is necessary to secure a charter, prepare and adopt bylaws, and arrange for the issuance of stock. These are legal matters. They should be handled by an attorney who is experienced in these fields.

In the operation of his business, the broker will be creating various types of contracts between buyers and sellers—offers to sell, offers to buy, leases, acceptances, escrows, binders, contracts for fees, deeds, title guarantees, and many other legal agreements. Many of these can be handled with standard legal forms, but variations will occur for which no standard form exists. Every standard form should be reviewed by an attorney before it is used in any deal to be sure that it actually fits the situation. The legal instruments required in special cases should be prepared by the attorney. It is, indeed, good policy to have the attorney prepare all legal papers.

Tax counsel

Almost without exception, real estate transfers involve consideration to and action upon important tax matters. These include such taxes as the transfer stamp tax, the federal and state income taxes, capital gains tax, *ad valorem* taxes, inheritance taxes, gift taxes which influence the decision of both seller and buyer. Many a real estate transaction is originated solely because either the seller or the buyer, or both, is seeking some sort of tax advantage.

The broker must be well informed about taxes. Since new tax regulations are created and old tax regulations are modified from time to time, the broker should keep his knowledge up to date. It is good policy to subscribe to a good tax service and study each bulletin with care. Knowledge of tax matters will often help the broker initiate lucrative, creative brokerage transactions. Even so, he may do well to employ a tax counselor on a retainer-fee basis for consultation and help. The tax counselor might be the broker's regular attorney. He can help the broker put together transactions that involve intricate tax considerations and can help him avoid costly mistakes.

Type of organization

One of the fundamental policy decisions to be made in planning a real estate brokerage career is whether to operate as a "loner," as a member of a partnership, as a principal in a corporation, or as one member of a group of associates not bound together by partnership agreement.

There are advantages and disadvantages to each type of organization. Which type is best suited to an individual planning a real estate brokerage career may depend upon one or more of several different factors. For example,

1. His personality
2. His available capital and credit
3. His previous knowledge of and experience in allied fields
4. His experience in selling real property
5. The character of the real estate markets in which he prefers to operate
6. The knowledge he already has of the territory he wants to cover
7. The availability of qualified associates.

Personality is an important factor. If he is self-assured, wants to make his own decisions, dislikes to take advice, and finds it difficult to work harmoniously with others, he had better try to work as an individual and operate a one-man office. The advantage is that he will have freedom of choice with unquestioned control of his own time and the kind of properties on which he prefers to concentrate his efforts. He avoids personal responsibility for the actions of others. He can enjoy greater satisfaction in consummating important deals, and he may get certain tax advantages. Furthermore, the relationship between the broker and the client is a personal one. Many clients prefer to deal with one individual in whom previous experience has given them implicit confidence rather than with an impersonal partnership or corporation.

In particular cases, however, there may be distinct disadvantages in "lone wolf" operations. Operating as an individual, the broker lacks the counsel and cooperation of close associates who may have supplementary knowledge and experience of great value in consummating an important transaction. Also, his office, its equipment, and his promotional activities must be limited by his own capital and credit.

Among the advantages of a partnership is the opportunity it affords for diversification of talent in the organization. One partner may specialize in residential properties, another in commercial properties, another in industrial properties, etc. Or each partner may head a different specialized department, such as a mortgage department, an insurance department, a sales department, an appraisal department. The merging of specializations into one unified organization broadens the scope of service that can be offered and should attract a greater number of clients. Also there is the advantage that one department can often "feed" opportunities into another department of the same firm.

Another advantage of the partnership is that by pooling the resources of two or more individuals it is possible to set up and maintain a more impressive office at less cost to each of the partners. The sharing of certain items of overhead may effect considerable economy for each of the partners. Each member of a partnership has personal liability for any loss or legal claim that may attach to it, and it may be disastrous for one partner when the other partners are unable to share the meeting of an obligation involving substantial sums of money.

A corporation, as the name implies, is a separate *corpus* (body). It is a legal person—a complete entity. In most states it has perpetual life. If the individuals serving as officers and employees pass away, the corporation still lives and can carry on the activities for which it was created. The prestige and public confidence in a real estate corporation, once developed, tends to survive after the original founders have passed away. Ownership of the corporation is represented by shares of stock. The shareholders (owners) have limited liability. Losses incurred by the corporation attach to its assets and not to the personal assets of the owners of the stock.

Location of the office

The broker's office should be located as closely as possible to the center of his field of operation. It should be easily accessible to clients and customers and not too far away from the properties he lists for sale or the properties on which he has management contracts. The office should be in the central part of the urban area if the broker deals in central business property, in outlying locations for chains, or in industrial property located in opposite directions from the central business area. In the central urban area, he is closer to key personnel of large commercial and industrial concerns that maintain offices in his city. He is more quickly and conveniently reached by out-of-town clients who may wish to engage his services. Also, he is closer to banks and financial institutions to which he may want to apply for loans. He can save time in going to the city hall and to the county building to look up records, and in going to and from outlying properties he may have for sale.

Unless he operates in a small city, the central business office may not be the best location for the broker who specializes in residential property, a particular neighborhood, or in business subcenters. His office, in any case, should be near the properties he handles and convenient to his clients and customers. Otherwise he is almost certain to lose many deals with clients and customers who will patronize a local office rather than take the time and trouble to travel some distance to a downtown office. Furthermore, the salesman cannot be truly productive in operating in a circle too far-flung from the office.

It is fundamentally important that the broker be thoroughly familiar at all times with the existing and potential opportunities for deals in his territory. To be well-equipped he needs to know significant facts about every property in the area—who the owner is, who the tenants are, what properties have been sold recently and by whom, sales prices and rents asked and paid, properties currently offered for sale or rent and why, and what properties are likely to come onto the market in the near future. He should know whether imbalance exists in land utilization in the area and why, and he should study ways and means of overcoming imbalances through creative brokerage deals. Such vital information cannot be secured or kept up to date in a territory so large that the broker and his salesmen cannot keep it well-covered. All of these matters are, or should be, influential in choosing a location for the main office and the location of branch offices, if any.

Having decided upon the specific district in which to locate his office, the broker should consider both ground floor at street level and an upper floor. If outside the central business district and in a neighborhood area, the office should be on the ground floor at street level, with window space where displays can be placed to be viewed by passers-by. The name of the firm on the door and on the display windows are valuable continuous institutional advertising. A street level entrance makes it easy for clients and customers to come into the office—no stairs to climb, no elevators to wait for. Convenience can add a significant percentage to the volume of business done in a year's time.

The rental value of ground floor space in the central business district, especially in the large cities, may be too high for real estate brokerage offices. Here it may be prudent to take space on the upper floor to get the benefit of lower rent. Offices on upper floors should be accessible by elevators or escalators, never only by stairs. The upper floor office does not have the advertising advantage of window displays or of having the name of the firm seen on the door and windows by passers-by. To attract customers and clients to upper floor offices, it is necessary to rely upon newspaper and direct-mail advertising plus personal contacts.

In transactions in chain store leasing, shopping center developments, subdivision acreage, or heavy-industry sites, office location is less important. The broker will go to the prospective client instead of waiting for him to come to the office. This is especially true of the broker who has not yet developed a clientele or established his reputation.

Experienced brokers, in general, consider the location of their offices of first importance in the planning of their operations. Brokers who specialize in commercial or industrial property prefer downtown locations. Brokers who specialize in residential properties usually locate their offices in residential areas in the city or in a suburb that appears to be in the path of residential development. The individual who is just beginning a real estate brokerage career may not have much choice. He is likely to be limited by availability of locations and by his financial resources. He may find it prudent to select a temporary location pending the time that he can build up greater financial reserves and find a location better suited to his field of activities.

Whether to rent office space or to own the property that houses his office operations is an important policy decision for the broker to make. His decision will be guided by his financial resources, his credit standing, and the scope of the operations he wants to develop.

Rented office space does not tie up substantial amounts of working capital that may be needed in current operations, such as office furniture and equipment, salaries of office personnel, advertising, and other necessary expenses. Also, the renter is not tied so closely to one specific location. He can shift his office to another location more quickly, perhaps, than an owner can if he needs to expand or to take advantage of a sudden new market development in another area.

The disadvantages of renting office space may include:

1. The duration of the tenancy is unstable. The landlord may sell the property to another owner who wants the space for some other purpose. Or the landlord, for some other reason, may be unwilling to renew the lease at all.
2. The level at which the rent will be fixed upon renewal of the lease is uncertain.
3. The broker has no control over the type and character of the tenants who may occupy adjacent space in the building. Undesirable neighbors can exert considerable adverse influence upon the prestige of the location.

Most brokers prefer to own their offices. They believe in private ownership and in the soundness of intelligent investments in real property. They know that prestige and public confidence attaches to real estate offices that are owner occupied.

Many brokers have purchased sites and improved them with buildings designed for their own purposes. Some have purchased improved properties, a part or all of which they have redesigned or remodeled to conform to their own specific needs. Usually the buildings contain excess space which is leased to selected tenants. Net revenue from rentals may in time recapture all of the capital invested in the property.

The more passers-by whose attention is attracted to the broker's office, the greater the number who will stop in for information and services—especially if the exterior indicates that the broker is a well-established and successful practitioner. For this reason many brokers prefer to own an attractive office with parking facilities and pleasing landscaping on a main thoroughfare. The design of the building and the landscaping have effective attention-getting power. In addition it is important to have an attractively designed sign on the building or appropriately displayed on the lawn to identify the firm and its type of business.

The broker who contemplates such a location will usually find it worthwhile to employ a local architect to design his building and to assist in the planning of the landscaping.

Some brokers who operate in and around business subcenters have purchased retail store property in which to locate their offices. A vacant retail store, or two adjacent retail stores, can often be remodeled to furnish excellent office facilities. The store windows provide good display space for showing photographs of properties the office has for sale or rent. These windows can be decorated attractively and draw many passers-by inside for information. If the gross floor area is adequate, the interior can be laid out into a reception area, a general office, and as many private offices as may be required. Careful attention should be given to the furnishings and decorations. The office interiors should be designed to convey an atmosphere of success and well-being.

Membership in associations and other organizations

The broker should seek membership in such organizations as the local real estate board, the state real estate association and the National Association of Real Estate Boards, the chamber of commerce, businessmen's luncheon clubs, a church of his choice, and, possibly, other important organizations dedicated to high standards of community life.

There are two major reasons why this is good policy. One reason is that the personal contacts that can be made through memberships can be a fruitful source of new business. A considerable volume of important business is being developed by real estate brokers through personal contacts with key personalities in their territories. Close association with fellow brokers and with specialists in the allied fields of appraising, property management, real estate finance, construction, and property insurance gives the broker valuable opportunities to make himself favorably known to such men and to develop their respect and confidence in his ability and competency. Wider contacts can be established through memberships in church, fraternal, civic, and neighborhood groups, including the PTA, lodges, property owners' associations, and other such organizations. If possible, the broker's firm should be represented in each important organization either by himself or by a principal officer of his firm or by a key employee of the firm.

So, from a purely selfish standpoint, it is good policy to establish and maintain these contacts and become known as an active participant in various community programs.

Such memberships are good policy because the broker, as a member of an organized vocation, owes a duty, both morally and ethically, to support them. This is especially true of the local real estate board and the state and national associations of real estate boards. These organizations are dedicated to the preservation of private property rights, to the up-building of their respective communities, and to the development of high standards of real estate practice and ethics. Their goals can be reached only by the unselfish and earnest teamwork of the members of the vocation. The broker has a duty to help in this important work by paying membership dues and by taking part in committee activities.

The broker's reference library

Nothing in the world—or the universe itself—is static. Changes are taking place constantly. Some changes are slow—evolutionary —almost imperceptible. Other changes are rapid—dramatic—revolutionary. Every community is at all times in a state of transition. So is the real estate vocation. It is profoundly affected by shifts in social standards, in economic trends, and in new political programs. It is affected also by the development of new techniques in real estate practice.

To achieve success and to maintain it, the broker must have

up-to-date information about these changes—where they are taking place. Why and at what rate? This means that he should equip himself with reliable bulletin services, with local newspapers and magazines, and with current books dealing with real estate. He should scan all such publications and study carefully the more critical developments reported in them. He should have and make use of a complete real estate library.

A further source of valuable information and ideas for new business can be found in the programs at real estate board meetings, at the annual conventions of the various state and national associations, and in the seminars and conferences on real estate subjects conducted by local, state, and the National Association of Real Estate Boards and by its various specialized institutes. These meetings are so numerous that the broker will not be able personally to attend them all, but he can see to it that his firm is represented at each such meeting by a partner, an officer of his corporation, or by one of his key employees. The information secured at each such meeting can be reported and discussed after the meeting is over.

CHAPTER SEVEN

Organization and equipment of the broker's office

The overall size of the broker's office is determined by the character and volume of activities to be conducted in it. Among the controlling principles to be observed in planning the size and layout of the office, especial attention should be given to the following:

1. Adequate working space for all officers and all employees
2. Adequate space for furniture, equipment, and supplies, with convenient access to all items
3. Convenient and comfortable working conditions
4. Furniture and decor designed to inspire the pride of all office personnel and to generate respect and confidence in clients and customers.

If the broker operates as a lone individual, he will need only a small office, consisting of a private room for himself, space and equipment for his secretary, and a small area for his files and other equipment. But if he conducts a departmentalized business and has salesmen and other specialists in his employ, he may need to have considerable floor space including several private offices and a great deal of appropriate equipment.

Some brokers prefer to limit private offices to the principal officers of the firm and to provide facilities for all employees, salesmen, and files in a large room serving as a general office. This policy has some advantages if the general office area is spacious enough to prevent crowding, to provide proper privacy for each desk, and is closely supervised by a competent office manager. But it has disadvantages since it does sacrifice privacy to a greater or lesser degree and makes it difficult to minimize distractions.

There are many successful brokers who are convinced that greater economy and efficiency of operations can be attained only if private offices are provided for all department heads and officers and for all key salesmen as well. They often limit the occupancy of the general office area to typists, clerks, stenographers, and files.

In planning the layout and equipment of a new office, consideration should be given to how many square feet of floor space to provide for each desk and for each officer, department head, salesman, and other employees. Some offices provide as little as 70 square feet of floor area per desk and as little as 50 square feet of floor area per employee. Other offices provide as much as 225 square feet of floor area per desk and 300 square feet per employee. These are extremes. The typical office provides about 130 square feet per desk and 125 square feet per employee. The aims should be to provide adequate space to permit freedom of movement and to keep employees far enough apart so that they do not interfere with each other in their work or waste time in extraneous conversations.

In addition to the providing of adequate work space for the various members and employees of the firm, good management of operations is concerned with the layout of functions within the office. Efficiency of operations is closely related to the flow of work from day to day and from hour to hour. The relative locations of receptionist, salesmen, clerks, typists, secretaries, files, interoffice communication equipment, conference room, supplies, and private offices can either hamper or expedite the flow of work. Everything should be placed in such a way as to facilitate movement and communication and to minimize waste of time and effort. Except in small offices it is often good economy to install an intercom system between the desks of the receptionist, the principal officers, and the key employees.

The reception area

First impressions are important. An individual who steps in the broker's office for the first time is either favorably or unfavorably impressed by what he sees and hears. The reception he gets and the atmosphere in which he receives it will condition his attitude positively or negatively toward the firm. This first impression is likely to be vivid and be long remembered. It may tend to arouse respect for and confidence in the firm or it may give rise to doubts that are difficult to overcome.

For these reasons, especial care should be taken in the planning and operation of the reception area. Ideally it should be in a separate room and not in an open space as part of the general office. It should be large enough to provide room for a switchboard, the receptionist's desk and chair, a table on which to keep copies of current newspapers and magazines, and chairs for callers who have to wait for interviews. The receptionist can double as a switchboard operator and typist. She must be neatly and tastefully dressed, attractive in appearance, friendly, and cheerful. Her personality is of prime importance.

The floor may be tiled or be covered by a rug or carpet, but whatever the material, it should be of top quality and be attractive in appearance. It should be kept conspicuously clean and fresh. It should be replaced as soon as it shows obvious signs of wear.

The walls and ceiling should be painted or papered in attractive colors, either plain or patterned. Appropriate pictures should be on the wall. Maps, especially aerial photographic maps of the local city or of sections of the local city, can add much to the attractiveness of the reception area.

The tables, the chairs, and the lighting fixtures should be pleasing in appearance. Extremes should be avoided. Coordination and unity should be the controlling principles in the selection of furnishings and decor.

Some brokers believe that it helps to develop a home-buying frame of mind to make the reception area in their offices resemble a living room in a private home. In such cases no office equipment is in sight. The room is carpeted. Davenports and overstuffed chairs are in evidence. There are tables and table lamps and floor lamps, but no overhead lighting. Such brokers have found that the homey atmosphere of the reception area does not hamper discussion of business matters with clients and customers. It tends to put them at ease during the initial interview and develop a favorable attitude that carries over when the discussions are transferred to one of the private offices or to the conference room.

Conference and closing room

Efficient operation of a brokerage business is sometimes aided by reserving one fair-sized room in the office suite for a conference room and closing room. Many deals involve several individuals. It may be, and usually is, necessary to get them together to discuss and agree upon some of the details of the transaction. Such conferences are often necessary in the planning of a project requiring the attendance of attorneys, sellers, buyers, and moneylenders. The closing of a deal usually requires the presence of several persons. They might be sellers, buyers, and their wives. Sometimes, also, it is necessary to have attorneys, moneylenders, and escrow agents present.

It is difficult to hold such meetings in the broker's private office unless it is large enough to contain a conference table and chairs for all in attendance. Conferences of such types should not be subject to interruptions or distractions. Privacy and noninterference are more likely to be secured in a separate conference room. Also, an appropriately equipped and attractive conference room can exert favorable psychological influences upon the persons who meet in it. It is good business policy to strive to achieve such an effect.

Ideally, the conference table should be of sturdy construction and large enough to seat 10 or 12 persons comfortably. The chairs should be comfortable also. The chairs known as captain armchairs are ideal.

To insure privacy in the conference room, some brokers do not include a telephone or an intercom connection in its equipment. An up-to-date large-scale map of the local area can be useful in conference and closing sessions.

Private offices

It is possible, of course, to do business in the general office if it is large enough to accommodate all needed desks, files, tables, chairs, and other equipment. But such a setup is poor economy since it sets the stage for confusion, distractions, loss of time, and interruptions. The modern broker who realizes the dollar-and-cents value of psychological influences upon officers and employees as well as upon clients and customers will provide the best possible working conditions in his office. This may mean a private office not only for each officer and department head but also for each salesman.

Each officer and each department head spends a sizable part of his working day in his office. He has a better attitude toward his job and can perform his duties more effectively if he feels a justifiable pride in his office and is glad to have it seen by clients, customers, close relatives, and friends. In a professional spirit he will equip his private office with attractive furnishings—one or more bookcases containing a professional reference library of his own, pictures on the wall, a wall map, perhaps, and possibly one or more "conversation" pieces such as a mounted game fish or something that reflects his chief hobby and may serve to "break the ice" for a friendly conversation with callers.

Some brokers have found that it pays to provide private offices for their key salesmen. The relationship between the salesman and his client or customer is a personal one. It usually involves some confidential information or personal problems which the client or customer is reluctant to have overheard by individuals who are not immediate parties to the transaction. In a private office the client and the customer can feel free to talk confidentially. Interviews are free from distraction. This may be important in leading the caller to the decision that the salesman wants made. An attractive private office tends to keep the salesman's morale high and stimulates him to put forth his best efforts to achieve a record number of sales.

Files

No equipment in the broker's office is more important than the files. They constitute a framework on and through which the entire office system depends. Multitudinous details intermittently come to the attention of the broker and to other members of the staff. They include emerging opportunities for current new business, various significant clues for future business, and items to be checked and followed up on past deals. Neither the broker nor any other member of the staff can keep all of these matters accurately in mind. That is not necessary, anyway, if there is a properly organized and efficiently maintained filing system. Such a system will make it possible quickly to review the history of any listing, any prospect, and the activity of each salesman. It will help the broker maintain a continuous control over budgetary matters and furnish information needed in the making of executive decisions in many different directions. Also the files can be made to be a rich depository of data that can be used in developing brokerage deals.

In the chapters on the executive control of listings and the executive control of prospects we shall discuss the detailed functions that the prospect and listing file can serve. At this point we shall limit discussion to the physical equipment of the filing section of the office.

The office must provide enough floor space for needed filing equipment. It should provide, in addition, a reasonable surplus space for expansion of the files as business volume increases. The files need not be given a prominent place in the office. They can be isolated in a remote area or be kept in a separate room. In the beginning, only a few files and a small floor area will be required. Their maintenance and operation, at first, will not require a full-time file clerk. The work can be done by the broker's secretary or by some other member of the clerical staff. The files should not be open to everyone in the office. The responsibility for placing material in the files and of taking material out of them should be limited to one person who is supervised by the broker himself or by the office manager if the firm and its activities are large enough to merit such an employee.

The filing equipment may include provisions for:

1. A listing file, with subdivisions
2. A prospect file, with subdivisions
3. A map file
4. An appraisal report file
5. A property brief file
6. A completed deal file
7. Bookkeeping files
8. "For Sale" signs file

9. "Sold" signs file
10. Cross-reference files
11. Stock files for forms of various kinds
12. Newspaper ads and clippings

The equipment may include four-drawer, or five-drawer letter files, files for legal documents, 3 x 5 card files, 4 x 6 card files, 5 x 8 card files, map files, and shelves on which to stack office supplies, forms, and other material needed in day-to-day operations.

Maps

Every broker's office should have at all times a substantial supply of maps of various kinds. Maps can be helpful to the broker and to members of his staff in many different ways. They can be useful in making economic surveys, in highest and best use studies, in the analysis of the various types of real estate markets, in securing listings at saleable prices, in presenting properties to prospective purchasers and lessees, and in many other ways. They can be convincing illustrations in sales briefs and in appraisal reports. They are valuable additions to the sales kits carried by the salesmen.

The broker will decide what maps should be used by his firm. He will determine how they are to be used. He will purchase them or have them made and printed. He will probably make his file clerk responsible for keeping them and disbursing them upon requisition to members of his firm.

A great variety of maps can be used in real estate brokerage. They include outline maps, zoning maps, ownership maps, occupancy maps, strip maps, street maps, soil maps, and many other types.

Outline maps are especially useful. They should be printed in black and white and should be drawn on a large enough scale to show every property in the area covered by the map. A series of such maps can cover the entire territory in which the broker operates. Many different kinds of useful data can be recorded on an outline map. Such data includes listings, properties that have been sold, rental data, lease expirations, properties listed by other brokers, and any other data which the broker deems significant to his operations.

Zoning maps may be available at the office of the local zoning authority, but one large zoning wall map at some appropriate place in the office may suffice. Zoning information can be shown on the black-and-white outline maps by cross-hatching or coloring the various areas.

In seeking locations for clients who want to build, it is important to know who owns vacant sites in the area and who owns sites that are not in their highest and best use. Properties that are in weak ownership, that are not currently on the market, but that are likely to be on the market within a year or so may be thought of as "critical" properties. The alert broker will watch such properties and try to figure out in advance where and how to find buyers for them when they do come onto the market. All such information can be shown on an ownership map and be available for quick reference and study from time to time as needed. They are not only time savers, they are also potent stimulators to creative thinking.

The principle of balance controls sound community development and the maintenance of property values. This means that the utilization of land in the area should be, in fact, it does tend to be, in equilibrium. Imbalance in utilization or occupancy immediately creates an opportunity for one or more brokerage deals. A map showing occupancy of every site in the area furnishes the basis for creative thinking on the part of the broker and may enable him to develop listings and make sales.

Strip maps are especially useful in dealing with retail store properties. Such a map is usually confined to just one street and shows every property on both sides of the street for from one or more blocks. It can show lot dimensions, names of occupants, types of stores, front-foot or square-foot rentals, lease expirations, ownership, and other matters deemed by the broker to be significant and of possible future value.

A general map of the area can show streets, lines of public transportation, schools, churches, recreational centers, racial distribution, and other data likely to be of interest to clients and customers and to members of the broker's firm.

Recording machines

Dictating machines are valuable items of equipment in busy offices. They are great conveniences in the office when stenographers are not immediately available. Often the busy broker or salesman finds it necessary to do paper work outside of office hours when there is no stenographer on duty. Letters, advertising drafts, or reports, can be put on a dictating machine and transcribed the following day by a typist. Some models of such machines can be carried into the field to make an on-the-spot recording of a full report while, or immediately after, checking the property to be sure that no significant detail is overlooked.

Some of these machines can double for the dictating of letters and reports and for recording conferences, discussions, and oral agreements later to be transcribed in typewritten form for the signatures of the parties concerned.

Duplicating equipment

It is frequently desirable, or even necessary, to get one or more duplicate copies of a letter, a memorandum, a bulletin, an advertisement, a report, an office form, or some longhand, typewritten, or printed material.

Reproductions can be made by a Mimeograph or similar machine that reproduces from prepared stencils. There are, however, also several machines on the market that will reproduce handwritten copy, typewritten copy, printed copy, photographs, and maps without the use of stencils. Such equipment secures good reproductions quickly and inexpensively.

Typewriters

It goes without saying that the broker's office should be equipped with an adequate number of good typewriters. It is also a good plan to have one or more portable typewriters for use outside the office.

Although the initial investment is higher, it is good policy to equip the office with electric typewriters. The electric machines usually make cleaner, more readable copy, straighter side margins, and have superior qualities for the cutting of stencils and for the making of a greater number of carbon copies.

Adding machines and comptometers

Many situations arise in the broker's office that involve arithmetical operations. Some of these may be lengthy and complicated. A good adding machine or a comptometer can save much time in making calculations and in avoiding costly errors.

Cameras and photographs

The alert broker will make extensive use of photographs. He should have photographs of every property he lists for sale, every property he serves as manager, every property he appraises, and every property on which he seeks to secure a mortgage loan.

These photographs, depending somewhat on the use to which they are to be put, may include front, rear, and side views of improvements; yards and landscaping; street views showing neighboring properties; interiors; comparable properties that are factors in appraisals or in the making of sales.

One or more high-grade cameras should be available for the taking of such pictures. At least one member of the firm should be skilled in the use of the cameras, in the development of the films, and in the printing of the pictures. If a Polaroid Land camera is used, several shots should be made of each view, or the office should be equipped with a Polaroid copier for making reproductions.

Signs

There are at least three kinds of signs that the broker will find useful. One of these is the "For Sale" sign. The sign should have the words "For Sale" in large letters; give the name and address and phone number of the broker; and, maybe, the words "Shown only by appointment." If the broker has a special emblem or slogan to identify his firm, it should be shown on the sign. Another sign that has good publicity value is the "Sold" sign. This sign should be placed on properties that the broker has sold and should be left on display for a limited period of time. The "For Sale" sign should be displayed with the prior consent of the seller, and the "Sold" sign should not be displayed without the consent of both seller and buyer.

"Vacancy" and "For Rent" signs are used by managers to let the public know that the property as a whole or that one or more units in the property are available for rent.

The purpose of all these signs is to attract attention—favorable attention—suggest action, and publicize the name of the broker. Each sign should bear the broker's name, his address, his phone number, and his emblem or slogan, if he has one. They should be clean, new looking, legible, neat, and use appropriate colors. They should be checked from time to time to be sure that they are in place, have not been defaced, and still have an attractive appearance.

An adequate supply of signs should be maintained in the office and kept in spic-and-span condition. To facilitate keeping track of them, they can be numbered and be checked out on requisitions. A record should be kept of the names of the individuals to whom the signs are issued and the addresses at which they are displayed. This can be the responsibility of the chief file clerk.

Library

An extremely valuable addition to the office equipment is a library of real estate literature and reference material. It is good management and executive policy and a good investment to build up a fairly complete real estate library in the broker's office. Most alert members of the firm will own and use personal libraries, but few of these individuals will be able to buy a complete stock of books or subscribe to all of the letter and bulletin services that are available.

The National Association of Real Estate Boards maintains a complete real estate library and is able and willing to supply brokers with up-to-date lists of available books and services. Such materials can be purchased from or through the book department of the Association.

There are excellent books available on selling, advertising, financing, management, construction, appraisals, real estate law, and other phases of the real estate business. In addition, there are several letter and bulletin services that publish significant news items and new ideas useful in developing deals and in managing brokerage operations. Such publications cover cost trends, building and sales trends, tax information, general business trends, and many other matters about which the broker and his staff should be constantly aware.

The library in the broker's office should be well-organized, indexed, and cross-indexed, and operated in accordance with modern library policies and procedures. Its contents should be listed in a mimeographed bulletin for the information of all members of the firm. New additions to the library should be promptly reported to all members of the firm. Rules governing the use of the library should be developed and copies placed in the hands of everyone in the office as well as displayed on the library bulletin board. Someone in the office should be designated as librarian and should keep a faithful record of the circulation of its contents.

Forms

It is difficult to operate a brokerage business without forms. Some of these can be standard forms that are in general use in the area and that can be procured from a local office supply agency, or that can be secured by mail from a source outside the local area. Other forms to fit special needs and conform to the broker's policies can be developed by him and be reproduced by a local printer or in his own office by the Mimeograph or other suitable reproduction device. Such forms include, but are by no means limited to:

1. Abstract receipt
2. Closing statement for seller
3. Closing statement for buyer
4. Closing worksheet
5. Direct-mail record card
6. Escrow receipt
7. Expense analysis sheet
8. Listing contract
9. Listing expiration card
10. Listing inspection report
11. New neighbor card
12. New neighbor letter
13. Newspaper advertising record sheet
14. Advertising schedule form
15. Offer to purchase form

16. Prospect card
17. Sign location card
18. Telephone call slip
19. Management agreement form
20. Salesman's report form
21. Contract for deed form
22. Report to owner forms
23. Requisition forms.

All forms should be given an identifying number. A list of all available forms should be reproduced and placed in the hands of all members of the firm. They can be disbursed upon requisition by the chief file clerk or the librarian.

The office manual

It is good management policy, even in small offices, to develop and adopt an office manual. See pages 95-98 for the important details about this.

CHAPTER EIGHT

Office personnel

The real estate broker has nothing to sell except personal services. Although his services are personal in character, he can rarely work alone. He must be able to analyze buyers and sellers, he must be able to understand them, he must be able to help them make decisions—the right decisions for them as well as for himself. Equally important he must get them to work with him. He works with people—not with real estate.

Except in isolated cases, the broker needs the help of one or more members of his office staff. His success in the long run depends upon the intelligent, competent, and loyal cooperation of office employees. Receptionists, secretaries, clerks, telephone operators, and others in the office are all members of his team. Each employee is either an asset or a liability. In a real sense, he is dependent upon his office personnel. They can make him or break him. They can make substantial contributions to the development of new business. They can be influential in the retention of clients and customers. They help to build good will and respect, or they tear down confidence in the competency and dependability of the firm.

Employees who are inefficient, who are discourteous, who are disloyal, who are not thoroughly sold on their jobs, are prone to make costly mistakes. They impair the confidence of the public in the competency and reliability of the firm. They alienate both clients and customers. They exert a deteriorating influence on other members of the office staff.

A lackadaisical or discourteous attitude on the part of the receptionist or the telephone operator, for example, is an effective deterrent to new business. Such an employee creates ill will on the part of clients and customers already being served by the firm. Even one loss from such a cause may be more in dollars and cents than the entire salary of the guilty employee for several years. No broker can afford to take chances with any but top-notch personnel in the reception area. The same is true of file clerks, bookkeepers, and other employees whose services must be depended upon for prompt and accurate performance of the duties assigned to them. Errors in bookkeeping and financial statements or in legal documents, misplaced files, poorly maintained office equipment, messy appearance of desks, inappropriate or slovenly dress—all are prolific breeders of disrespect and indifferent attitudes. Such conditions are money losers and should not be tolerated by the executive who is responsible for the effective operation of the business.

Sources of new employees

When a new position is created in the office, or when a vacancy occurs in an established position, it may be possible to fill it by promoting and advancing some one who is already an employee of the firm. This makes it necessary to find a new employee to fill the vacancy created by the transfer, but this is often the best policy. Upward movement within the office staff is an important means of developing and maintaining morale. *Esprit de corps* is a valuable factor in promoting long-range personnel satisfaction.

Most employees have a circle of friends and acquaintances outside the firm with similar educational and experience backgrounds. One or more of these may have the qualifications needed for the position to be filled and may be interested in the job. It is often good procedure, therefore, to seek the help of existing personnel in finding a new employee.

Help-wanted ads in the newspapers is another source of employees. Ads should be specific in stating the requirements for the position so as to assist in weeding out unqualified applicants. This is not usually a good source, since persons who read help-wanted ads in searching for a job are either unemployed or are dissatisfied with the jobs they have. Unemployed but experienced persons may have been let out of their latest positions for inefficiency or some other detrimental reason. Employed persons responding to help-wanted ads are dissatisfied with their present positions, and perhaps not for good reasons. Often the readers of help-wanted ads are persons who are never satisfied but are always looking for "greener pastures." Such a person is unlikely to become a permanent employee of the broker but will leave at the first opportunity to graze in a greener pasture. Employee turnover is time-consuming because of interviewing and training and is otherwise expensive. It should be avoided if at all possible.

Employment agencies are another source of new employees, but persons who register with employment agencies are in much the same category as readers of help-wanted ads. They are often chronic job-changers. This, of course, is not true of all persons who read help-wanted ads or who register with employment agencies, but the fact that it is true of many, makes it advisable for the broker to be careful in his investigation of applicants from either of these two sources. When seeking the help of an employment agency in finding new personnel, the broker should interview the job counsellor at the agency to make his requirements perfectly clear and to insist that each referral is one that conforms to the job specifications as to experience, education, personality, salary expectations, etc.

Probably the best-qualified person for the new job or replacement is already employed in an allied field and not looking for a change of employment but willing to consider an attractive offer. It is not recommended that the broker pursue a policy of pirating the employees of competing brokers, but if he can offer working conditions and a salary that are substantially more desirable and the position he wishes to fill is a permanent one, he should give the matter appropriate and careful consideration. The broker is a business man usually faced by spirited and competent competition. Without being unethical, he must do the best he can to build and keep a highly efficient working staff.

The broker should always keep in mind that each employee is a person, a human being who has cost-of-living expenses, who is striving for economic security, who is devoting a large share of his or her life to the job—an indispensible member of the broker's business team, and entitled to sympathetic understanding and assistance in shaping a successful career. The broker has an ethical and moral obligation to each employee.

Selection of new employees

It is important in the saving of time and money to contact fruitful sources of new personnel when a position in the office is to be filled. Of even greater importance is the selection of the best-qualified person for the job from among applicants furnished by these sources.

First of all, each person seeking employment with the firm should be required to fill out and file a detailed application form. This form should include such items as:

1. Name in full
2. Address
3. Phone number
4. Place and date of birth
5. National origin
6. Number and ages of dependents
7. Academic record
    a. Grade school
    b. High school
    c. College
    d. Major sequence of college subjects and degrees
    e. Extracurricular activities while in college
8. A full chronological record of employment since leaving school
    a. Name and address of employer
    b. Positions held and duties
    c. Salaries received
    d. Reason for leaving each job
9. Church affiliation and activities
10. Club memberships and activities
11. Hobbies
12. Starting salary expected
13. Earliest date available for work
14. Comments.

In addition to the filing of a formal detailed application, it is desirable to require the applicant to write a covering letter to supplement and amplify the information given on the form. A letter can do much to reveal the personality, attitude, ambition, and ability in self-expression of the applicant.

A satisfactory personal interview should be an indispensable prerequisite for employment. One feature of this interview should be a review of the information given on the application form. Another feature should be a review of the duties to be performed. This enables the applicant to decide whether he or she is qualified to do the work. Office policy pertaining to the job should be stated and explained. This includes rules governing vacations, sick leave, overtime, coffee breaks, office hours, health insurance, social security and income tax deductions, paydays, and promotion schedule. An interview gives the employing officer the opportunity to note the reactions of the applicant to the various duties involved in the job, the dress and grooming of the applicant, the attitude of the applicant, and the applicant's personality and facility of speech. He must decide whether the applicant is a person who is likely to "fit in" with his office staff—whether conformity and cooperation can be expected or whether there is a likelihood of a clash of personalities. He should make it clear that the job is for life and not a temporary job. Unless he is convinced that the applicant wants a permanent connection, he should terminate the interview and seek someone else for the job.

It is often good policy to interview the applicant a second time before deciding to offer employment. This second interview, in many instances, should be in the applicant's home, to note standard of living, and the manner in which the home is maintained. Home conditions exert a powerful influence upon the attitude, ambition, and personality of the individual. They also reflect his or her tastes, attitudes, and personality. All of these matters may be important factors in harmonious office relationships and in the personal relationship between the employee and the broker.

Training and supervision

It is essential that the new employee be properly oriented and instructed in the duties to be performed, in office policy, in lines of authority, and in procedures to be followed. It is good management to have a standard operating procedure for each job insofar as possible. This should list in proper sequence the various steps to be taken in carrying out each project for which the employee is responsible. It should be in typewritten form, including a "flow chart" if possible. A copy should be maintained in the master office manual and a copy should be at the desk of the employee for quick reference as needed.

Ordinarily, the new employee should be given one day or more after reporting for duty to study the standard operating procedure, to become acquainted with the office staff, to learn the office geography of equipment and personnel, and to receive necessary instruction. This will require the close personal attention of the broker, or of the office manager, or of some other member of the staff who is properly qualified to give the instruction. The instruction given to the new employee should not be of the hit-and-miss or haphazard variety. It should be carefully planned in advance, systematic, and thorough. Instruction and training is time-consuming at the beginning of the employee's period of service, but it saves time in the long run. It forestalls interruptions to answer questions, to explain procedures, and to give demonstrations from time to time. Also it is insurance against errors, which may be costly, and against personal embarrassments.

The broker might well have a personal conference with each employee—and especially with new employees—on a regular periodic basis to discuss personal office problems and performance of duties. Conferences are valuable in maintaining morale and personal efficiency. They help to iron out misunderstandings and personality conflicts before they become insurmountably serious. A staff conference of the entire office force at least once a month, or once each week, is good office management policy. At such staff conferences, each employee reports on current status of work underway so that all employees are fully informed on activities and are better able to function as an integrated team. At these meetings, opportunities are afforded for helpful suggestions on baffling problems that may arise from time to time.

Employee records

It is suggested that the broker or the office manager—if there is one—keep and maintain an up-to-date confidential personnel file on each office employee. Included in this file will be the original application, reference letters, and a sheet or large card on which is kept a chronological service record. This record may include such items as the following:

1. Date of original employment
2. Starting salary
3. Dates and amounts of pay increases
4. Dates of vacations taken
5. Dates and amount of overtime
6. Dates and duration of sick leaves
7. Date of entry into the retirement pension plan, if any
8. Record of entry into and payments on group health insurance
9. Social security number
10. Deductions from salary for social security, income tax withholding, etc.
11. Efficiency rating

Office rules

No office can function well on a haphazard basis. Neither can it operate efficiently if rigidly regimented to set routines. Unexpected emergencies will arise. New business opportunities for which advance preparations could not be made may suddenly appear. Office procedures must be flexible and adjustable, but they should be systematized and conducted in reasonable conformity to established rules set forth in the office manual. These rules may include:

1. Specific hours for opening and closing the office. A rigid time-clock system is not required. The broker's office is not a factory, and his employees are not paid on an hourly basis. But it is good management to require all employees to sign in and out on a daily register kept on the desk of the receptionist. Under some conditions this might apply to the lunch hour and to coffee breaks. An in-and-out register tends to keep all employees alert to duties. It identifies individuals who are habitually late in arriving to work and who squander time during lunch and coffee breaks.

2. Rules concerning overtime. A record of overtime spent by each employee should be kept. It is the basis for overtime compensation and may be required by law. Over a period of time such a record may reveal a need for extra part-time or full-time employees. It may reveal the fact that an individual employee who piles up a continual record of overtime is a dilatory worker during office hours or deliberately works slowly in order to augment salary payments with compensation for overtime.
3. There must be a definite rule respecting the lunch hour. A specific time should be set, if feasible, for each employee to go to lunch and return to work. No variation should be permitted, except by approval of the office manager. In order to ensure the presence of an adequate skeleton office staff during the noon hour, staggered time periods should be set up and apportioned among individual employees. A record should be made by the receptionist or telephone operator of all telephone calls and personal callers coming in to individual employees who are out to lunch and brought to their immediate attention when they return to the office.
4. Many offices now permit employees to take coffee breaks in the forenoon and in the afternoon. Such brief periods of relaxation and refreshment make for efficiency and are good for office morale. When such a policy is in force, care must be taken to see that it is not abused. The entire office force should not, ordinarily, take a coffee break at the same time. The time allowed for such a recess should be limited to not more than a certain number of minutes and should be scheduled in such a way as to avoid bringing the work of the entire office to a standstill.
5. Every employee is subject to illness. Except in periods of epidemic it is likely that only one or two will be sick at the same time. But over a long period of time it is probable that no member of the office staff will escape brief absences due to illness. A sick person is certainly not up to par efficiency as a worker. Furthermore, if the illness is of the contagious kind, there is danger that it may be spread throughout the office. The employee who becomes sick should be relieved from duty and stay home until well enough to return to work. Short periods of illness should not result in docking of pay, unless

chronic and sufficiently frequent seriously to jeopardize the work. In such a situation, the employee, if a good one, might be given an extended leave of absence without pay. Rules governing sick leave are not easy to draw or to administer, but there should be such rules and they should be stated in the office manual. Enough elasticity in the administration of these rules should be permitted to avoid unfairness either to the employee or to the firm.

6. In general, it may be said that vacations are indispensable to the health, efficiency, and morale of the office worker. The length of the vacation is usually related to the years of service. It seems to be general policy to grant a two-week vacation at the end of each of the first 5 to 10 years of employment, three weeks at the end of each subsequent year of service up to 15 or 20 years, and four weeks per year thereafter. The policy varies with different firms. Whatever it is, it should be clear-cut and stated in the office manual. Some employees whose duties have made it necessary to work overtime prefer an extension of their vacations, equal to the overtime served, in lieu of monetary compensation.

7. Manuals are especially valuable for the instruction and guidance of new employees. Since memories are often faulty, office manuals are valuable references for veteran employees and officers of the firm. This is especially true of matters that arise infrequently. Manuals help to prevent misunderstandings and in resolving controversies. They serve to keep all members of the office team on the beam and in harmony with each other and with their employer.

Office manuals are likely to be growing documents. They are sure to need additions and revisions from time to time. Parts may become obsolete, outdated, no longer necessary. These parts should be deleted. No manual is apt to be perfect in the first draft. It must be lived with and adapted to the growth of the firm, to changing times, and to improvements in procedures and policies.

The manual may be typewritten or mimeographed. It should be loose-leaf, neat, clear, and attractively put together. It should be easy to revise, part by part, and every member of the office staff should have a copy.

The contents of the manual should include:

1. A clear statement of the basic policies of the firm
2. Standard operating procedures for each type of work
3. Job specifications for each position in the firm
4. Rules governing office hours, lunch periods, coffee breaks, vacations, sick leave, overtime, personal use of the telephone, and other matters about which questions arise from time to time
5. Storage, requisition, and use of supplies, equipment, and signs
6. Office housekeeping rules
7. Names, addresses, and phone numbers of local, state, and federal officials with whom the firm maintains business contacts
8. Vacation schedules
9. Names, addresses, and phone numbers of all members of the firm
10. Miscellaneous data that may be needed from time to time for reference purposes.

Incentives and morale

Salaries

Self-preservation (the desire for personal security) is a basic instinct. It is a strong motivating force in the life of every person. It exerts a controlling influence upon the individual in choosing a career, in accepting a job, and in staying in a position. The employee wants and must have an income that is sufficient to meet necessary living expenses, and, if possible, sufficient to cover the cost of recreation, amusements, social activities, and savings. For this reason, the individual, ordinarily, will not accept a position that pays a lower salary than can be secured elsewhere, or that does not offer a reasonable prospect for advancement. If the salary is not in conformity with the employee's standard of living or if the position offers no prospects of advancement, the employee will consider the job a temporary one and will be constantly alert to find a more satisfactory position elsewhere.

For these reasons, starting salaries and pay increases should conform to local market standards. In fact, it is good business policy to pay salaries somewhat above the general local level of salary schedules. This cuts down employee turnover and is a potent factor in maintaining loyalty and morale.

The broker-executive can secure from the government an authentic official salary schedule for civil service employees. From local employment agencies and other sources he can secure salary ranges that are current for various types of jobs.

In the light of current market conditions for employment, the broker-executive should establish a minimum-maximum salary range for each job in his office. This should be reviewed annually and revised to conform to changed conditions. It is good policy to start a new employee at the lowest level consistent with the market and grant a reasonable pay increase each year until the maximum level for the job in question has been reached.

Health and hospital insurance

There are many sources from which group health and hospital insurance can be secured. Group life insurance also is available. One of the best of these is sponsored by and can be secured through the National Association of Real Estate Boards. In addition, there is the Blue Cross and the Blue Shield, as well as group policies written by several of the well-established insurance companies doing a nationwide business.

Every broker's office should have group insurance if it is able to qualify. It is an inducement in attracting serious-minded employees, and it helps to maintain their sense of security. The premiums on such policies are met in part by deductions from the salaries of the employees and in a larger part by contributions of the employer.

Retirement insurance

It is to the best interest of the brokerage firm to keep good employees as permanent members of the office staff. One of the most powerful inducements to get employees to stay with the firm permanently is a good retirement insurance plan. Group insurance of this type is available from several different companies. A part of the premium is deducted from the salaries of the employees who enter the plan, and the balance (usually about twice as much) is paid by the employer.

Other morale-building devices

A spirit of comradeship is important in developing loyalty and teamwork. Any brokerage firm that lacks *esprit de corps* in its office force is on a shaky footing and at a tremendous disadvantage in competing with other brokers in the area. There are many different ways of creating and maintaining this valuable asset. Reliance should not rest on any one of them. As many as possible should be used. Among them are:

1. Office membership in a bowling league
2. Office teams in marathon bridge tournaments
3. Annual outings, planned and conducted by the employees
4. Christmas parties
5. Annual bonuses
6. Flowers and messages to sick employees, plus a personal visit by the broker if the illness continues for a week or more
7. Birthday cards
8. Appropriate recognition of births, marriages, deaths, and other important occurrences in the families of employees
9. Office bulletins or house organs containing news and snapshots of employees
10. Luncheon celebrations of employment anniversaries with appropriate gifts from the firm, say at the end of 5-year, 10-year, or longer periods of employment service.

There is nothing more important in developing loyalty and maintaining employee satisfaction than the knowledge on the part of the employee that good work is appreciated by the broker. Commendation should be quickly given for work especially well done. Also it pays rich dividends in employee satisfaction if the employer shows a friendly interest in the personal work and out-of-the-office problems of his employees. He should make it a point each day to greet each employee with a cordial salutation and take the time for a brief friendly chat whenever possible.

CHAPTER NINE

Selection of salesmen

Importance of selection

Except in the small one-man real estate brokerage office, good salesmen constitute the broker's most valuable asset. Without sales, there will be no income. Without income, the broker cannot stay in business. The broker himself can and will make sales, but substantial income, ordinarily, is dependent upon substantial sales volume. Except for the completion of transactions on extremely high-valued properties, this can be achieved only through the productive efforts of salesmen to supplement the work of the broker.

Good salesmen, except in a static market, make a lucrative income for themselves and in doing so add to the net income of the broker. Poor salesmen, as a rule, are economic failures. They are soon forced by lack of income to leave the firm and seek employment in some other field of endeavor. They are a liability to the broker. Their productivity may not be enough to cover overhead costs of desk space, telephone charges, drawing accounts, and the valuable time spent in training and supervising them. Moreover, their ineffective and perhaps unethical activities may bring disrepute upon the firm. The salesman is the personal representative of the firm. In the eyes of the client or customer, he is the firm. For these reasons, the broker cannot afford to employ incompetent or unethical salesmen or to keep such salesmen in his firm. He must use special care to employ top-notch salesmen and to discharge those who are incompetent and cannot or will not conform to his standards.

Sources of new salesmen

The finding and employment of good salesmen is one of the broker's most difficult problems. When he needs or wants a new salesman, he must consider the sources from which they might be found. There are at least six such sources.

Unsolicited applications in the broker's "Hold" file are one source. In most urban areas there are apt to be several individuals who for one reason or another desire a career in real estate selling and who take the initiative in seeking employment. They are likely to seek personal interviews with brokers in the area. When no position is open at the time and the applicant seems to have a good potential, he is usually asked to file an application for future consideration. Others may not come to the office in person but may write letters to the broker, asking for an interview or actually applying for a position. Sometimes a really good salesman comes to the broker in this way. Letters and applications from individuals seeking careers in real estate selling should be kept in the broker's "Prospective Salesmen" file and should be reviewed when the need for new sales personnel arises.

Responses to advertisements is another source from which new sales personnel may be obtained. The broker can advertise in the classified columns of local newspapers, in real estate magazines, and in bulletins that are distributed to real estate offices. Ads may produce a considerable number of responses. Most, if not all, of these responses will be from individuals who are not well-qualified. On the other hand, there may be one or more responses from persons who would be long-range assets to the firm. When seeking new salesmen from this source, all applicants must be carefully screened and investigated. This may be time-consuming but, if fruitful, will be time well spent.

Recommendations from associates and friends is another source to be considered. When the broker wants to employ one or more new salesmen, it is sometimes well to make it known to his associates, his employees, and to friends outside the office. This may produce no leads at all, or it may produce the names of one or more good prospects. Prospects derived from this source must be handled with tact and diplomacy to avoid offending the individuals who recommended them, but it is a source that should not be neglected.

Universities and colleges constitute another good source. Many of these institutions offer a series of courses in real estate on their campuses for both undergraduates and post-graduate students. Some of them offer evening classes for part-time students through their extension divisions. Individuals completing these courses are already well aware of the importance of real estate as a career and are ambitious for opportunities for employment in the vocation. They have been well-grounded in fundamental theories and from an academic standpoint have become familiar with procedures employed in real estate practice. Names and addresses of individuals completing these courses can be obtained from school officials. A record of the grades on the final examinations can also be secured. Students completing the on-the-campus courses for academic degrees are usually young and with little or no experience in business. Some of them have great native ability and can be developed into productive salesmen. Individuals completing the courses in evening classes are usually much older, have had business experience of some kind or other, and are likely to be already employed, although dissatisfied with their jobs. The fact that they took the time and spent the energy and money to complete evening courses is indicative of ambition and ability, but they are likely to need practical training and close supervision during the first few months of their employment as real estate salesmen.

Retired executives constitute another source for real estate salesmen. Throughout the country there are a great many retired men and women who are in good health, who have superior talents, and who are eager to engage in remunerative activities. These include executives from the armed forces, from industry, from commerce, from financial institutions, and from the field of education. These individuals, in general, are far above the average in intelligence, in forceful personality, and in ability to deal with people. Some, but not all, have the attributes necessary to become productive salesmen. These individuals who do have native sales ability are easily trained. With proper supervision and incentives, they can become extremely valuable additions to the broker's sales force.

Another source of real estate salesmen can sometimes be found in the professions, such as law, engineering, and teaching. Not infrequently there are individuals in professional fields who, for one reason or another, find that they are like square pegs in round holes. They are failing to make good or they are unhappy in the vocations they have chosen. They did qualify to enter these professions but found it difficult to succeed or be happy in practice—maybe because of personal attitudes and temperament. Usually that is it. They have good educational backgrounds and have been faithful workers in meeting the requirements for their academic degrees and for their licenses. But, after all this work, they are not in the right vocations to be truly productive and satisfied. Some of these individuals may have exceptional sales ability when properly motivated.

The selection process

The first step in selection is the decision as to which source of supply is most likely to be fruitful. Items to be considered in making this decision include the type of property to be sold; which advertising medium is most likely to reach the type of salesman desired; whether or not the firm has an employee in another department who can qualify as a salesman; and whether applications, if any, filed during the past year include one or more worthy of consideration.

The second step is to secure written applications and supplementary letters from all individuals who want to be considered for employment. It is unlikely that any real estate brokerage firm needs to have printed application forms, unless it is an unusually large one with a large expansion program or with a rapid turnover of the sales force. A mimeographed form or list of items to be covered in writing by the applicant should suffice.

The following items might be included in the application, together with any others about which the broker desires information.

1. Name in full
2. Address and phone number

3. Date of birth
4. Place of birth
5. Citizenship
6. Social Security Number
7. National origin
8. Knowledge of foreign languages
9. Political affiliation
10. Church affiliation
11. Marital and family status
    a. Male or female
    b. Single or married
    c. Widow or widower
    d. Divorced
    e. Alimony payments
    f. Number, sex, and ages of dependent children
    g. Other dependents
12. Height
13. Weight
14. Serious illnesses during past five years
15. Life insurance carried
16. Health and accident insurance carried
17. Residence
    a. If homeowner, your amount of debt on home
    b. If renter, amount of monthly rent
    c. Do you live with parents or other relatives?
18. Automobile
    a. Make
    b. Type
    c. Year
    d. Miles driven
    e. Paid for or amount of monthly payments
19. Chronological record of places and duration of residence
20. What real property, if any, do you own? Describe
21. For how long can you finance yourself?
22. Other income, if any
    a. Sources
    b. Amount
23. List and explain debts and financial obligations
24. Have you ever been arrested? If so, explain

25. Can you accept full-time employment?
26. When can you report for duty?
27. Is your spouse employed? If so, where, by whom, and what kind of work?
28. Are you related to anyone in the real estate vocation? If so, who and how?
29. Have you served in the armed forces? If so, give details.
30. Nature and date of discharge.
31. Are you a member of the reserves or of the National Guard? If so, describe.
32. Draft status
33. Are you employed at present? If so, by whom, for how long, position held, and reason for seeking a change.
34. Give a chronological record of past employment since leaving school. State reason for leaving each job.
35. Have you ever held a real estate salesman's or broker's license?
36. List clubs, societies, and other organizations in which you have held or now hold membership and state positions held in each.
37. What are your hobbies? How many hours per week do you devote to them?
38. Give a history of your academic background.
39. Describe your extracurricular activities while in school.
40. What real estate books and magazines do you read?
41. What real estate courses of study have you completed?
42. What annual income do you hope to develop as a real estate salesman?

Another major step in the selection process is composed of three personal interviews. The first interview is for the purpose of forming a preliminary estimate of the fitness of the candidate and of explaining the purpose and importance of the written application. This interview can be quite brief. It is an initial screening to eliminate individuals who are obviously unqualified and to encourage those who appear to have adequate talents, including sincerity of purpose, to file an elaborate application in written form, and to return for an extended interview at a later date.

The second interview with the prospective salesman is for the purpose of reviewing and discussing the application in detail, item by item. The interviewing officer should make careful advance preparation for the interview. He should go over each item in the application and note the questions, if any, that he thinks should be asked when that item is being discussed in the interview. This second interview should be unhurried and free from interruptions by telephone, callers, or office staff. The applicant should be made to feel at ease, relaxed, and in a position to talk freely and confidentially about his background, experience, ambition, and personal affairs. The interviewer should radiate friendliness and a genuine desire to help the applicant develop a long-time successful career in the real estate vocation. No item in the application should be slighted. Each one is important. Any one of them may have to do with a factor that makes the difference between success and failure. The applicant's answers and comments may reflect personal bias, prejudice, judgment, and ethical character. During the interview the broker should refer to a typewritten list of questions he has prepared to be sure no significant matter is overlooked.

The importance of most of the items listed in the written application are obvious and require no explanation, but the significance of some of these items may not be immediately apparent to the inexperienced interviewer. The type of property on which the salesman is to devote most of his time is an example. The salesman of rural properties, for instance, should have an agricultural background. The experience of having lived and worked on a farm is a valuable asset. Courses of study in an agricultural school are excellent preparation for the salesman of rural properties. Such a background enables the salesman to talk the language that the prospective purchasers of rural property understand. Such a salesman knows a lot about the problems that must be met by the users of rural property. He is in a better position to be of service to them than is the salesman who lacks a knowledge of farms and ranches.

The salesman of industrial properties needs a broad experience with and a wide knowledge of the problems of users of that type of property. An engineering background, either academic or practical, is helpful. He needs to know a great deal about such matters as sources of raw materials, labor and unions, transportation, climate and weather affecting production processes, zoning, markets for finished products, and many other factors affecting the desirability of site location for various kinds of industry.

The salesman of investment properties should be well informed about the capitalization processes, rates of return on invested capital, depreciation, taxes, alternate investments, competing properties, general business trends, area trends, and other factors affecting the net productivity of the property he offers for sale.

National origin and knowledge of a foreign language may be of prime importance to the salesman. This is true if he attempts to sell properties in an area inhabited predominately by first and second generation Italians, Poles, Swedes, Chinese, French, or other segregated populations that adhere strongly to the language and customs that characterize their native lands.

The hobbies of the applicant are often revealing reflections of the temperament, stability of character, social acceptability and ability to work with people, range of acquaintanceships, and spending habits. Devotion to certain hobbies may be commendable. Other hobbies involving heavy expenses or that consume a great amount of time are danger signals to be heeded when employing a salesman. This is especially true if the applicant is addicted to gambling or to playing the stock market.

It is well to be wary of the applicant who has a record of change of employment at relatively frequent intervals, unless the changes brought about substantial increases in responsibility and income. A change of employment may be due to lack of competency, inability to work harmoniously with employers or with fellow workers, incapacity for loyalty or for withstanding disappointments. The real estate salesman must have patience and strength of will not to be defeated by failures to close deals. He must be able to preserve an optimistic outlook, to profit by his mistakes and failures, and to have the will to keep right on trying.

The applicant's attitude toward study and self-improvement is an important matter for consideration. The man who feels that he already knows everything worthwhile in his vocation is not likely to make a good salesman. Social, economic, and political forces are in a constant state of transition. New methods and techniques are always being developed. New governmental rules and regulations affecting real property are promulgated from time to time. To keep abreast of these changes the salesman must read extensively, attend real estate board meetings, seminars, conventions, and other programs of an educational character. He must be eager to put forth personal effort to improve his knowledge and skills if he hopes to compete with alert salesmen in his own and in other brokerage firms.

The salesman must be able to command the respect and confidence of sellers and buyers. They will not deal with him if they doubt his sincerity, his ethics, or his competency. His ability to command confidence and respect may be reflected in his record of leadership in school, in church activities, in social clubs, and in his achievements with previous employers. Evidence of such talent weighs heavily in his favor when being considered for employment.

A real estate salesman must be familiar with the factors that create, modify, and destroy values and that influence the marketability of property. He must know the essentials of contracts, agencies, escrows, options, leases, titles, deeds, mortgages, and construction costs. The applicant is sometimes well-grounded in such fundamentals. If he is not, he must be a self-starter and not have to be pushed into study programs. Furthermore, he must be able and willing on his own initiative to make a constant study of the real estate geography of his territory. He must know its status and its trends.

The second interview may convince the broker that the applicant has the qualifications for the job. But the broker should know that to be productive, the salesman must have confidence in the firm, must be satisfied with arrangements for compensation, must be willing to conform to rules and working conditions, and must be eager to devote himself diligently and loyally to the job. It is important, therefore, not only that the applicant sell himself to the broker but also that the broker sell the firm and the job to the applicant. With this in mind, the broker should state and explain the rules and regulations of the firm that apply to salesmen. This may include such matters as the equipment to be furnished to the salesman, group insurance, deductions from pay, vacation, what the salesman needs to know about office routine, drawing accounts, salary and commissions, sales contests and quotas, sales meetings, floor duty, training programs, reports to be made by the salesman, cooperation between salesmen and between salesman and the sales manager, and other pertinent matters.

As the broker states and explains these matters, the applicant should be encouraged to ask questions and make comments. The broker will note carefully the nature of the questions asked, the quality of the comments, and to what extent that the questions, comments, and mannerisms reflect mental reservations and doubts. If the broker is satisfied that the applicant is eager to have the job and that he is well-qualified, it is often good policy to withhold commitment for a few days until there is opportunity to visit the applicant in his home for a third and final interview.

Prior to the date of the second interview, the broker may do well to get a confidential credit report on the applicant. It may be well also to get confidential letters or comments from previous employers and from others who have knowledge of the applicant's character and past activities.

In addition to careful attention to each item in the application, the broker, during the second interview, should note and make mental evaluations about ambition, sincerity, enthusiasm, dress and grooming, maturity of the applicant.

The applicant should be encouraged to talk freely not only on matters covered in the application, but also about current events. This will give the broker an opportunity to note the applicant's facility and ease of expression and whether he appears to have sound judgment. Important information not possible to discover in the written application may be secured in this face-to-face interview.

If the applicant survives the second interview, he should be visited in his home for the final interview. Here, the broker will note significant home conditions, standard of living, attitudes of members of the family, living habits, and other matters that have significant influence upon the character and personality of the applicant and that may affect his productivity as a salesman.

CHAPTER TEN

Training and the sales force

Basic policies

The first phase of the training program is instruction in company and office policy. It is important that in the very beginning the new salesman be fully informed about these policies, that he understands them, and that he is willing to conform to them. Otherwise, he may unintentionally violate them and bring embarrassment upon members of the firm as well as himself. Without such an understanding he is likely to be ineffective as a salesman and unable to render the fullest measure of cooperation that the broker expects. He should be made to feel that he belongs, that he is trusted and depended upon, and that in his contacts with clients and customers he does indeed represent the firm.

These basic policies may include:

1. Demarcation of the territory in which the firm operates
2. The type or types of properties handled by the firm
3. The specific type of property assigned to the salesman—i.e., whether he is to specialize
4. What specialities are included in the firm's activities and who is in charge of them
5. Rules governing office hours, vacations, holidays, floor duty, drawing accounts, division of commissions, cooperation with competing firms, expense accounts, and reports

112   *Modern real estate practice*

6. Membership in clubs and the real estate board and who pays the costs involved
7. Group insurance
8. Sales quotas
9. Advertising
10. Open houses
11. Other basic policies and rules which have a bearing upon the salesman's work.

Most of these policies will be covered in general terms at the time the salesman is interviewed, but they should all be covered in detail as soon as the salesman reports for duty. This instruction period, while time-consuming, is an investment that will pay off. This instruction should be given, if possible, by the broker himself. It should be followed by an oral examination to be sure that the salesman does comprehend the policies and rules that are in force.

Office procedures

The second phase of the training program should be instruction in office procedures. The new salesman should be introduced to each member of the firm and to each employee. He should be made familiar, in general, with the duties and authority of each individual in the office. He should be given time to read the office manual and the standard operating procedures. He should be made familiar with the office forms, files, and equipment. This period of training should be followed by an oral examination.

Real estate fundamentals

The third phase of the training program should be instruction in real estate fundamentals. The range of subject matter covered by this instruction includes the principles of land utilization, the appraisal process, the essentials of contracts and agency, titles and deeds, financial instruments, private and public restrictions, and other matters of which the new salesman may have insufficient knowledge.

Some new salesmen will already be well-grounded in these fundamental theories through having completed real estate courses, through independent study, or through several years practical experience in related fields or with other brokers. Even then, however, it is usually desirable to require the new salesman to review this basic subject matter during the first few weeks of his employment. The new employee without such knowledge should be required to devote himself to a diligent study of the subject matter, either by enrolling in evening classes, by independent study, or by attending evening or early morning classes conducted in the broker's office. Deadline dates should be set for completion of the study program and passing grades on written examinations should be a condition for advancement, special privileges, or even for continued employment.

There are many excellent textbooks available for these study programs. Detailed course outlines, textbooks, and other reading matter can be secured from the Education Committee of the National Association of Real Estate Boards. This material in up-to-date form should be maintained in the office library of the broker firm. The sales manager should be responsible for planning and supervising these study programs. Since all salesmen do not have the same academic and experience backgrounds, their need for instruction varies. For this reason, it is desirable that this particular phase of the training program be tailored to fit the specific needs of individual employees.

Weekly class meetings in the broker's office can be quite effective. These might take the form of a series of lessons on real estate law, or on appraising, or on principles of land utilization, or on finance. Guest speakers can usually be secured for such meetings from local law offices, financial institutions, title companies, local colleges, and local governmental agencies.

Territorial analysis

The third phase of the training program is instruction in the real estate geography and related factors of the territory in which the salesman is to work. The firm should have in its stockroom a supply of maps covering the territory in detail. One map should cover the entire territory, showing streets, lines of transportation, and points of major community interest, such as schools, churches, parks, and cemeteries. There should also be zoning maps and a series of maps in outline form drawn to a scale large enough to show the outlines of all individual lots.

It will help the new salesman to become thoroughly familiar with his territory if he is required to study it block by block. A separate large-scale map of each block can show the dimensions of every lot in it. The salesman should make an exterior inspection of each property in the block he is studying and fill in data on his outline map to show the type of improvement, the name of the owner, and the name of the tenant if the property is rented. He can contact the owner or tenant in person as he makes the study, saying that he is making a survey of the area and asking for cooperation in compiling information about it. In these personal interviews he can ask such questions as:

1. How old is the improvement?
2. How long have you owned the property?
3. What is the rental and how long is the lease, if it is tenant-occupied?
4. Would you consider selling?
5. What do you like about the location? About the property?
6. What do you dislike about the location? About the property?
7. What further improvements, if any, do you plan to make?

The sales manager directing this phase of the training program will suggest other questions that can be put to the owner and to the tenant.

All this and other valuable information can be secured in personal interviews if the salesman is friendly and tactful. He should make it clear as he begins the interview that he is not at the time soliciting a listing or seeking a prospect to buy some other property. He should stress the fact that the purpose of the interview is to gather information needed in a community survey of conditions and trends. When the salesman introduces himself he should state his name, the name of his firm, and give the interviewee one of his business cards. If available, he should leave a printed folder or brochure that explains the services offered by his firm—brokerage sales, mortgage financing, insurance, appraisals, or management.

There is a dual purpose in having the salesman make a survey. It makes him familiar with the land and buildings in his territory, but, more importantly, it acquaints him with the people in the area. In order to list properties he must deal with people. He must know people. He must find out if they are dissatisfied with the properties they own or rent and why. He must learn what kind of real estate they would like to have. He must evaluate their needs and capabilities. All this and more he can learn in making a block-by-block survey of his territory. He should avoid trying to list or sell properties during the initial contacts, but the contacts he makes pave the way for later solicitation of listings and for the development of prospective buyers.

The block-by-block survey of his territory will be time-consuming. It will not be practical to debar the salesman from taking listings and making sales until the entire survey has been completed. He should have an approved time schedule for completing the work which provides intervals during which he is free to secure listings and make sales in areas he has studied. He might well devote his full time to the survey until he has covered several blocks in which he has uncovered a few opportunities for deals. Thereafter he can continue the survey on a part-time basis until the entire territory has been covered.

In many built-up areas will be found vacant lots, overimprovements, underimprovements, or misplaced improvements, indicating a lack of balance in utilization. These properties present opportunities for creative brokerage. If the salesman is well-informed on the principles of land utilization, if he has vision and imagination, and if he has good judgment, he may be able to spot opportunities and develop lucrative deals. He can be a community builder, earn a substantial income, and derive deep personal satisfaction if he is able to find and develop creative deals.

Other important data developed in the survey include the various types of real estate markets that exist in the territory, which markets are active, which markets are dormant, which properties may be classified as "critical" properties, which properties have been sold or rented in recent months (at which price levels and by whom the deals were made), which properties are currently listed for sale or rent (at what asking prices, and with whom listed).

The well-established and alert real estate office will probably have a data file containing pertinent information about every property in the territory. Even so, the new salesman should make a personal field survey to see the properties and other physical aspects of the area and to make personal contacts with potential clients and customers. Some of the information he gathers will duplicate data already on file. Some of the data on file may be obsolete and in need of revision. Neighborhoods are always in a state of transition. The new data gathered by the salesman can be used to up-date the files.

The salesman should record the data he gathers on his outline maps and on appropriate property data sheets. He should check these records against the office files. Then he should review and discuss his findings at frequent intervals with the sales manager, who will assist him in its evaluation and disposition.

Training in getting listings

In general it can be said that the broker cannot stay in business without properties to sell. He must have listings, unless he specializes exclusively in serving buyers. Some listings may come to him without solicitation, but they are likely to be few in number and probably only from individuals for whom he has rendered satisfactory service in the past—or from their relatives or friends. To develop and maintain an adequate volume of listings it is necessary to go get them, and to keep right on going after them. For the most part the broker must depend upon his salesmen to do this work.

It is an axiom that properties properly listed are already half sold. They are unlikely to be sold at all unless they are properly listed at salable asking prices and with the cooperation of the owners.

Improper listings clutter up the files with deadwood, waste the time of both the sales force and the office staff, and incur the ill will of owners who depend upon the firm to find buyers promptly. It is important, therefore, that the salesmen be well-trained before they are permitted to solicit listings. The new salesman should be thoroughly instructed on the various forms of listing contracts used by the firm, how to estimate market sales prices, sources of listings, and the techniques of negotiating with owners to secure listings at saleable prices. The training program might include the reading of the listing contracts followed by an oral test to make sure that the contracts are fully understood. The reading of available books and articles dealing with listings can be instructive. Close observation of an experienced salesman's work in securing listings can be helpful. A series of question-and-answer conference periods with the sales manager is an essential part of the training program.

It is a good idea to require the inexperienced salesman to produce a few acceptable listings before he is permitted to do any selling. Before making any contacts to secure listings, he should prepare a plan for approval of the sales manager or his broker. He should make a daily report to the sales manager for the purpose of discussing his findings and experience with individuals whose properties he has sought to list. In conferences the sales manager will discover what mistakes and errors in judgment have been committed and instruct the salesman how to avoid them in the future. Good work by the salesman should be commended. Personal cooperation in handling additional interviews should be promptly given if needed. These daily conferences constitute an extremely valuable part of the training program.

Training the salesman to get prospects

It does no good to get listings if prospects for the purchase of the properties cannot be found. Some unsolicited prospects will come to the office to seek help in finding locations and types of properties they want to buy or rent, but they are likely to be few in number. When a property is listed, the broker has an obligation to the owner of finding prospects and of making a sale. This he must do within the time period specified in the listing contract. He may already have the names of one or more logical prospects in his office files. More likely, he will have to seek prospects by advertising, by a sign on the property, or by canvassing in the area where the property is located.

The three major functions of the salesman are to list properties, to find prospects, and to make sales. He should have training in each of these functions. He should constantly seek prospects not only for properties that have been listed, but also for properties that have not yet been listed. He should be instructed on sources

118 *Modern real estate practice*

of prospects, on methods of tapping these sources, on what information to get about each prospect, and on how to record, file, and follow up the information he secures.

Sources from which the names of actual prospects and of potential prospects can be derived include the following:

1. Classified advertising
2. Display advertising
3. Direct-mail advertising
4. Signs on property
5. Radio advertising and news stories
6. Television advertising and news stories
7. Neighbors
8. Foreclosures
9. Recommendations of clients
10. Re-sales
11. Personal contacts
12. Houses open for inspection
13. Window displays
14. Apartment dwellers
15. Owners of listed property who want to change locations
16. Recent sellers of property
17. Items in the local newspaper
18. Architects
19. Bankers
20. Civil engineers
21. Assessment rolls
22. Membership rosters of clubs.

An important part of the training program is to make the inexperienced salesman familiar with these and other sources and to instruct him how to make use of them.

Prospects may be classified by type. All types have certain characteristics in common, but no two types are exactly alike. Recognition of the distinguishing characteristics of each type is helpful in selecting sources in which to seek buyers for specific kinds of property. This is also helpful in selecting properties for specific buyers. The following incomplete list of various types of prospects is suggestive.

1. The new resident
2. Middle-aged and elderly couples in a large house when their children marry and move away
3. Newlyweds
4. Divorcees
5. The socially ambitious
6. Individuals who suffer financial reverses
7. Individuals whose mortgages have been foreclosed
8. The spendthrift
9. Frugal individuals
10. The industrial worker
11. The office worker

12. The tourist
13. The invalid
14. The foreign born
15. The executive
16. The professional
17. The investor
18. The speculator
19. Individuals with outdoor hobbies.

The inexperienced salesman can be benefited by instruction in the characteristics of various types of prospects, where to seek them, how to analyze them, how to approach them, and how to negotiate with them. Even though the instruction is in the realm of theory and numerous exceptions to general rules are admitted, the knowledge acquired through instruction by an experienced sales manager will help the salesman interpret and profit by the experience he has with prospects.

One midwestern Realtor has a policy of requiring each salesman every day to meet and become acquainted with at least one person whom he has not known before. This policy is part of that Realtor's initial and continuing training program. The salesman is instructed on where to look for new acquaintances, how to approach them, what information to seek in conversations with them, how to be friendly and cordial, and how to pave the way for subsequent contacts. Dale Carnegie's book *How To Make Friends and Influence People* is valuable supplementary reading for salesmen.

Daily or weekly reports on these contacts should be made to the sales manager. The salesman should check the names of his new contacts against the office listings, prospects, and appraisal files to find out whether any of them are already in the office files and whether any of them are already clients or customers of other members of the firm. No office records of the new acquaintances should be placed in the files, except those whom the salesman believes to be prospects for some service of the firm within a reasonable period of time. These individuals should be discussed with the sales manager, and plans should be made to cultivate them for the purpose of developing business.

The salesman should be instructed also in how to find prospective sellers and buyers by scanning news items in the local papers. Deaths, births, marriages, divorces, promotions, newcomers into the territory, and transfers out of the territory are often followed by the necessity of selling, leasing, or buying real estate. An appropriate investigation of the real estate needs of individuals featured in such news stories can be a fruitful source of prospects.

Kibitzing actual sales

The inexperienced salesman can learn by observing the work of a veteran salesman. If the new salesman accompanies the experienced salesman when listings are being solicited, when prospects are being interviewed, when properties are being shown, and when deals are being closed, he can see and hear sales theories and principles put into practice. This is one good way to learn. It is case-study demonstration. Following the demonstration of each step in the sales process, the new salesman should be given the opportunity in a private conference of asking questions and discussing what he has seen and heard.

Coaching through actual deals

The inexperienced salesman is helped by coaching through a few actual deals. This should be the task of the broker or the sales manager. Such procedure requires the salesman to plan each step in detail and to discuss plans with his tutor before he makes face-to-face contact with the owner or the prospective purchaser. The tutor will give suggestions and instructions on each item in the plan. It may be desirable for the tutor to accompany his pupil when the owner or the prospect is being interviewed to observe the work and later to discuss strong and weak points in the interviews that the salesman has conducted.

Training of experienced salesmen

The sales force may include three different kinds of experienced salesmen: (1) individuals who have had a long period of sales experience with their present employer, (2) individuals who have had sales experience with other real estate brokerage firms, and (3) individuals who have had sales experience outside of the real estate vocation.

To varying degrees they all need continuous training and supervision. This is especially true of individuals whose sales experience has not been in the real estate brokerage field. It is true to a lesser degree of those whose experience has been with other real estate brokerage firms, and even those who have had a long period of experience with their present employer may need supervision to keep them up to maximum efficiency and fully aware of changing conditions.

The objectives and policies of the firm will be amplified and revised from time to time as the scope of its activities expands and as additional personnel is added to the staff. Population shifts and changes in business conditions in the area must be noted and interpreted. New sales situations develop, and the various real estate markets fluctuate.

All of these, and other matters, affecting the needs and capabilities of owners and of users of real estate during transition periods make constant study a mandatory policy. Salesmen should not be left to their own individual initiative to keep up to date on general business trends, on changing conditions in the city and the neighborhood, or on the development and use of new methods. Their comprehension and thinking should be stimulated and directed through an on-the-job training program.

We have pointed out before (see pp. 85-86) how important books and other types of publications are for the salesmen.

The on-the-job training program should include regularly scheduled sales conferences. All salesmen should be required to attend and take part in the programs. These conferences should be held frequently, perhaps daily for one hour at the beginning of the day's work. The programs should not be merely academic in character. They should deal with current market conditions, with company sales policies and short-range objectives, with rules governing sales contests, with knotty problems attending the sale of specific properties, and with other practical matters about which the company or the salesmen are concerned.

Attendance at real estate conventions, seminars, clinics, real estate board meetings, and association sales conferences is another excellent way to keep salesmen informed and inspired. The alert salesman at such meetings will establish personal contacts that may be helpful in developing new business. He can pick up new ideas and learn about new methods that he can use in his own

122 *Modern real estate practice*

work. Time and money spent in attending such meetings are good investments.

Functions of supervision

Supervision is an essential part of the training program. If left entirely to its own initiative, the sales force is not likely to attain maximum sales volume or to maintain it. Effective use of time must be made by each salesman. There can be no loafing on the job. Day after day, each salesman must be hunting for listings, interviewing prospects, showing property, or closing deals. Maximum sales volume requires coordinated effort. It means avoiding time spent on unsalable properties and time wasted on unqualified prospects. Supervision can insure that time is not wasted, that effective sales techniques are being used, that opportunities are not being overlooked or neglected. Maximum sales volume depends in part upon sustained motivation and inspiration. One function of the supervisor is to furnish sustained motivation and inspiration.

Long-range prestige and public confidence in the competency and reliability of the firm requires unfailing adherence to ethical standards. Under the stress of economic pressure, or for other reasons, a salesman may be guilty of misrepresentation in dealing with an owner or prospect. Through the use of high-pressure tactics he may commit an owner or a prospect to a deal that should not be made. Or he may step out of bounds in his relationship with fellow salesmen or with members of competing firms. Proper supervision can forestall many of these occurrences and take proper steps to remedy damages caused by such conduct when violation of ethical standards do occur.

To exercise effective executive control, the broker or his sales manager needs to know from day to day the exact status of all pending deals and of all deals that are in progress. This knowledge cannot be had without supervision. The executive is not in full control unless he does know where and how time is being spent and whether the selling techniques being used are effective. It often happens that even an experienced salesman will lose a deal that could have been made. This may be because he lacked certain information, because he made the wrong approach, because he overlooked or neglected some important detail, or because he was not diligent in processing the deal. One of the most important functions of the supervisor is to save deals that are in danger of being lost.

Without unswerving loyalty on the part of the salesman, the fullest measure of success cannot be achieved by the brokerage firm. The supervisor has the responsibility of developing and maintaining loyalty. To do this it helps to show a sincere sympathetic and helpful interest in the personal problems of each salesman. Effective supervision means effective leadership. The supervisor must not only be an executive, but also a leader. He must keep his salesmen inspired and eager to work. He must make them realize that he is ready to help them consummate difficult deals. He must see to it that each salesman is given fair treatment in all of his dealings with fellow salesmen and with the firm.

Technique of supervision

Perhaps the first requirement in the supervisory training program is the submission of daily reports by every salesman. These reports should be in written form. They can be memoranda and informal in character. Each report should show such items as (1) time spent on the job; (2) names, identity, and address of persons contacted or interviewed; (3) purpose of the interview; (4) results of the interview; (5) special problems encountered; (6) suggestions, recommendations, and requests for help; (7) reports and comments on other matters deemed to be of interest to the firm; and (8) requests for personal conferences with the broker or sales manager.

The salesman should make it a practice to write out his report at the end of his working day and have it on the desk of the supervisor for immediate attention the next morning. The fact that he is required to submit a written report keeps the salesman alert throughout his working day and is a safeguard against his overlooking significant details. If the supervisor is at his desk 15 or 30 minutes before the office opens for business, he can read the reports, decide whether personal conferences are desirable or needed, and make plans accordingly. Reports are valuable in many ways, not the least of which is a record for future reference.

Personal conferences constitute another supervisory training technique. The need for conferences may be revealed in the daily reports submitted by the salesman, but even when the daily report does not disclose the need for help, it is smart policy for the supervisor to have short, personal conferences with each salesman. The supervisor is not omnipotent. He does not know everything. He is not a mind reader. The salesman in his daily contacts is almost sure to discover valuable information that his supervisor does not have and which might be important to the firm. Friendly discussion of the salesman's experience and information he has secured in the field helps to build morale as well as keep the executive officers of the firm informed. The sales force can constitute an extremely valuable real estate intelligence staff, as valuable to the boss as is the G-2 staff of an army commander.

The sales manager, or supervisor, can learn a great deal about each salesman by observing his behavior closely. Does he report for work on time? Is he cheerful? Is he downcast? Is he irritable? Do members of the office staff and other salesmen like him? Is he self-assured or is he easily confused? His attitude, his dress, his speech, his facial expression, his tone of voice, and other aspects of his personality and behavior may be revealing reflections of his ability to withstand disappointments and utilize unexpected opportunities.

Another technique of supervision is the establishment of sales quotas. There is a minimum income which the salesman must make in order to stay on the job. Not only from the standpoint of the firm, but from a purely personal standpoint. This minimum will vary among salesmen, since their personal needs vary. The salesman and the supervisor should have a clear understanding of these minimum requirements. This means the establishment of a sales quota below which the salesman must not fall. A quota keeps the salesman on his toes, makes him willing to receive instruction when needed. The quotas of productive salesmen can be revised upward to reasonable and attainable levels periodically to stimulate them to put forth their best efforts.

Sales contests in themselves are not supervisory techniques, but they are good methods of stimulating production, and they do require supervision. They give the supervisor the opportunity of observing the behavior of each salesman under pressure, of identifying special talents, of discovering weaknesses of individual salesmen, and of developing teamwork and *esprit de corps* in his sales staff.

Each sales contest should be thoroughly planned with careful and thoughtful attention to every detail. It should be closely supervised to make sure that pressure of competition does not result in unethical conduct.

The basic purpose of supervision is to help each salesman become and remain a top-notch producer. If the salesman produces a high-level income for himself, he will be happy and the firm will be prosperous. The welfare and personal economic status of the salesmen should have first priority in the thinking of the supervisor. Such an attitude on the part of the supervisor helps to maintain a low level of salesman turnover.

CHAPTER ELEVEN

Compensation of the sales force

The real estate broker operates in a dual capacity. He is both a professional man and a business man. He is a professional man in the sense that he renders a personal, expert, and technical service to individuals who are in need of such services but who are not able themselves to perform them. He is a professional man in the sense that what he has to sell is personal knowledge and skill rather than a commodity which he himself owns and on which he expects to make a profit. He is a business man in the sense that he acts as an agent in a business deal on a commission basis to buy or to sell a commodity for others. The professional man works for a fee which is paid whether or not his service is satisfactory to the client. The business man works for a profit or for a commission which he receives only if his service is satisfactory to his client or to his customer, as the case may be. The professional man does not advertise aggressively or solicit clients or customers. As a business man, the broker must make use of business methods in (1) the hiring, the training, and the supervision of personnel; (2) selling his services to the public; (3) making a profit on the work of his sales organization, his management department, his insurance department, his mortgage department, and on whatever other activities he may carry on in related fields.

As a business man, the primary purpose of employing salesmen is to make a profit on their activities. Each salesman must produce enough to support himself plus enough to cover all overhead of the firm chargeable to him and plus a satisfactory net to his employer. In fixing the compensation of salesmen, therefore, the broker has these three requirements in mind: First of all, the salesman must make a satisfactory living for himself and family, plus enough to provide for savings and contingencies. Second, the salesman must produce enough to cover the overhead costs of the firm chargeable to him—such as a pro rata share of rent on office space, bookkeeping, telephone, receptionist, advertising, equipment furnished by the firm, social security, insurance, and other expenses incurred by the firm by reason of his affiliation and activities with it. Third, the salesman must produce enough in addition to give the broker a satisfactory profit or net income on his activities.

The compensation of salesmen is a problem that every real estate broker faces and must solve on a mutually satisfactory basis if he expects to stay in business with the help of a sales force. Policies and methods of compensating salesmen vary widely throughout the country. They may vary within a local area, depending upon specializations, competition between brokerage firms to attract and hold good salesmen, the business philosophy of the brokers, and personal relationship between the broker and his salesmen. It is false economy for a broker to compensate his salesmen at a lower level than is maintained by competing firms. To attract and hold the best men, he should make the compensation he pays to his salesmen more attractive than the compensation offered by his competitors.

Many brokerage firms have a mandatory policy that requires a new salesman to have enough personal capital to finance himself through a specified period of time—perhaps for three months or longer. During such a period the salesman is getting ready to sell by learning his territory, local markets, and company policies and methods. He must, if necessary, be able to support himself even though he makes no sales at all.

In addition, the new salesman is generally required to own a comparatively new automobile. Some firms require the salesman to pay all costs of repair, maintenance, and operation of his automobile. Other firms pay costs in whole or in part. It is important that there be a definite understanding between the broker and the

Compensation of the sales force   129

salesman with respect to compensation for services and what expenses will be paid by the firm. It is good policy to cover all of these matters in a clearly worded contract between the broker and the salesman to avoid future misunderstandings and dissatisfaction.

Real estate brokers have been experimenting for many years with various methods of compensating salesmen. There is still no one method in universal use. The salary plan has been tried, but it has usually failed. This is primarily because the broker cannot afford to pay more than a meager salary to an untried salesman. As soon as the salesman makes a few good deals he realizes that his income would have been much greater if he had been on a commission basis rather than on a salary. Flushed with success by a few good deals, he is optimistic and expects to continue making sales. So, he is not satisfied with a salary, unless it is raised substantially. Unless he gets a big raise, he is likely to ask for a transfer to a commission basis or to seek employment with another broker. Or, even, to try to set himself up as an independent broker if he can qualify for a broker's license.

Some brokers have been successful with drawing accounts and advances made against future commissions, but this method has often resulted in substantial losses to the broker. There are many salesmen who are glad enough to avail themselves of drawing accounts during preliminary training periods but who find themselves heavily in debt to the broker when they do get into production. Then when a substantial deal is made and all or a large part of the salesman's commission goes to pay his debt to the broker, he is dissatisfied. Even after a few such deals, the debt generally has not been fully paid off, and the salesman thinks of resigning if he can find a position with another broker. He has already learned his territory and the local markets. He has been trained to the point that he can and does make sales. Another broker employing him does not have to wait through a long training period to get him into production and can afford to offer an attractive compensation plan. The broker who has trained him at a considerable expense in time and money may lose him. These disappointing instances have discouraged brokers from giving drawing accounts or advances, except in very special cases where the conditions convince the broker that he is justified in taking a calculated risk.

The business of selling real estate cannot be learned quickly.

Every salesman must serve his period of apprenticeship. No matter how well equipped an office may be or how many splendid listings it may have in its files, the new salesman cannot be effective until he becomes familiar with a large number of properties, all of which he has personally inspected. He must have talked with owners and equipped himself with a vast amount of information. Most professions require a training period of several years and the expenditure of a considerable amount of money before a man entering as a member is qualified to do business with the public. It is foolish to expect a man coming fresh into the real estate vocation to produce during the first few months. He may be lucky enough to make a sale or two within the first 60 to 90 days, but that is not likely. Usually a much longer period is required to get into production. This is the reason newly employed salesmen are usually required to finance themselves during the apprenticeship period. Unless they are able and willing to put in their time and pay their own way against the training they will receive from the broker, they ought not to enter the business.

As a general rule, the basis for compensating salesmen is a split of the total commission with half to the salesman and half to the broker. Some brokers pay more—sometimes 60 percent or more to the salesman, but the commissions are usually split on a 50-50 basis. The broker pays all overhead expenses and the salesman pays his own expenses, including maintenance and operation of his automobile.

The broker may not be ambitious to build up an organization large enough to support a sales manager; so he employs only experienced salesmen who handle most of their deals from start to finish without help. They require little if any supervision. The broker may then pay a higher commission rate, and because the rate is high, he may require the salesman to pay all or part of advertising costs and certain other items of expense.

Most salesmen working on a 50-50 basis are satisfied that they earn more during the year with the help of the broker or sales manager than they would on a higher percentage of the commission with little or no help from the firm in developing listings or prospects or in handling the complexities of closing deals. The smart broker will not leave even the experienced salesman entirely on his own but will keep himself informed on the progress being made on every deal and be ready to pitch in and help to save any deal that seems likely to be in danger of being lost.

Some firms operate under a plan which gives the better producers a bonus at the end of the year. It is believed that this plan keeps the salesmen alert and constantly diligent in sales activities. Whether such a plan is successful depends upon the attitude of the salesmen and upon the leadership and inspiration furnished by the broker.

Other firms follow a plan under which a salesman starts out on a 50-50 percentage basis and gets a raise in the commission rate if and when he has earned a certain agreed-upon amount of commissions for himself. Under this plan the higher rate of commission is retroactive to the beginning of the year. Many brokers prefer this plan to the bonus plan. It gives a strong incentive to the salesman and tends to keep him constantly active.

Although strong incentives are helpful in developing and maintaining maximum sales volume, special care should be taken by the broker to make sure that no salesman is guilty of sharp practices, of misrepresentations, or of unethical conduct in his zeal to make additional commissions. Every deal should be fair to both seller and buyer and leave each of them fully satisfied. Sellers and buyers who are dissatisfied harbor deep resentment toward the firm. The ill will which results from high pressure or questionable sales tactics tends to spread throughout the community and destroy public confidence in the integrity of the firm.

Some of the larger brokerage firms divide their territories up into districts and assign each district to a specific salesman who becomes responsible for developing listings and making sales within the area. Under this plan it has been found desirable to protect the salesman with a certain percentage of the total commission when a property he has listed is sold by another salesman or when a prospect he has developed is sold by another salesman in the firm. This commission may be 10 percent of the total commission and be deducted from the commission earned by the salesman who completes the deal. Since he has complete information put into his hands by the salesman who developed the listing or the prospect, he is relieved from the necessity of spending much time in working up the deal. He is, therefore, quite willing to pay part of his commission to the salesman who produced the listing or the prospect. Such an arrangement encourages the listing salesman to have all listings in his district in complete, up-to-date form. Likewise he is stimulated to have complete information available on each prospect he has contacted even though he is unable to give the prospect immediate service.

Cooperation among salesmen is sometimes necessary in order to make a deal. Cooperation should be encouraged by the broker, since it may save deals that would otherwise be lost. Both of the cooperating salesmen can be encouraged by having a fair share in the commission, and there should be a definite understanding between the salesmen as to the part each is to play in working up the deal and as to the division of commission. If this situation is not specifically covered in the established rules of the firm, the understanding between the salesmen should be approved in advance by the broker in order to avoid later controversy and ill feelings.

New salesmen should understand and fully appreciate the fact that on a 50-50 commission split basis the broker cannot make a single dollar until the salesman has earned many dollars. The reason for this is that the broker is paying all overhead costs out of his 50 percent, and his half of the commission must be substantial to cover the overhead and leave any net income. If a sales manager is employed, he is generally placed on an overriding basis, and his compensation is part of the overhead that comes out of the broker's half of the commission. The salesman should realize that it is to the broker's advantage to get him into production as soon as possible and to see to it that the salesman constantly increases his sales volume. The only way that the salesman's services can be profitable to the broker is to produce a substantial income for the salesman himself.

Brokers who pay listing commissions to salesmen should make it a rule to pay commissions only where the listings have not expired. When the listing contract has expired and has not been renewed by the salesman who originated it, he loses all rights to participate in the commission if the property is sold by another salesman. An old, neglected listing which has to be revitalized and rechecked should not entitle the listing salesman to a commission when the property is sold by another person.

The broker should make such rules governing the division of commissions between salesmen as can be mutually agreed upon by him and his sales force. Division of commissions in unusual situations should be covered if possible. Every effort should be made to see that commissions are paid to the salesman who earns them and in proportion to his efforts. Such rules avoid misunderstandings and forestall deterioration of morale in the sales force.

Commissions on prospects

It is not always possible for the individual salesman to sell every property he lists because of lack of time. Some of his listings can and should be turned over to other salesmen in the firm who are in a position immediately to service the owners. Also it is not always possible for the individual salesman to locate a satisfactory property for every prospect he finds. Some of his prospects can and should be turned over to other salesmen in the firm who for one reason or another are in a position to render immediate service.

The salesman who produces a listing that is sold before the listing contract expires by another salesman is entitled to part of the commission. So also is the salesman entitled to part of the commission earned by a second salesman who makes a sale to a prospect produced by the first salesman. Specific rules governing all such circumstances should be established by the broker and should be understood and agreed upon by the sales force.

The brokerage firm cannot do business without listings. There must always be enough to keep all salesmen busy—but not too many. Ordinarily no salesman can handle more than six or seven listings effectively. Neither can a brokerage firm do business without prospects. There should always be enough to keep all salesmen busy—but not too many. Some salesmen can service more prospects than other salesmen can. The number that an individual salesman can service simultaneously he must learn by experience. It depends to a great extent upon the type of property involved and the condition of the market. The salesman should not attempt to service more prospects that he can handle. Otherwise he cannot do effective work either for the prospects or for the firm. Under pressure that is greater than he can surmount, he is certain to neglect significant details and lose deals that might have been made if he had given complete attention and constant effort to them.

One of the primary responsibilities of the salesman is to find and qualify prospects. This means being constantly alert in the study and cultivation of the various sources from which prospects may be derived. He will usually find more prospects than he is able to serve. This is because it takes time to get fully informed about an individual prospect's needs, desires, and capabilities, some individuals are merely curious with no financial ability to buy. For every real prospect that the salesman encounters he is likely to come into contact with dozens of "suspects" who are interested in looking but who cannot qualify as purchasers. It takes time to screen out the real prospects from the much larger group of "suspects." It takes time to show properties, to negotiate deals, and to close deals. No real prospect should be lost through negligence. Each salesman has the responsibility of finding not only all of the prospects which he himself can service, but also the responsibility of finding additional prospects to be developed and serviced by other members of the sales force. As an incentive to do this, he should be assured that he can participate in the commissions earned on sales by other salesmen to prospects he himself has found and turned over to other salesmen. It is through such cooperative efforts that the brokerage firm approaches or arrives at its maximum volume of business and that all members of the sales force develop high-level incomes for themselves.

The name of and pertinent information about each prospect originated by a salesman should be registered promptly in the office files after a check has been made to be sure that the files do not already contain the name of the prospect. Such a register is a protection to the salesman who discovered the prospect. It avoids duplication and controversies. A check of the files may reveal the fact that it already contains the name of the prospect and that some other salesman has prior claim on him.

Some brokers have found it good policy to limit the protection given to a salesman who originates a prospect to a certain time period. If such a period is 30 days, for example, the salesman who produces the prospect has exclusive rights during that period in locating a satisfactory property and making the sale. But if the salesman is unsuccessful in making a sale within the time period covered by the rule, the prospect is made available to some other member of the sales force and the originating salesman is given an agreed-upon percentage of the commission earned by the salesman who actually closes the deal.

There may be several conditions under which a salesman can earn commissions.

1. Securing salable listings on properties which he himself sells without assistance. Here he is paid for making the sale, but not an additional amount for securing the listing.
2. Securing salable listings on properties which are sold by someone else in the company. Here he is paid a percentage of the commission earned by the salesman who closes the deal.
3. Securing salable listings on properties which are sold by someone in a competing firm on a cooperative basis. His employing broker gets, as a rule, one half of the total commission, and the originating salesman gets an agreed-upon percentage of his employer's share in this transaction.
4. Selling properties listed by someone else in his own company. He usually gets one half of the total commission less an agreed-upon percentage paid to the listing salesman.
5. Selling properties on a cooperative basis that have been listed originally with a competing brokerage firm. Here 50 percent of the total commission is split with his employer.
6. Developing leads that result in management contracts, leases, or mortgage loans. He is paid for his services in accordance with advance agreements between himself and his employer.

For each and every service performed by the salesman that adds to the income of the firm, he is entitled to proper compensation. To be the most successful, the salesman needs to know precisely what services he is authorized to perform, when and how to render them, and what compensation he may expect for each.

The compensations earned by the salesman should be paid to him at regular intervals. At least once every two weeks or once a month, depending upon the payday schedule for salaried office personnel. He should be paid by check to which a voucher is attached showing not only what specific services are being compensated and in what amounts, but also what deductions have been made to cover withholding taxes, social security, group insurance, reimbursements to drawing accounts or advances, and other items.

CHAPTER TWELVE

Types and sources of listings

The term "listing" is used in three different ways: (1) it is used to refer to a contract between an owner who wants to sell a real property and a broker who agrees to act as that owner's agent in selling it, (2) it is used to refer to the property identified in the contract, and (3) it is used to refer to the file card or to the data sheet which records detailed information about the property.

A listing contract is a legally enforceable instrument designating a broker to act as the agent of the owner under certain stated conditions in selling a specified parcel of real estate. The owner on his part agrees to sell the property at a stated price, provided that certain stated financial terms are satisfactorily met by a buyer and provided further that the broker produces a buyer within a certain specified period of time. The owner also agrees to pay the broker a specified commission for his services in making the sale. The broker on his part agrees to put forth his best efforts to find a qualified buyer and to negotiate the sale in accordance with the conditions stated in the contract.

The essential elements of the listing contract include:

1. The names and addresses of the contracting parties.
2. The date on which the contract becomes effective.
3. The date on which the contract will expire.

4. The identity of the property offered for sale.
5. The price which the owner will accept.
6. The conditions of the sale, such as the down payment required and other financial terms.
7. The commission to be received by the broker.
8. Items deemed important by the contracting parties.

Various "standard" listing contract forms have been developed by attorneys and are offered for sale by some real estate boards and by some stationery stores. Such forms are timesavers in negotiating the terms of the listing agreement. They safeguard both parties against overlooking important details. They facilitate the meeting of the minds with respect to essential details to be included in the contract. The fact that it is a standard form approved by the local real estate board and in general use by other owners and brokers should convince the owner that it is adequate and fair. The form must have legal approval and be drawn by a practicing attorney.

There are four types of listing contracts in general use: (1) the open listing, (2) the exclusive listing, (3) the exclusive right to sell, and (4) the multiple listing.

The open listing commits the owner to sell a specified property at a stated price if a buyer is produced before a stated date and to pay the procuring broker a stated commission for his services. It leaves the owner free to list the property with other brokers if he wishes. Also the owner is free to sell the property himself to any buyer not produced by a broker who is a party to the listing contract, in which case the broker does not receive a commission.

Some owners prefer the open listing and will sign no other type of contract. This is because they believe that the property will be sold more quickly when several rather than just one broker are seeking buyers. Also some owners may hope that they will be fortunate enough themselves to find buyers and thus be able to save the money that would otherwise be paid as a commission to a procuring broker.

There are some brokers who prefer the open listing because they do not want to assume the obligation of spending time and money in trying to make a sale which they would feel obliged to do under an exclusive contract. Such brokers like to build up a large file of open listings and wait for buyers to take the initiative in seeking properties they want to acquire. They will often take a listing at any price, regardless of the current market conditions. Their policy is to wait for a prospect to make an offer, any offer, for consideration by the owner. These brokers are reluctant to accept responsibilities. They want to avoid hard work. They are content to drift and wait for buyers to turn up and make offers. They rarely, if ever, achieve top-ranking prestige in their communities.

The disadvantage of an open listing to the owner is that rarely will any broker who is a party to the contract make much effort to find a buyer and make a sale. A considerable period of time may elapse before the property is sold.

The disadvantage of the open listing to the broker is that he may spend time and money in finding a prospect, showing the property, and negotiating the sale only to find before the sales contract is signed that some other broker has completed the deal or that the owner himself has committed himself to a buyer. Then the broker has wasted his time and money. That is why most brokers will not accept open listings. When a broker has an open listing, he can protect himself to some extent by reporting in writing to the owner the name of each prospect to whom he shows the property and the date on which the property was shown. The report should be in duplicate, the original to the owner and the copy retained in the broker's file. If no other broker has shown the property to the same prospect on a prior date, the broker is entitled to a commission even though the prospect in question buys the property from another broker or from the owner directly.

The exclusive listing gives the broker the exclusive right to sell a specified property during a stated period of time. It excludes all other brokers during the term of the contract but does not debar the owner himself from selling the property to any prospect not produced by the broker.

The advantage of the exclusive contract to the owner is that he has the right to expect the contracting broker to devote himself diligently to whatever sales effort may be necessary to effect a sale, but he is himself free to sell the property on his own without having to pay the broker a commission. As in the open listing, the broker should report in writing to the owner the name of each prospect to whom he shows the property and state in his report the date on which the property was shown. This protects the broker if the owner himself makes the sale to a prospect that the broker produced. Also it keeps the owner aware of the fact that the broker is actually making efforts to sell the property.

Another type of listing is the exclusive right to sell contract. Many brokers prefer this type and will accept no other. Under such a contract no one other than the contracting broker—not even the owner—has the right to sell the property. The contracting broker is legally entitled to the commission if anyone sells the property during the period of time specified in the contract.

Another type of listing is the multiple listing. The details of this plan vary in different local areas. Usually it gives the listing broker exclusive rights for a stated period of time, after which for another stated period of time the property is listed with all other brokers who hold membership in the multiple listing plan. During the first period of time, the listing broker has exclusive rights to the commission. During the subsequent period of time, the listing broker receives a certain percentage of the commission if the property is sold by another member of the multiple listing plan. Some real estate boards operate a multiple listing service. Membership in the plan may be optional or mandatory for members of the real estate board. The real estate board participates in the commission. It takes a stated percentage of the commission deemed adequate to cover the expenses of keeping records, circulating information about the listings, and paying the costs of other office overhead. In addition, some real estate boards charge a membership fee for participation in the plan.

In some communities several real estate brokers have created and operate a private multiple listing system, independently of the real estate board. Membership is usually by invitation and is designed to exclude conflicting personalities and brokers who cannot be depended upon for wholehearted cooperation. The success of either plan depends upon the rules governing the operation, the objective enforcement of the rules, the attitudes and personalities of the members, and the spirit of cooperation that characterizes them.

The advantage of the multiple listing plan to the owner is that it stimulates the listing broker to be diligent in his efforts to make a sale before the exclusive period of time expires, and it commands the services of many brokers if the property is not sold by the listing broker during the first time period. The disadvantage is that if the property is not sold during the first time period, it becomes, in effect, an open listing without definite protection to any member of the plan who worked on making a sale which is finally made by another broker.

The advantage of the multiple listing plan to the broker is twofold. He may find it easier to get a listing under this plan because he can promise the owner multiple services in finding a buyer, and if he is unable to sell the property himself during the time he has exclusive rights, he may be able to participate in the commission if the property is sold by another member of the plan after his exclusive rights have expired.

Sources of listings

Listings are made by owners who, for one reason or another, are dissatisfied with their properties or with some condition associated with their ownerships or occupancies. They may be dissatisfied with changed conditions in the neighborhood. They may find themselves in situations they do not like. They want to rid themselves of the dissatisfactions they feel by substituting situations that are more to their liking. In seeking to list a property, the alert broker will find out, if he can, just why the owner is dissatisfied and what improvement he hopes to achieve by selling his property. Why does the owner want to sell? Is there a deadline date by which the sale must be made? What will the owner do with the money he gets from the sale of the property? Correct answers to these questions may help the broker get the listing and, perhaps, sell another property to the client.

The reasons owners want to sell are many. Dissatisfaction develops from changes in family affairs, from changed economic status of owners, from changed social composition of neighborhoods, from opportunities for more attractive investments, by need for expansion, by need for contraction, and from developments that convince owners they need the capital represented by the properties they own for some other purpose.

Every owner of a real property is a potential seller. Except for strong sentimental reasons, almost any owner will sell if offered a high enough price. Because owners are mortal and cannot take their properties with them when they die, the titles to property rights are inevitably transferred when the owners die; so, eventually, every property in the broker's territory is a potential listing. The broker, with the help of his sales force, should be familiar with every property in his territory. He should have a record of the ownership of each property. He should have a fair idea of which properties are in strong hands and which are in weak hands. Such knowledge is valuable in revealing sources from which listings may be secured. Every property in weak ownership is a "critical" property, and its potentials should be reviewed by the broker from time to time. These properties are likely to come onto the market at any time. The alert broker will watch them and be prepared promptly to service their owners when the time comes to convert the properties to other uses and to other ownerships.

One source of listings is a canvass of all owners in the territory. This may be done by personal contact, house to house, property to property, pushing doorbells for personal interviews. This is an assignment often given to new salesmen to get them familiar with their territories. It is the most effective method for an initial survey of the market potential insofar as owners who wish to sell is concerned. It is well worth the cost in time and money. It gives a fairly accurate understanding of the market potential during the immediate future. But the contacts thus established and the information secured need to be renewed at appropriate intervals in order to keep up-to-date understanding of the market and to be sure that opportunities are not overlooked.

Some brokers place considerable reliance upon telephone canvasses to find listings or to supplement other efforts to get them. This method usually produces new leads for listings but it is less effective than face-to-face interviews with owners. Many owners resent telephone calls coming from individuals with whom they are not acquainted and which interrupt meals, social parties, television shows, or other activities in which they are engaged at the time the call is made. Telephone canvassing must be carefully planned and skillfully conducted to be fruitful. A complete canvass will include every owner, house by house, block by block, skipping owners known not to be in the market. The owners to be called may compose a specially prepared list of "suspects" gleaned from the office records and from news items in the local papers or from rosters of local clubs. An appropriate day of the week and hour in the day should be chosen in the hope of finding the persons called available to answer the calls and in the mood for conversation. Exceedingly important is the personality and the voice quality of the person making the call. The first few sentences spoken by the caller are important. One approach that has been found effective is "We may have a client who wants to buy a property in your neighborhood, and we wonder if you would consider selling yours?" If the reply is in the affirmative, the way is open to arrange for an inspection of the property and a face-to-face interview of the owner.

Another canvassing method is direct-mail solicitation. It, as well as the telephone approach, is best used in seeking listings of single-family homes. There are other more fruitful methods of developing listings of commercial, industrial, and rural properties. The well-equipped office of the broker who deals in single-family dwellings will have the names, addresses, and phone numbers of all owners in his territory. A suitable mailing piece with a return coupon or postcard that is sent to all owners in the territory at least once a year is good institutional advertising. Such mailings help to produce leads for listings, insurance, management, appraisals, and mortgages.

Another source of listings is the "Property for Sale" ads by owners in the classified columns of the local papers. The commission for the sale of a property is often several thousand dollars. Many owners seek to save the commission by trying themselves to sell their properties. They may advertise in the local newspapers and put "For Sale by Owner" signs on their properties. Some buyers think that they can purchase at a lower price by dealing with the owner direct and they are attracted by such ads and signs. Unfortunately, many uninformed sellers and buyers, alike, are distrustful of real estate brokers and are reluctant to deal with them. It is up to the broker to convince such persons that in handling real estate deals on their own, there is danger of making costly mistakes that may well be greater than the amount of the commission.

The alert broker watches for "For Sale by Owner" signs on properties and in the classified columns of the local papers. A properly conducted interview with these owners often results in the securement of listings. The broker's task is to convince the owner that the complicated ramifications of a real estate sale can be better handled by an experienced expert who is familiar with selling techniques, with essential legal instruments, and with sources and methods of financing. When the owner realizes that he can save time, worry, and money, and avoid costly risks by using the services of a skilled negotiator, he is often quite willing to sign a listing contract with the broker. Where the owner wants to get his money out of his property in order to buy another, the broker has the opportunity of making two deals. Sometimes the owner will trade his property for one that the broker has already listed to sell for another owner or for one that the broker can find without too much delay.

Opportunities for deals with owners who are themselves trying to find buyers should be promptly and thoroughly investigated. It is wise to work out several standard "canned" approaches for use in contacting and interviewing these owners. Such approaches should be carefully reviewed, in the light of what may be known about a specific owner, to decide which one or more of the approaches should be used in asking for the interview and in conducting it once it has been granted. It may well be that more than one interview will be necessary to enable the broker to sell his services to a doubtful owner. The initial interview, therefore, should be conducted and ended in a manner that leaves the way open for further discussion at a later but an early date.

Another source of leads for listings are the news columns of local papers. Reports of divorces may be followed by the sale of a dwelling and, possibly, by the purchase of another. The death of a spouse may make it desirable or necessary for the survivor to sell one or more properties and enter the market for the purchase of another. Parents in a large house left alone by the marriage of their children may want to sell and buy a smaller dwelling. The birth of children to parents in a small dwelling may make it necessary to sell and buy a larger house. The transfers of executives, salesmen, college professors, officers in the armed forces, and civil service employees to other locations often create opportunities for brokers to get listings.

Promotion of executives to positions commanding substantially higher salaries may lead them to seek larger and more pretentious dwellings in a more exclusive neighborhood, providing they can sell properties that they already own.

Urban renewal projects, slum clearance programs, widening of streets, construction of new highways, and other public improvement or defense projects that displace occupants of either residential, commercial, or industrial properties are replete with opportunities for the broker to develop listings and prospects. Since everyone must use real estate and must pay for such use, whether as an owner or as a tenant, any event that makes a change of location desirable or necessary creates an opportunity for the services of the real estate broker.

In a metropolitan area there is hardly any issue of a daily newspaper that does not contain news items revealing the names of potential sellers and buyers of real estate. For this reason it is good policy for the broker to see to it that someone in his office scans the news columns of every local newspaper in search of items, clips them out of the paper, and brings them to his attention.

Another source of listings consists of individuals who contact the broker's office without solicitation to seek help in finding buyers for their properties. These individuals may be former clients or customers. They may be persons who have learned about the broker through recommendations of friends and acquaintances. Perhaps they have received a direct-mail institutional advertising piece at some time in the past, or have noted the broker's ads in the newspapers, or have seen his signs on properties for sale. Maybe they have been attracted by the displays in his office windows. They may make a telephone call asking for information, or they may come to the office to request an interview with the broker. The well-established brokerage office with a good reputation gets an increasing number of unsolicited listings and prospects as time goes on. This is why the development of an unblemished reputation for competency, integrity, and fair dealing should be one of the primary objectives of the broker. Unsolicited listings sometimes constitute a major source of income for the real estate brokerage firm. This desirable situation comes about through years of satisfactory service to sellers and buyers, persistent institutional advertising, and continuous favorable publicity through the various local media.

CHAPTER THIRTEEN

Condominiums

The usual concept of real estate is that property rights in land are on the surface of the land or in the ground. Prior to 1961 in the United States, little attention had been given to the property right which exists above the surface of the land otherwise known as *air rights*. With the enactment of *condominium* or *horizontal property* laws in many of the states, the conception of property rights on the land has changed and *living* in and *owning* a part of the sky has become a reality.

A concept of ownership

Condominium ownership is not new in this world. Since the 6th century B.C. Romans *living together* has been a legal concept of ownership and in Europe today, the fee simple ownership of a single unit of land and building plus the common ownership of land and building areas is prevalent. Puerto Rico was the first part of the United States to adopt a condominium law and has used it extensively in the construction and sale of apartment and commercial buildings during the past number of years. Since July of 1961, Hawaii, Florida, Arizona, California, and other states have passed condominium or horizontal property ownership acts. Under their provisions, brokers and land developers have been active in the construction of new buildings and the conversion of existing properties. The Federal Housing Authority was authorized to insure mortgages for condominiums under Section 234 of the National Housing Act on June 30, 1961.

Eligible property

Under the condominium and horizontal property acts in effect in the United States and Puerto Rico, all classes of property are eligible. Land, apartments, office buildings, commercial and industrial properties are acceptable for recording of a declaration placing the property under the law of the particular state or commonwealth. The legal use of the property is at the will of the owner. A declaration may be recorded with a special use in mind, but may be changed as physical conversion and sales progress. Use of the property will be governed by provisions in the declaration, zoning ordinances, and restrictive covenants. Use under the declaration may be changed by action of the association formed by the condominium owners as provided in the declaration and the association's by-laws.

Units are allocated according to a recorded plat which clearly outlines the apartments, offices, or square footage of the units and the common areas. The percentage of unit ownership and common area ownership is derived from the relative percentage of single unit sale price to the total sale price of all units or by square foot area of the single unit to the total saleable square foot area.

The size of units in commercial and industrial properties may be shifted according to the requirement of purchasers. Additional space for expansion by existing unit owners presents a problem unless adjacent space is available. In medical buildings, due to plumbing and electrical equipment future space requirements create critical situations. Industrial properties have the problem of providing additional space within a given area for an expanding user. A growing company may provide for expansion by purchasing additional space and renting it until needed. The problem of space is no different to a condominium owner than to a renter who requires either additional space or to make a change of location.

Office buildings used for multiple use such as banks, medical services, lawyers, and general office space are to be found in many cities. The advantages of owning over renting are the same in all types of use.

Procedures

Procedure in all project types for establishing a condominium is the same except for legal requirements of the various states. As apartment condominiums are the most prevalent type, they will be discussed in detail.

Many people visualize a condominium as a high rise building fashioned after the cooperative type of ownership. In operation, it is analogous, but in legal ownership, it is quite different. The co-op is usually owned by a corporation which sells stock to the prospective purchaser and grants a proprietary lease for occupancy. In the co-op, the management of the building is vested in corporate officers, who may employ a management agent. A first underlying mortgage and junior mortgages may be used for financing the entire property and the corporation or owning entity is obligated on the mortgage or mortgages. Each stockholder is assessed a percentage share of the operating expenses, insurance, taxes, and mortgage obligation, but is not personally liable on the mortgage. In case of default of the underlying mortgage or mortgages, the owner of the stock which gives the holder the proprietary interest and leasing right may find himself faced with the loss of his investment. In condominium ownership, each owner receives a deed to his unit, occupies it by the right of possession granted by fee simple title ownership, and has the right of use of the common areas by the right of common ownership. Each unit is financed either free of mortgage or by an individual mortgage. The security is the fee simple title ownership of the legally described unit plus the ownership of a pro-rata share of the common areas. Default of the mortgage on a single unit is default on that single unit and not on the entire property. This type of ownership, with the ability to make a mortgage for an amount required by the purchasers, lends liquidity and marketability to the unit.

The financial advantages of condominium ownership are becoming more and more attractive to present and prospective owners of free standing homes. The reduced personal care, expense of maintenance, lower taxes, and apartment living that offers home amenities appeal to many people. The market is broadening and resales and conversions are becoming an increasingly active segment of residential sales.

Developers create the condominium declaration before first sales. It is desirable that the declaration, which creates the legal entity according to state law[1] provide for condominium ownership to be effective when 51%[2] or more of the units are sold. The possibility of a project becoming a rental project is always present. Sponsorship responsibility, appeal of the project, and many unknown factors will cause a proposed project to be a success or failure.

Condominium management

Management of a condominium is very much the same as a co-op. A board of managers or a board of trustees under the declaration created by state law and the by-laws may appoint a member of the board as the manager of the project, or may engage professional management. The expenses of the common areas such as heating, if central heat is used, janitors, and other items of general expense are allocated to the units according to the percentage of ownership. Taxes are levied against the individual units by the tax assessor and the unit owner pays taxes on his unit and his proportionate share of the common areas. The common area taxes are generally billed by the board of managers and included in the monthly maintenance bill to the unit owners.

The percentage of common area ownership is based on the percentage of each unit space to total saleable space, or the percentage of common area ownership may be allocated according to the sales price or value of the unit related to the total sales price of the project. If a project is valued at $100,000.00 and the sales price or value of a unit is $10,000.00, the percentage is 10 percent. All items of expense allocated to the common area will carry a 10 percent charge to the unit valued at $10,000.00. A percentage change must be approved by all owners of the units, or, if so pro-

---

1/ The laws on "condominium" and "horizontal property" vary in the states and attorneys familiar with the law should be consulted when a condominium is proposed.
2/ Consult Federal Housing Administration rules for guidelines.

vided, by agreement with a majority or more of the unit owners. Voting rights may be established by percentage of common area ownership or by one vote to one unit.

The success of a condominium project lies in several factors. In analyzing the market, it can be said affirmatively that a high rise condominium unit must offer more in amenities than an apartment unit with the same occupancy charge. The permanency of home ownership makes a person feel that there are many advantages to ownership other than the purpose of shelter. As owner of a home in the sky he must feel that he is purchasing the same amenities of home ownership plus the financial advantages to the owner of a single family home. In a condominium, these amenities are found in location, view, size of rooms, convenience of transportation, and freedom from maintenance of yards, walks, snow removal, and other chores of home ownership—plus the advantage of income tax deductions for interest and property taxes. The accrual of equity through mortgage reduction gives the condominium owner an investment advantage over renting, and a hedge against inflation. The purchaser will, however, carefully consider whether the purchase is permanent and weigh the cost of equity down payment against the terminal lease.

Financing

In financing a high rise development, the sponsor has a horizontal subdivision and sales may occur inversely to construction progress. Financing is, therefore, different from that of the townhouse developer who may release land or units from a blanket encumbrance as sales are made. In a single family, townhouse, or free-standing house, conventional home financing is available. In the high rise development, the method of physical construction requires an analysis of the ability of the sponsor to provide more equity funds for construction purposes and imposes different mortgage payout and release procedures.

The sponsor of a condominium project must be aware of the difference in promoting a building for the rental market and a promotion in the sales market. People who rent are transient minded and moving is a way of life. They do not, therefore, expect the permanency or stability in their living that the home owner demands. The condominium sponsor must be home ownership oriented. Recognition of this will make him knowledgeable in creating the project.

Real estate developers must know the basic qualities that make a condominium project successful. The procedure is both legal and practical and must be understood so that the broker or counselor may present to a client some of the problems which may occur in analysis and promotion. The two types, namely high rise and town or free-standing house, will bear some discussion.

Analysis of the proposal

The first analysis of a proposed high rise condominium project must consider whether it meets the qualifications of the condominium concept of "A Home in the Sky." This expression was coined some years ago and holds good today in the minds of those who have promoted condominium projects and those who have bought them. When we speak of "A Home in the Sky," the unit is exactly that. The design, architecture, and construction of the building must be other than "just another high rise apartment building."

In analysis of the proposal, the important ingredients may be placed in the following order:

1. Location.—The location must have special amenities in:
    a. Size of the ground with provision for light, air, and views which are attractive.
    b. Offer access by public transportation or highways, expressways, or boulevards which make traveling to work, shopping, or recreation convenient.
    c. Neighborhoods which have status appeal.
    d. Convenience of schools, churches, and other cultural activities which have appeal to the home owner.
3. Architecture and livability
    a. Attractive exterior appearance and lobby decor.
    b. Large and livable rooms with at least 20 percent more square feet per room than commensurate apartment size.
    c. Large closets with at least one walk-in closet and one storage closet within the apartment area. Laundry facilities either within the unit or on the same floor.

d. Foyer in units.
   e. In a high rise luxury building, a swimming pool or a recreation room suitable for either individual owner parties or community gatherings by owners within the building.
3. Engineering and construction
   a. Fireproof and noise resistant walls between units.
   b. Individual heating and air conditioning within units.
   c. Apartments not to exceed four units to a floor per elevator.
   d. Soundproof elevator operation in high rise building.
   e. Refuse depository from each unit or each floor to basement.
   f. Open or enclosed porches depending on climate.
   g. One bathroom for each bedroom plus one powder room for each unit.
   h. Wind and sun resistant windows and frames.
   i. Garage facilities of one or one and one-half spaces per unit depending on location.
   j. Provision for both passenger and service elevators in high rise buildings.

As a general comment, consideration must be given to the status appeal of the building so that, regardless of the number of rooms per unit or the variance in price of the units, the same feeling of economic importance is conveyed by the amenities of living.

The appraisal report

The appraisal report on a new condominium will require two final opinions of value. The apartment building can be appraised by the conventional methods of reproduction cost, market comparison, and capitalization. A condominium project is appraised by the cost approach to ascertain a basis for one of the upper limits of value. The capitalization method is used for mortgage purposes and construction financing. Rental units which may or may not be condominium owned may be used to establish gross income. The market approach can be used after sufficient competing comparable properties are available. The value of air rights will present a "good guess" until units are sold or a second sale takes place. View, height, location of a unit in the building in relation to stairways, elevators, and mechanical equipment will affect the saleability of a unit. As comparable properties become available and sufficient units are sold and resold, the market approach will have greater validity.

The analysis of a low rise or garden type project is not as difficult as the high rise. When each unit is attached to the ground, the problem of valuing air rights is not present. Each unit has space on the ground and the common areas are ground areas. Walks, gardens, pool, and access streets or parking areas are common areas. The assignment of space for parking presents no problem and is often a part of the common access area to the unit.

Garden type condominium projects are attractive to people who wish to live in a country environment. New condominiums and conversions in close-in urban renewal areas for city dwellers will have cultural, educational, and employment advantages.

Mortgages

The mortgage application for a condominium construction project need not vary from the application for either a single family or rental apartment building mortgage. The appraisal process may differ in the apartment building; namely, the project is valued as an investment property or as a condominium project. In either case, the method of payout will follow the requirement that equity funds be disbursed before opening the mortgage and that mortgage funds will complete the building. In the condominium construction mortgage, payouts may present greater risk than in the investment apartment building mortgage. The condominium project may have multiple owners and some may desire changes in specifications on their individual units. These changes are agreed to between sponsor and purchaser, but may or may not be paid for at the time of approval. The mortgagee may or may not be aware of changes and additional costs may not be covered in the mortgage proceeds. To cover these possibilities, inspections must be made more frequently and affidavits obtained from the sponsor, architect, and unit owners at each payout to avoid controversy at a later date. The purchasers should make payment for extras to either the mortgagee or the sponsor when changes or extras are ordered.

Payout precautions

The opening of the loan is the crucial time for the mortgagee to be sure that all contracts are firm, that no hidden financial arrangements have been made between the sponsor, general contractor, or subcontractors for an equity interest or some secondary security for payment of their contract. When controversies arise unrevealed subterfuges are brought out in the open. The problem is compounded by the number of persons involved and all become individually concerned with their position.

To emphasize the difference between payouts in a condominium project and an investment project, the investment project has one owner who may be sponsor as an individual, corporation, partnership, or any other form of legal entity, whereas the condominium project has one sponsor builder with many individuals vitally interested in their particular unit, each with the thought of personal homeownership. All condominium purchasers do not make changes, but whether it be none or all, the problem of change orders is present. Structural changes affect the timetable of construction. Changes cause additional costs and expense for interest, insurance, and taxes during construction. In large projects this can amount to a considerable sum and require changes in cost estimates made in the mortgage application and necessitate revised construction cost statements before making advances from the mortgage proceeds.

Protection from possible liens may be overcome by completion bonds binding not only on the general contractor but also the subcontractors. Payouts may be made through a title company who will examine individual contracts at each payout and guarantee against liens up to the time of payout. This procedure may or may not be full protection as extras are not always accounted for and the title insuring company may have no means to be aware of them. Affidavits are good legal documents but are not protection against law suits or the stoppage of construction if a contractor or subcontractor has found that he is not being paid for work done. Nor is the contract made in the first instance assurance of the cost to complete. Rising labor and material costs are difficult to meet in times of rising prices and no contractor will stand still for a contract that he cannot fulfill because of conditions beyond his control.

When two or more mortgagees join in a construction loan, the procedure for making payouts must be varied. One of the mortgagees may act as the payout agent for the project and the participating mortgagees reimburse the paying agent after each partial payment or at the completion of the project. If one mortgagee does not undertake the responsibility to act as principal, or the loan exceeds the legal limit of one lender to act, the participating mortgagees may join in an escrow agreement with a title company and the title company becomes the payout agent. When the mortgagor makes a request to the title company for a partial payment the title company orders an inspection, obtains the necessary orders, waivers, and inspection reports on progress of construction from the architect, sponsor, and general contractor. Upon approval of the necessary documents, the title company makes a request to the participating mortgagees for their share of the payment and disbursement is made.

Mortgage participation by a number of mortgage lenders has many advantages. The risk of high concentration of funds is limited, the problems of inspection, approval, and liens are lessened and bring mortgagees together in more uniform processing and analysis of risk. If an examiner finds documents in good order in the files of one participant further examination could be waived by other participants.

During the period of payouts many mortgagees require a later date of the guarantee title (or abstract) as a check on encumbrances which may have been recorded between payouts. When a title or escrow company makes disbursements, this procedure may not be necessary. Before final disbursement is made, it is advisable to escrow the final disbursement and make a final search. If disputes arise for payment for changes or extras, this procedure will not protect against possible liens.

When individual mortgages are placed on the units, the procedure for payout is modified. Before a first advance on an individual unit is made the disbursing agent must ascertain the cost to complete the unit and the common areas. As work progresses partial payments are made. This procedure allows larger payments from individual mortgages on work completed, but does not require the holdback of proportionately more of the total common area cost. In multiple horizontal projects, supervision must be more intensive and the allocation of funds estimated more accurately and with greater knowledge of construction costs. The advantage of unit mortgages to the sponsor is the use of unit mortgage funds, and, in some instances, the use of funds deposited by the purchaser. Authorization must be obtained from unit owners to use unit owner's mortgage funds. When the unit owner permits the use of his individual mortgage funds, he assumes risk of completion of his unit and the common areas, and must rely to a greater degree on the sponsors' responsibility.

Insurance

Fire and hazard insurance on a condominium property is placed by the board of trustees or managers. The entire property, which includes all units and the common areas, is covered by one policy. The reproduction cost of the physical property less depreciation is the basis for insurance. Public liability and other hazard insurance is placed at the will of the managers for an amount considered to be adequate for the risk involved. The sponsor places insurance for the protection of the mortgagee who has made a construction mortgage. As sales are made, insurance certificates are issued to individual mortgagees who have negotiated mortgages to unit owners. Unsold units remain insured either as individual units or under a blanket policy and the mortgage clause remains in effect.

The unit owner under a multiunit mortgage is protected by the issuance of a certificate for his unit. No specified amount is named in the certificate as the blanket policy covers the individual units and the building as a whole. The unit owner, in addition to the general coverage, should carry additional insurance on his unit for the cost of additional items which he may attach personally within the unit. Special wall covering or decorating, light fixtures, extra size stoves, refrigerators and kitchen equipment, if attached to the property and considered real estate, should be covered at cost. Personal property, such as furniture, rugs, and personal property, not considered real estate should be covered in a separate personal property policy. Insurance may be obtained on additional items and for personal property by an attachment to the building policy. A separate endorsement and certificate of insurance is issued. This insurance may be obtained at favorable rates and is paid by the unit owner.

Losses are adjusted by the board of managers. It is the duty of the board of managers to make adjustments which will protect the individual unit owner and the common ownership of the property. A knowledgeable insurance broker should be consulted and a thorough understanding agreed upon before placing the insurance.

Profit opportunities in conversions

The conversion of existing apartments or commercial buildings to condominium ownership presents profit opportunities to real estate brokers. The broker can earn a commission by the sale of the existing building, retain the building for sale as a condominium, and earn a commission on each sale, and, finally, be employed as the manager of the property for the condominium association or trustees.

There are many reasons for conversion of an existing building to condominium ownership. Rising operating costs, taxes, and management problems have resulted in unprofitable operation of some investment properties. The reduced net income and cash flow is discouraging to property owners who see no relief from a burdensome investment. To convert, therefore, relieves the owner of unprofitable ownership.

All buildings are not suitable for conversion. A market survey should be conducted before a conversion should be attempted. It must be determined that there is a strong demand for the units being offered and the building must be in a neighborhood which has appeal to renters and buyers. The test of neighborhood desirability and apartment or condominium demand is existing vacancies. Under normal economic conditions, a neighborhood with a high percentage of vacancies is an indication of undesirability. It is obvious that a declining neighborhood would have little appeal to the prospective condominium owner. The decline may be caused by age, lowering of economic status, or undesirable elements entering a neighborhood. A conversion is most likely to be successful in neighborhoods of strong rental demand. The owner must be in a position to notify a tenant that it is his intention to convert and to offer the apartment to the tenants. The tenants will weigh the advantage of owning to renting, and, if the rental market is strong and he finds it difficult to relocate, he may purchase.

An existing building can be offered at a more attractive price than a new building. The profit margin to the owner lies in his ability to offer a lower competitive price for the older unit. The profit to the owner is due to his lower original cost for the building.

The advice of an attorney should be obtained on occupancy problems. Legal advice also should be obtained as to zoning eligibility and title restrictions. The existing leases may be a deterrent to immediate sale and tenant objections may cause delays in sales and closing of contracts. An architect should be consulted on remodeling or rehabilitation as the proposal may be found to be either impractical or too expensive. Although sales prices per unit may be doubled above the value as a rental project, the cost of acquisition, loss of rents, legal expenses, cost of conversion—including architects' fees, interest during conversion, and sales costs—may render the project unprofitable. It is not necessary to convert a building within a given time. Existing leases may be allowed to terminate and conversion take place at a future date.

Many luxury apartment buildings and office-apartment buildings have been offered for condominium purchase to their tenants. The most outstanding of these projects was the John Hancock Building in Chicago which is a commercial office building and apartment complex. Many tenants accepted the conversion in order to obtain ownership at prices less than a comparable new structure in a comparable location. Condominium conversions will continue as the pressure for desirable apartment living becomes more acute. To the broker there are many financial advantages in this new market for real estate.

Prospects of success

Analysis of the prospects of success or failure of a condominium development lies in two directions of equal importance. Location and sponsorship will spell success or failure before an existing building is purchased or a shovel is put in the ground on a new development. It is difficult to state which is the more important. In weighing one against the other, location may be more important because a good location and a relatively well designed building will pull inept sponsorship out of an otherwise bad situation.

In selection of a location, the project must either have established prestige or the project be of sufficient size to create its own environment. The most successful condominiums have been cluster and high-rise housing. The market has greatest appeal to medium- and high-income families forced to move by increasing rents. In suburban areas, many medium priced condominiums have been successful because of their appeal to a middle-income group of singles and couples whose children have grown who are attracted by the desirability of owning against renting. Price has been the principal influence in these cases. Location has had appeal and new neighborhoods have been created. In conversions, the normal apartment location must be avoided. Location does not always weigh too heavily in the minds of middle-income families as rents in rental property compete with condominium carrying charges. However, tax advantages are lost to the renter.

Sponsorship entails analysis of know how and financial responsibility. A sponsor must have development experience. Condominium development requires analysis of markets, neighborhood appeal, economic and social status, architectural vision, and use of new products. The apartment building concept is not acceptable to the condominium buyer. He expects new design, the feeling of possession, greater feeling of livability by better use of space, and more attractive views and vistas created by either height or landscaping. Without something different to offer in living, the financial advantages are not sufficient to overcome "just another apartment." To the public, the attractiveness of a condominium lies in its superior architectural appeal, the size and equipment of the units, and location.

Financial responsibility of the sponsor is required for two reasons. Mortgage financing requires that equity be sufficient to complete the common areas. The purchasers' mortgages cannot be opened until the building is substantially completed for occupancy. Sales may occur in different locations and no uniformity of completion can be scheduled to take care of the various units which have been sold and possibly ready for occupancy. Lower floor apartments may be completed, but until the elevators or services for the entire building are completed a purchaser and the mortgagee take great risk in advancing funds on individual mortgages.

Until sufficient apartments are sold to assure the project as a condominium, the risk that it may remain a rental project is present. The construction loan must, therefore, be processed as an investment property. As the construction cost of a condominium is greater than an apartment property, the rents assigned as an investment property do not support the higher cost. The amenities built into a condominium are similar to those of home ownership. Unless a low capitalization rate is used, similar to the capitalization rate on a residence, the capitalized value of the units does not equal sales prices. The difference, therefore, between cost and economic value must be absorbed in equity. The difference in valuation will cause an increase in equity of from 10 percent to 15 percent or the reduction in the mortgage from 80 percent of cost to 65 percent to 70 percent.

The profit to the high rise condominium sponsor does not accrue in parcels as in a townhouse development. Townhouse development can be completed in units and the recapture of cost and profits can progress as homes or developed lots are completed. Because the high rise condominium units are horizontal and the common areas require completion in full before complete recapture of invested capital and profit, the equity must remain for longer periods.

Without real estate development experience or know how and financial responsibility, a condominium project can be disastrous. By the same token, a sponsor possessing know how and financial responsibility can be successful and the project profitable.

Mortgage lenders will find the following outline of procedures in application, inspecting and final payout, a guide to the analysis peculiar to condominium lending.

Construction lending procedure for condominium projects

1. Application information and initial interview
    a. Location plat
    b. Plans and specifications
    c. Title policy
    d. Pro forma financial statement
    e. Financial statements of borrowers, corporate, partnership, or individuals
    f. Architects knowledge of condominium construction
    g. Sponsor's experience in condominium promotion
    h. Sales programe and management
    i. Trustee—board of managers—owners participation
    j. Unit pricing and financing
    k. Proposed declaration and unit percentage interests
    l. Type of construction financing—single or unit mortgages
    m. Mortgage amount, term, method of repayment
    n. Attorney knowledgeable in condominium law and procedures including declaration
2. Appraisal request
    a. Value as apartment rental project and value as condominium unit sales prices.
    b. Statement of breakdown by trades and residual square foot and cubic foot cost.
    c. Feasibility opinion by appraiser (advisable before final request for appraisal)
3. Commitment
    a. Mortgage amount
        (1) As apartment project based on capitalization approach to value
        (2) As condominium project based on sales prices of units
            (a) Sum of total units
            (b) As individual units and sales to purchasers
    b. Payout and repayment procedure
        (1) First payment
        (2) Monthly and/or lump sums
4. Title
    a. Single title policy for property
    b. Individual policies for units based on declaration

c. Examination of title by attorney and opinion of attorney
   d. Preparation of and signing of mortgage documents
      (1) Mortgage
      (2) Note
      (3) Assignment of rents
      (4) Waiver of right of redemption
      (5) Release clauses
         (a) Amount per unit
         (b) Before completion for unit mortgage
         (c) Final completion
   e. Contractors' statement
5. Insurance
   a. Total construction
   b. Common areas by sponsor and board of managers
   c. Unit by owners
   d. Liability and property damage
   e. Provision for assumption by condominium board of trustees or managing agent
      (1) Single control—managing agent
      (2) Board control
6. Equity
   a. Ascertain source of equity
      (1) Contractor participation
      (2) Cash
      (3) Land
      (4) Sales deposits
         (a) Agreement to use
      (5) Architect fees
      (6) Profit
7. Procedure prior to approval to proceed
   a. Location of building on lot by survey
   b. Final signature to plans and specifications with architect and superintendent of construction of general contractor
   c. Understanding on extras and payment for same
      (1) Approval by sponsor, architect, and general contractor and subcontractor
8. Payout procedure
   a. Use of title company as escrow agent or direct payments by mortgagee
   b. Signatures on payout orders

Modern real estate practice

       (1) General contractor
       (2) Architect
       (3) Sponsor or superintendent
       (4) Mortgagee's inspector or
       (5) Title company officer
   c. Agreement on dates for payouts
   d. Agreement on inspectors' review of construction
   e. Periodic inspection by mortgagee's inspector
   f. Change approvals
   g. Deposits for extras and method of charge to sponsor or unit owner
9. Final payout
   a. Final inspection
       (1) By sponsor and representative of mortgagee
       (2) Approval of purchaser where necessary or if changes have been made
       (3) Withholding of funds for uncompleted items
       (4) Final waiver of liens and statement of payment in full from general contractor and subcontractors
   b. Approval of board of trustees, purchaser, or managers if direct payment has been made from individual mortgages
   c. Final affidavits

CHECKLIST FOR DEVELOPING A CONDOMINIUM PROJECT

1. **Investigating the project**

    a. Where is the location plat?
    b. Have final plans and specifications been drawn up?
    c. What is in the title policy? Who are the owners? What are the zoning and other restrictions?
    d. Has pro forma financial statement been prepared?
    e. Are there financial statements available on all individuals and companies involved?
    f. How much do the architects know about condominium construction?
    g. How much experience have the sponsors had in condominium promotion?
    h. What are the plans for promoting and selling the project?
    i. How actively will the trustees, owners, and other principals participate in the planning and promoting of the project?
    j. How will the units be priced and financed?
    k. Has the declaration been prepared and agreed to by all parties?
    l. How will the construction be financed?
    m. What is the amount of the mortgage? What are the terms? What is the method of repayment?
    n. How much does the attorney know about condominium law and procedures including declaration?

2. **Appraising the project**

    a. What is the value as apartment rental project? What is the value as condominium project?
    b. What are the cost breakdowns by trades and residual square feet and cubic feet?
    c. Does the appraiser think the project is feasible?

3. **Financing the project**

    a. How much can be financed by a mortgage?
        (1) As apartment project based on capitalization approach to value?

(2) As condominium project based on sales prices of units?
  (a) As total units?
  (b) As individual units and sales to purchasers?
  b. What are repayment procedures?
    (1) When will the first payment be due?
    (2) Will the payments be monthly?

4. **Obtaining the title**
  a. Can you obtain a single title policy for the property?
  b. Can you obtain individual policies for units based on declaration?
  c. Have the attorneys for all parties examined the titles?
  d. Have the following documents been drawn up?
    (1) Mortgage
    (2) Note
    (3) Assignment of rents
    (4) Waiver of right of redemption
    (5) Release clauses
      (a) Amount per unit
      (b) Before completion for unit mortgage
      (c) Final completion
  e. Has a contractor's statement been filed?

5. **Insuring the project**
  a. What is the total value of units?
  b. What common areas of coverage have been agreed to by all parties?
  c. What coverage will the unit owners be responsible for?
  d. What are the extents and limits to coverage for liability and property damage?
  e. What provision has been made for assumption by Condominium Board of Trustees or by the managing agent?

6. **Participating in the equity**
  a. What are the sources of equity?

(1) Contractor participation
(2) Cash
(3) Land
(4) Sales deposits
   (*a*) Agreement to use
(5) Architect fees
(6) Profit

7. **Checking prior to proceeding**

   a. Has a survey been made?
   b. Have final agreements to plans and specifications with all parties been written and signed by all parties?
   c. Is there an understanding on extras and payment for same?

8. **What are the payout procedures?**

   a. Will you use title company as escrow agent or will direct payments be made by mortgagee?
   b. Do you have the signatures on payout orders of:
   (1) General contractor?
   (2) Architect?
   (3) Developer or superintendent?
   (4) Mortgagee's inspector?
   (5) Title company officer?
   c. Do you have an agreement on dates for payouts?
   d. Do you have an agreement on inspectors' review of construction?
   e. Will there be deposits for extras and method of charge to sponsor or unit purchaser?

9. **Completion of project**

   a. Has a final inspection of the project been made by all parties?
   b. Have you an approval of purchaser where necessary if changes have been made?
   c. Are you withholding funds for uncompleted items?
   d. Have you obtained final waiver of liens and statement of

payment in full from general contractor and subcontractors?
- e. Do you have approval of Board of Trustees, purchaser or managers if direct payment has been made from individual mortgages?
- f. Have final affidavits been signed?
- g. Has date of first meeting of owners been set for election of Board of Trustees and selection of manager?
- h. Has date been set for control and operating of property by owners and release of developer?

CHAPTER FOURTEEN

Executive control of listings

In one sense the real estate broker is a merchant. He maintains a stock of commodities—listings—which he offers for sale. Unlike other merchants he does not own his stock of goods and he must sell each item in his stock within a specified time period, else it may be taken out of his stock by its owner. Within the time periods stipulated in the listing contracts, the commodities constitute merchandise that he is authorized to sell at fixed prices. He gets his profits in the form of commissions.

Like other merchants, his fullest measure of success is dependent upon executive control of his inventory. This includes the acquisition and maintenance of an adequate stock of salable listings, knowledge of what he has to sell, and the use of appropriate economical methods of effecting turnover of stock.

The first step in effecting a sale is to make sure that the listing is salable. Of course, the owner wants to get the highest possible price for his property. He wants to recover what he paid to acquire ownership, plus the costs of all improvements he has made subsequent to its acquisition, plus a profit. That is what he wants. It is sometimes possible to do this, because of inflationary trends, pressure of expanding population, or because ownership was acquired at a price substantially below market value. But such fortunate circumstances may not exist. Whether they do or not, it is unlikely that any property can be sold in competition with similar properties at a price much higher than other properties are offered.

In considering a potential listing, therefore, the broker should compare the property with similar properties that have been sold recently and with similar properties that are currently offered for sale. It should never be his policy to beat down the owner's asking price purely to get the listing for a quick sale. His experience and his knowledge of market prices plus his understanding of the supply and demand factors in the area should enable him to make a fairly close estimate of the price at which the property can be sold. He should decline to list the property at a substantially higher price. The owner may be willing to have an appraisal made by an independent valuator in order to set a fair price on the property for sales purposes.

A careful broker will not commit himself to a listing contract until he has inspected the property and found it to be in salable condition compatible with the asking price. To be prepared to present the property to a prospective buyer, he needs to have complete information about it, including the sales points likely to appeal to prospective buyers and defects that may arouse sales resistance. The information for these purposes varies with the type and class of property, whether single-family dwellings, apartment buildings, commercial property, industrial property, or rural property.

It is a good idea to have available a comprehensive checklist of items on each type of property as a guide when inspecting a prospective listing and compiling information about it. Most brokerage offices are equipped with standard listing forms on which to record information. Sometimes these information blanks are on printed or mimeographed cards, sometimes they are on 8 1/2 x 11 sheets, or even on four-page folders. Whatever the size and style of the form used, it should be adequate to record all essential information thoroughly to understand the property, to prepare advertising copy, and to equip the salesman to show the property to a prospective buyer.

A checklist on single-family dwellings, for example, without regard to sequence and arrangement on the record form, might include:

1. Property address
2. Price asked
3. Ownership
    a. Name
    b. Address
    c. Phone number
    d. Names and addresses of all parties whose signatures are necessary on the sales contract
4. Type of architecture and design
5. When built
6. Lot shape and dimensions
7. Exterior material
8. Foundation
9. Roof
10. Basement
11. Garage or carport
12. Side drive
13. Heat (Type)
14. First floor rooms (Number and type)
15. Upper floor rooms (Number and type)
16. Recreation room
17. Solarium
18. Breakfast nook
19. Fireplace
20. Baths (Number)
21. Closets (Number)
22. Kitchen
23. Laundry
24. Sleeping rooms (Number)
25. Swimming pool
26. Decorations
27. Insulation
28. Carpets and flooring material
29. Screens
30. Storm windows
31. Gas
32. Water (Municipal or well)
33. Water heater (Gas or electric)

34. Sewer
35. Electric power and outlets (100 amp.–220 v., etc.)
36. Bedrooms (Number)
37. Alley
38. Sidewalk
39. Curbs
40. Lawns
41. Plantings
42. Drainage
43. Fencing
44. Taxes
45. Price paid by owner
46. Cost of improvements added by owner
47. Mortgage
    a. Original amount
    b. Mortgages (Date and due date)
    c. Unpaid balance
    d. Interest rate
    e. Monthly payments
48. Unpaid special assessments
49. Current occupancy
50. Occupants of neighboring houses
51. Owner's motive for selling
52. Distance to public transportation
53. Distance to schools
54. Distance to shops
55. Legal description
56. Down payment required
57. Zoning
58. Deed restrictions
59. Title and ownership policies
60. Liens
61. Name of owner's attorney
62. Defects and cost to cure
63. Sales points to stress in selling
64. Special features
65. Date of listing
66. Expiration date of listing
67. Type of listing (open, exclusive, or multiple)

68. May a sign be placed on property?
69. Limitations on showing
70. When available to buyer
71. Floor plans
72. Photographs
73. Plot plan
74. Lot, building location on lot.

The information needed in listing a retail store and preparing to sell it may include:

1. Ownership
    a. Name
    b. Address
    c. Phone number
    d. Individuals whose signatures are necessary on sales contract
    e. Owner's attorney
2. Address of the property
3. Legal description
4. Lot
    a. Shape
    b. Dimensions
    c. Area not covered by building
    d. Parking facilities
5. Alley
6. Building
    a. Date of construction
    b. Basement
    c. Dimensions and square-foot area of floors
    d. Type of construction
    e. Type and age of floorings
    f. Utilities
    g. Roof
    h. Special features
7. Highest and best use of the site
8. Location in the block
9. Strip map showing occupancy of both sides of the street in the block and adjacent blocks
10. Occupancy history of the property

11. Taxes
12. Mortgage
    a. Mortgagee
    b. Date of mortgage
    c. Expiration date of mortgage
    d. Amount of the mortgage
    e. Unpaid balance
    f. Interest rate
13. Asking price and terms of sale
14. Type and length of lease offered
15. Rental history
16. Rental comparison with similar properties in area
17. Date present ownership was acquired
18. Depreciation history of improvements
19. Type of tenancy for which best suited
20. Rental potential
21. Width of street fronting property
22. On sunny or shady side of the street?
23. Pedestrian traffic
    a. Volume by hours in the day
    b. Volume by days in the week
    c. Direction of traffic flow
    d. Destination of pedestrians
    e. Quality of purchasing power in area
24. Public transportation
25. Private deed restrictions
26. Public restrictions
27. Size and quality of the trade area

The foregoing suggested checklists may be expanded, compressed, and otherwise revised both as to content and sequence of items. These are intended to suggest the scope of data that may be needed properly to serve both seller and buyer. Each broker will work up his own checklists and forms to reflect his individual preferences, experience with the market, and his executive ability. It is recommended that in the interest of effective executive control the broker needs to have these lists and forms on all types of property with which he deals. There are thousands of real estate deals that are lost every year because the broker or the salesman did not have complete enough information to present the property to prospects.

It is one thing to assemble comprehensive data about properties listed for sale. It is another thing to record and file such data in conveniently useable form for ready study and reference purposes. To achieve efficient executive control there must be a properly organized and administered filing system. There are four types of listing files: (1) card files, (2) record sheet files, (3) property folder files, and (4) master cross-reference files. The same office may use all four files to accommodate different types and classes of listings.

The card file may consist of 3 x 5 cards, 4 x 6 cards, or 5 x 8 cards. They may be vertical files or be housed in visual Kardex-type pull-out drawers. They may be arranged by types and classes of property and also by street addresses. There can be, for example, a section of files devoted exclusively to single-family dwellings. This section can be subdivided into groups of two-bedroom, three-bedroom, and four-bedroom houses. Or the cards may be subdivided by price range, or by streets, or by neighborhoods. The advantage of the card file is that it is easier to file and re-file in it and to use it in finding quickly pertinent data on a particular kind of listing. The disadvantage is that the space on a card is limited and may be inadequate. Each card should have attached to it a companion card for control purposes. On this control card should be recorded summary data such as:

1. The date of the listing
2. The expiration date of the listing
3. The type of listing
4. The name of the salesman to whom the listing has been assigned
5. Dates of ads run and the media used. Also costs
6. The names of prospects to whom the property has been shown
7. The dates of the showings
8. Objections encountered
9. Other pertinent data

The record sheet file may be made up of 8 1/2 x 11 sheets of heavy paper stock to prevent crumpling in the file drawer. These sheets should have provision for all of the essential information recorded on file cards plus other pertinent data. The control record can also be made on the reverse side of the sheet, unless both sides are needed to record data about the property. If more recording space is needed for control purposes, a separate sheet should be attached. The organization of these files may follow the same pattern as suggested for the card files.

The property folder files may be in a heavy file folder or in a heavy envelope, either large enough to accommodate 8 1/2 x 11 sheets without folding. This file may contain the listing record sheet, the listing contract, a file copy of the property brief, a copy of an appraisal report on the property, memoranda, correspondence, and other related material. It should also contain a control card or sheet to show for quick reference the history of efforts that have been made to sell the property.

The master cross-reference file may be 3 x 5 cards. It should contain a summary record of every listing in the office and indicate the location of the card, record sheet, or property folder where detailed information about the listing can be found. This is especially helpful if the same listing has been filed in more than once place, such as by type and class of property, by price range, by street address, or by type of listing.

The filing system can be arranged and administered so that it shows at a glance the degree of urgency for each listing. Colored tabs can be attached to the cards, the sheets, or the folders showing expiration dates pending negotiations with prospects, problem listings on which additional data is needed, and other important matters to which attention must be given by certain deadline dates.

The broker's office should maintain a "Dead" file for listings that have expired and for properties that have been sold. No data on any listed property should ever be discarded. Expired listings are subject to renewal. Properties that have been sold may come on the market again at unexpected times. Information about any property, once assembled, may be extremely valuable in saving time at a future time for listing purposes, and for comparison with other properties in sales, appraisals, management, or mortgage loans. When a listing has expired or the property has been sold, all information about it should be assembled and put into the "Dead" file. The active files and the "Dead" files together constitute a data bank of great value. One of the administrative objectives of the broker should be eventually to have a file on every property in his territory.

Some owners who are reluctant to pay a commission will agree to sign a net listing. Such a listing is one which gives the owner his asking price in full without the payment of a commission and gives the broker the difference between the owner's asking price and the price at which the property is sold. Thus, if the owner's asking price is $25,000 and the broker sells the property for $27,500, the owner gets the $25,000 he wanted for the property and the broker gets $2,500 for his services in selling it. Net listings are unprofessional and are considered to be unethical by reputable brokers. In some states they are prohibited by law.

It is an executive function of the broker to decide what volume of listings can be handled by individual salesmen. The number that can be serviced properly by an individual salesman depends upon the type and class of property, the price range, the current demand level for the type and class of property, the length of the time period for which the property is listed, and the skill and diligence of the salesman.

The individual salesman will sign up listings through his own efforts. Other listings will come to the office as a result of institutional advertising. Owners will sometimes come to the office without solicitation to list their properties. Listings not produced by individual salesmen will be assigned by the broker to salesmen not already heavily loaded with listings and considered to be particularly adept in selling the type and class of property offered.

Frequent contact should be made with each owner who has listed property with the firm to keep him informed about sales efforts that have been made and about the results. When a listing expires before a sale can be made, the broker himself should review the history of the case to find out why it was not sold. He will want to know the answers to such questions as:

1. What ads were used? Where and when?
2. What response was made to the ads?
3. What did the ads cost?
4. To what prospects was the property shown?

5. What objections were encountered?
6. What offers were made?
7. How were the objections answered?
8. Which salesman had the assignment?
9. How diligent were his efforts?
10. Was the time period of the listing too short?
11. Can or should the listing be renewed? If so, by whom should the approach to the owner be made?

The broker should watch the properties listed with his competitors. He should compare their ads and their signs on properties with his own. He should note how effective his competitors are in making sales. Constant attention to the methods and techniques employed by his competitors may enable him to improve his own. In addition it helps him to keep informed about the supply of properties on the market, how rapidly they are being absorbed, and whether the trend is up or down as compared with previous periods of time.

With the owner's permission, as soon as a property is listed, a "For Sale" sign, with the broker's name, address, and phone number should be put on the property in plain view of passers-by. This accomplishes two purposes. It advertises the property and may produce a purchaser. It publicizes the name of the broker and may bring him other listings as well as prospects for other properties. The signs should be attractive, in good taste, look like new, and be kept in good condition and firmly in place. The file clerk should keep an accurate record of the location of all signs, who put them up, and when. She should see to it that the signs are returned to stock as soon as the listings expire or the properties are sold.

So that the broker, as chief executive of the firm, may at all times know the exact status of his inventory, he may well require a weekly, or even a daily, report from the chief clerk or from the sales manager to show:

1. The number of live listings in the file, by types of property.
2. The names of salesmen to whom assigned
3. The number of listings acquired since the last report, and to whom assigned
4. The number of listings that have expired since the last report, by types of property

5. The properties that have been sold, by whom, and at what prices
6. Other related matters

These reports tend to keep the sales force alert and diligent. They are a spur to keep the filing department up to date on its work and constantly aware of what data is available and where to find it. They let the chief executive know whether current conditions are satisfactory or what executive action is needed to correct situations that appear to be getting out of hand.

Some brokerage offices make a practice of making a pictorial display of their listings. When the number of listings is greater than available display space, photographs of typical listings are put on display. The display may be, in part, in the windows facing the street to be viewed by passers-by. Large bulletin boards can be set up in an appropriate part of the office, and photographs of the properties for sale put on it. The clerk responsible for the listing files can be assigned the mounting of photographs and of returning them to the files when the listings have expired or the properties have been sold. Some firms affix a "sold" sticker on photographs of properties that have been sold and leave them on display for a few days. This practice is intended to reveal the fact that the firm is successful in making sales and to encourage others to list their properties with the firm. The photographs selected for display should be chosen by the broker or by his sales manager with an eye to attracting attention and to advertising properties the sale of which is most urgent.

CHAPTER FIFTEEN

Executive control of prospects

The real estate broker's business is to sell properties. He cannot do business without properties to sell. He cannot do business without purchasers. He needs listings and he needs prospects. He needs an inventory of both. To achieve maximum income he must exercise intelligent executive control over both inventories. Unlike other merchants who stock standard, staple commodities, he is seldom an ordertaker. He must use negotiating and sales techniques to do business. Not only must he have a stock of listings, he must also have a stock of prospective buyers, actual and potential, or be able to find them without undue delay. Just as his stock of listings should be classified and administered in a systematic way, so should his stock of prospects.

The broker must realize that people do not buy real estate primarily to get the physical property itself. They buy because of what real estate will do for them. The buyer of a single-family residence buys it because he wants the shelter, the security, the convenience, or, maybe, the prestige that goes with its ownership. The buyer of an apartment building buys it because of the income he expects to get from it. The buyer of an industrial site buys it because it offers him facilities for manufacturing some product he can sell at a profit. The type and class of property for sale determines the type and class of buyers who need or want it.

Broadly speaking, all prospects can be classified into groups by types and classes of property that they desire.

1. Prospects for single-family dwellings
    a. Low-income groups
    b. Intermediate-income groups
    c. High-income groups
2. Prospects for investment properties may want:
    a. Residential
    b. Transient and resort housing
    c. Commercial property
3. Prospects for special purpose properties.

There are other ways to classify prospects. The categories may include:

1. Persons who need property for occupancy and use
2. Persons who seek maximum safety for accumulated savings, without regard to income
3. Persons seeking long-term investments in income-producing properties
4. Persons with risk capital, wishing to speculate
5. Persons desiring specific properties for sentimental reasons or to gratify their ownership instincts.

Executive control of real estate prospects begins with an understanding of just what a prospect is. Not every one is, or can be, a prospective purchaser of real property. Even though nearly everyone is interested in real estate to some degree, there are many persons who are merely curious about it. There are many who want to own real property but lack the financial resources to acquire it. They may like to look; they may inspect model homes; they may attend home-show exhibitions; they may answer ads. They lack purchasing power, and therefore they are not prospects. Collectively they can consume a vast amount of the broker's time. There are others who do have adequate financial resources, who would be benefited by properties the broker has for sale or by properties that he can find for them, but who have no intention of buying. These are potential prospects. They should be identified and cultivated. There are others still who have ample financial capacity and who are eager to buy if and when they are shown property that meets their needs—real or fancied. They are real prospects. They should have the immediate attention of the broker and command his most diligent efforts for service.

A real estate prospect, then, is a person who would be benefited by ownership and who is financially able to buy. He will buy only because of what the property will do for him. He has certain needs or desires which can be satisfied by the ownership of a certain type and class of real estate. He is subject to classification with a group of other individuals having similar needs, desires, and financial capacities.

The broker may, and usually does, get listings for which he has no immediate prospects. Then he must get busy to find one or more logical buyers. Many deals are made in just this way. But the alert and well-established broker will have at all times an inventory of potential prospects in his files. These files should be classified according to types and classes.

There are at least six important essential features of executive control of the inventory of prospects. The first essential phase of executive control is the planning and organization of the prospect files—of the inventory of potential buyers. This involves:

1. Deciding whether to use cards, record sheets, dossiers, or a combination of two or more methods of recording data
2. Deciding what size cards, record sheets, and dossiers to stock
3. Deciding what information to have recorded about prospects
4. Deciding what classifications to use for filing purposes
5. Setting up an appropriate cross-reference system
6. Establishing a follow-up and periodic review routine to keep files up to date

The second essential is the development of an adequate inventory of prospects. This inventory is of two kinds: groups of individuals definitely known to be desirous of buying or leasing real property; and groups of individuals who are potential prospects for specific types and classes of property. Individuals in the first category have made contact with the broker's office in response to ads offering specific properties for sale or they are persons who have contacted the office without solicitation to seek help in finding a certain type or class of property which they want to buy or lease. Persons in both these categories are real, active prospects.

Appropriate records of all these persons should be made immediately for the inventory of prospects, and of course, appropriate action should be taken promptly to serve them.

The third essential phase of executive control of prospects is to screen all inquiries about purchasing and leasing that are made in response to ads and that come into the office without solicitation to identify individuals who really are actual prospects and who are merely potential prospects. This should be done to eliminate individuals who do not qualify either as actual or as potential buyers.

A reservoir of potential prospects includes rosters of clubs, rosters of trade associations, lists of chain store executives, lists of known investors, lists of land developers, lists of speculators, and other lists. These individuals can be contacted by telephone or by direct mail when the broker has a listing for which he has no specific prospect and which he thinks has special benefits for persons of the type included in one or more of his rosters. For example, he may have a listing of a property which he considers to be ideally suited for a gasoline service station. But he has no immediate prospect for that kind of property. Then he proceeds to contact appropriate executives of oil companies to find one that wants a new location. This he can do by telephone, by personal contact, or by direct mail.

The alert broker will become personally acquainted with key executives of all chain store organizations that operate in his territory, or that can reasonably be expected to be interested in securing outlets in it. Periodic contacts with executives will keep the broker up to date on their needs for expansion. Once he has made one satisfactory deal for one of them he is likely to have priority on securing future locations for the chain in his territory and in adjacent areas. He becomes, in effect, the purchasing agent for the chain.

The fourth phase of executive control of prospects is to record the preliminary data about the prospects at the time of the initial contact and place it in the follow-up file for an investigation of the needs, desires, and capabilities of the individual.

The fifth phase of executive control is to assign the prospect to an appropriate salesman who will contact the prospect and secure and record detailed data about him as well as take the necessary steps to find and show properties, to negotiate the sale, and to close the deal.

The sixth phase of executive control of prospects is to require the salesman to submit a written report on each interview and each showing of a property to the prospect. This will not only keep the salesman diligent but will also keep the broker informed on what progress is being made and whether the salesman is in need of help to make a deal.

The seventh phase of executive control of prospects is the decision as to what disposition should be made of the records when the prospect buys or leases a property or when it is definite that no deal with him can be made in the foreseeable future. The buyer or lessee with whom the broker has made a satisfactory deal is a good prospect for another deal, either in the immediate future or at some point more remote in time. The records on the individual with whom a deal has been made should be saved and kept in an appropriate filing classification for future contacts. The records on the prospect with whom it has not been possible to deal may or may not be saved. The decision should be made by the broker or by the sales manager and will depend upon the needs and capabilities of the prospect, upon the type and class of property in which he was interested, and upon the probability that such a property will come onto the market within a reasonable period of time.

Although it is good business policy to develop and save comprehensive information about potential prospects, it is poor housekeeping to let the files become cluttered up with "deadwood." From time to time data that have been useful are not worth saving, even in the "dead" files. This is true of data on deceased persons and on persons who have permanently left the territory.

This brings us to the eighth phase of executive control of prospects, which is periodic review of the files. This should be done to eliminate data that has no further value, to ascertain what reclassification of prospects should be made to keep the records up to date, to discover opportunities that may have been neglected or overlooked, and to check upon the progress that has been made in serving active prospects.

Sources of prospects

When it is necessary to find a buyer for a specific property and the potential prospect cannot be found in the files, a search must be made to locate one. To facilitate a search and to be sure that no possible source is overlooked a comprehensive checklist of sources is helpful. The broker will do well to have copies of this list in the hands of all salesmen. It can be the basis for discussion at a sales meeting when the office is hard pressed to find a buyer for an important property. It will stimulate the thinking of every salesman who needs to hunt for prospects. There follows here a brief discussion of some of the items that belong in a checklist of sources of prospects.

1. The man next door

People who live in or who own property adjacent to or near property for sale have a genuine interest in who buys or leases it. Often they are glad to suggest names of friends they would like to have as neighbors. This is true of any type of class of property. Sometimes the man next door would like to add to his holding, or he might want to purchase it as an investment, since he probably already believes in the economic soundness and future of his own location. He may want to exercise control over the character and type of his future next door neighbor.

2. Friends and acquaintances

The real estate man who has been in business over a period of several years has developed a wide circle of friends and acquaintances. He is likely to know a great deal about the investment policies and about the real estate needs of many of these persons. With such a background, the broker or the salesman may be able to find a good prospect for the particular property he has for sale if he will spend some time in a mental review of the probable real estate needs of all the persons he knows.

3. Persons who have listed properties for sale

Frequently the person who has listed his property for sale has done so in order to secure the capital necessary to acquire a different location or a different type or class of property. Such a person might well be a good prospect for a trade and be quite willing to exchange his property for another that more fully satisfies his needs or desires. Or, if unwilling to trade, he may easily be interested in buying another property as soon as he sells the one he has listed for sale.

4. Persons who have recently sold property

The names of these persons can be secured from newspaper stories or from the recorder's office. They have had ownership experience. They have money derived from their recent sales. Some of them may be good prospects for the purchase of other property. It is good business policy to watch for their names, to contact them promptly, to find out about their real estate needs and plans, and to offer expert service in helping them get maximum benefits in the ownership of another property.

5. The columns of local newspapers

It is difficult to find a single issue of a daily paper that does not contain information pointing to a real or to a potential prospect for some type and class of real estate. Births, engagements, marriages, divorces, deaths, promotions, transfers, formation of new business firms, foreclosures, opening of branch manufacturing plants or business offices, and many other news items are often leads to sales.

6. Arrivals and moves in the city

In addition to newspaper items as leads to sales, it often happens that good leads can be secured from moving, storage, telephone, gas, and fuel oil companies. The secretary of the local chamber of commerce may be able to furnish profitable leads, since he is likely to know about new industries moving into the area and about local firms that establish branches elsewhere.

7. Directories and rosters

Membership rosters of clubs and fraternal organizations are not *per se* lists of prospects, but they are composed of persons having similar social or business interests and on about the same economic level. Such rosters or directories may contain names of excellent potential prospects for some kind of real estate service.

It is worthwhile to keep up-to-date directories in the reference library and to scan them carefully when in search of a person who can be benefited by ownership of a particular property. It may be profitable to circularize some of these lists with an appropriate institutional direct-mail advertising folder about once a year. A direct-mail folder on an industrial property mailed to members of an industrial club or to members of the industrial division of the local chamber of commerce may produce a buyer.

8. Apartment dwellers

Changing economic conditions, social composition, and change in family relations often induce apartment dwellers to consider buying a home. The alert management department of a real estate broker's office may know about renters who are good potential or actual prospects.

9. Former customers and clients

The purchaser or the seller of real estate may know of a friend or an acquaintance who is a potential prospect. Requests for names should be made of each customer and client as soon as the deal with him has been closed. A satisfied customer or client will have a friendly attitude toward the firm and will be pleased to have the opportunity to cooperate upon request.

10. Lists of payers of high income taxes

It is reasonable to assume that any group of persons who are in high income tax brackets include many individuals who are able to make investments in real estate. With care and effort a list of these persons in the local area can be compiled, or it may be possible to purchase a list from a local company that makes a business of compiling mailing lists for use in direct-mail campaigns.

11. List of owners of large properties

By consulting tax records as well as other sources, a list of owners of large real estate holdings can be compiled. They are already sold on the value of real property as investments and some may be quickly interested in buying additional property. In nearly every sizable community can be found one or more persons who take great pride in owning a great deal of real property. They are canny buyers, but they are likely to be easily approachable by the broker when he has a good buy to offer.

12. Investors

In almost every sizable community there are also many persons who are buying stocks and bonds but who do not own real estate as investments. This may be because they do not understand the peculiar advantages of real estate investments and have not been properly solicited by well-informed and reputable brokers. It is difficult quickly to compile a list, but it can be built up over a period of time through personal contacts with leading business and professional men in the area. Prominent physicians, surgeons, lawyers, and stars in the field of entertainment and sports are included in this list.

13. Other real estate brokers

The broker who specializes in a particular type of property, such as industrial property or country estates, may have a customer or client who wants to buy a home or some other type of property that he does not handle. It is worthwhile to establish and maintain friendly relations with all specialists. To earn a split in a commission, if for no other reason, a specialist may be in a position from time to time to refer business deals to other brokers.

This is not an exhaustive list. There are many other sources, some of which follow here without comment.

1. Visitors at own-your-home shows
2. Callers at homes open for inspection
3. Courthouse and municipal records
4. Other prospects
5. Window displays
6. Signs on property
7. Clipping bureaus

8. The telephone
9. Firms operating at capacity and interested in expansion
10. Chain stores
11. Business firms whose leases expire
12. Individuals required to move to make way for urban renewal or slum clearance projects
13. Individuals adversely affected by construction of new highways or street widening projects
14. Ambitious employees of established firms
15. Advertising in its various forms
16. Employees in the broker's own office
17. Building and loan associations

The real estate broker in his capacity as company executive will be familiar with all of the sources mentioned in this chapter. He will do well to instruct his sales force and other employees in the potentials of each source. He should conduct training sessions on how to tap these sources and what disposition to make of the names of new prospects as they are discovered. He should provide a well-organized filing system for preserving the names of prospects with appropriate information about each. He should supervise the use of the files to be sure they are kept in efficient working order and that they are overhauled from time to time to keep them up to date.

Analysis of prospects

It should be remembered that the buyer of real estate wants the property for what it can do for him. He has certain needs or desires that he wants to satisfy by acquiring the ownership or possession by lease of a certain type and class of real estate, usually in a specific geographical area. His needs, his desires, and his financial capabilities are reflected by his background, by his current environment, by his social and economic status, and by his ambitions. In order to serve him properly the broker needs to know a great deal about him. The broker acts as the agent of the prospect as well as the agent of the seller. To a great extent, from an ethical standpoint, the relationship is a professional one, especially when the prospect is a client rather than a customer. The broker is fully justified in asking his prospect for detailed information concerning his status, his needs, his desires, and his financial capabilities. The broker should lead the prospect to understand that he can furnish the fullest measure of service only if he is provided with necessary detailed confidential information.

In the potential prospect files a rather brief summary of data will be quite sufficient. But considerable additional information is needed on the active prospect. This detailed data can be recorded on 8 1/2 x 11 record sheets or even on a four-page folder. It may be practical to develop a printed or mimeographed form for the recording of such detailed data. The importance of the prospect sometimes justifies the development of a comprehensive dossier.

It is often a waste of time to show properties to a prospect who has not been thoroughly analyzed in advance to make sure that the properties offered to him actually match his needs or desires. The overlooking or the neglect of only one important detail may lose a sale. That is why the analysis should be thorough and complete. To avoid overlooking important details it is good practice to have a comprehensive checklist at hand when the prospect is interviewed. Any one of the following suggested items may be important.

1. Name of the prospect in full
2. Addresses and phone numbers of business and residence
3. Date of initial contact
4. Type and class of property desired
5. Motive for buying
6. Location desired
7. Occupational history
8. Position held—present and past
9. Income bracket of prospect
10. Marital status of prospect
11. Cash available for down payment
12. Financial terms desired
13. Property now owned by prospect
14. Current debts of prospects
15. Source of the prospect
16. Children, by sex and age
17. Church affiliation

18. School facilities needed or desired
19. Racial origin
20. Hobbies
21. Club and other significant memberships
22. Where to contact prospect
23. When to contact prospect
24. Salesman to whom prospect is assigned
25. Processing
    a. Dates of calls
        1) By telephone
        2) In person
    b. Properties shown
        1) Dates
        2) Locations
        3) Results

CHAPTER SIXTEEN

The management of real property

Management is a new science in the business of real estate investment and has taken its place in the educational process.

An investment in real estate may have one or many purposes: the purchase of land for enhancement in value, the purchase of land for development, the purchase of existing property for rehabilitation, the purchase of a new building for security and income, the purchase for use, or any other reason of the purchaser for either investment income or the satisfaction of ownership which the amenities of the property may render.

No matter what the reason for ownership, the management of the property will be important to the success or failure of the investment.

Owners' objectives and interests

The management of a property must not only satisfy the investment purpose of the owner, but also serve the purpose of the user, whether he be the owner or tenant. The objectives of an owner and his interests are:

1. Preservation of capital
2. Reasonable return
3. Enhancement in value
4. Prestige of ownership

Discussing these objectives in order, first and foremost among the owner's aims is to maintain the value of his investment so that when the time comes to sell, either by necessity or desire, the owner can recoup his original investment. To attain this objective, the manager and owner must have a close relationship and a program of management and an orderly plan. Physical property deteriorates with the passage of time and requires constant attention to retain its value.

Second, the owner is entitled to a reasonable return, in either interest on his investment or the return of amenities by occupancy. A property bought for investment requires an adequate gross rental with a program of expenditures which will leave a net return on the investment and retire the investment over a given period of time. Amenity income to an owner-occupant is measured in the satisfaction of ownership. An owner-occupant may have a special use for the property or gain satisfaction from ownership which fulfills his personal desires. The advertising value of a home office created by distinctive architecture, location, height, or recreation facilities for employees may give an owner-occupant satisfaction profitable to him, but not measurable in direct financial return.

Third, the enhancement in value of a property is a distinct desire of an owner. When, through astute management, net income is increased, the value of the property is enhanced. Net income to the owner is the measure of value, and sales prices will fluctuate with the net income produced by the property. Management can cause an increase in net income by: (*a*) an increase in gross income; (*b*) a reduction of expenses and taxes; (*c*) rehabilitation resulting in an increase of net income or sales price. Although rehabilitation for condominium sales does not produce greater net income, an enhancement in value is obtained, and the investment becomes profitable through capital value enhancement.

Fourth, the ownership of real estate renders prestige and is the fulfillment of the desire of every property owner. The owner of profitable income property feels that he has reached the ultimate success in real estate investment. The owner of income property has established prestige and is looked upon as a leader in the community. The managers of property must, therefore, maintain the properties they manage so the owners can have pride in their possession. To allow deterioration of the property reflects on the personality of the owner, and he can lose the respect of his friends and associates. To him, good maintenance is also a good investment and pays dividends in his pride of ownership.

The protection of these ideals of the owner is the responsibility of the manager. The successful execution of the directives of the owner is the duty of the manager.

The property owner has responsibilities to his tenants and seeks relief from these responsibilities by employing a property manager.

Tenants' rights and interests

The tenant has interests and rights to which he is entitled when he contracts to pay rent. The owner binds himself by contract to conditions in a lease and grants to the tenant certain rights to which, by common law, he is entitled.

These rights and interests are:

a. A tenant is entitled to the security and safety of his person and property. The owner must give protection from entry and seizure by having security devices in good repair and providing personnel for protection. Security encompasses more than personal protection of person and goods, including protection from vermin, leaky roofs, inadequate heat, or property conditions unsafe for human habitation.

Tenant organizations and consumer groups are organized for enforcement of tenants' rights and must be reckoned with by management.

b. The tenant pays for comfort and convenience. Upon inspection of the premises, he becomes acquainted with the property to which he is entitled. The rooms are of a certain size, the arrangement of rooms is established, and light and air is noted. Of these physical characteristics, he is aware. The maintenance of the property in good repair is the duty of the owner. Attention to complaints is appreciated by tenants and courteous attention establishes a relationship leading to a long tenancy which is profitable to the owner. The manager can establish this relationship.

c. A tenant is entitled to peace in the occupancy of his quarters. To be annoyed by other tenants, to have noisy and unruly children disturb his quest for quiet, to have clattering air-bound radiators disturb his sleep, violate his right to peace and comfort. Noisy and party-giving tenants do not enhance the reputation of a building as a desirable place to live. The manager is responsible for the control of these undesirable conditions, and must give prompt attention to complaints of tenants, and demand that the rules of the building and the lease be obeyed.

d. When a person rents, he pays a rental within his ability to pay. To him, his pride of possession is as important as the owner's pride of ownership. He is entitled to no more than what he pays for, but for what he pays, he is entitled to. To the tenant, the premises are his image to his friends and associates. He has set up status and a standard of living for all to observe.

The manager has the obligation to provide the amenities to which the tenant is entitled. The tenant is entitled to a well-maintained property, clean halls, prompt garbage collection, lighted entrances and stairwells, safe porches, and clean yards. These items of physical care are image makers for the tenant.

The owner-tenant relationship is becoming increasingly a social and socio-economic relationship, with the manager intimately involved.

Managers' rights and duties

The relationship between the owner and manager must be clearly defined. This is by contract between owner and manager with clauses to delineate rights of the owner in the management of his property to the manager. These rights are summarily the right to create and collect income and the right to preserve the property through expenditures which preserve the physical property and maintain its operating functions.

Leasing program requirements

The right to create income gives the manager rights to lease the premises and contract for rent over a period of time. The leasing process requires preparation in establishing rents. This function of the manager necessitates the following research:

1. Economic survey of the neighborhood.
2. Physical inspection of the property.

3. Analysis of the relationship of the property to the neighborhood.
4. Budgeting of income and expenses.

Within these four categories of analysis lies the basic knowledge required to set up a leasing program.

The economic analysis of a neighborhood appears to be a simple task, but is fraught with possible erroneous conclusions. Neighborhoods have physical boundaries which often cause neighborhoods within neighborhoods. The status appeal of streets, parks, schools, boulevards, transportation, and age mix of existing buildings will cause a diversity of income in renters. This diversity of income will occur in changing neighborhoods where areas are limited in their appeal. The change from the brownstone to the luxury highrise, from the status multiroom residence to the luxury condominium are examples of economic mix. An economic survey is also a social survey. The researcher must be aware of the desire by people to live within a social-economic group of their own status.

Income levels create ability to pay, and once the income bracket is established, the ability to pay is established. The neighborhood economic survey will establish upper limits of rent applicable to the accommodations. As the survey reveals existing rents, ratios of rent to income can be established, and brackets of income become valid; thus the rents may reveal a ratio of one to four or one to five of annual rent to annual income, or income to rent-paying ability. A family earning $10,000 per year may be able to pay $2,500 annual rent, or a family annual income of $15,000 may pay an annual rent of $3,000. As a general rule, the higher the income of a family, the wider the ratio, such as 4 to 1–$10,000 to $2,500 and 5 to 1–$15,000 to $3,000. The census tracts are an excellent source of income and employment statistics. In addition to the economic study, social statistics are important in the study of a neighborhood. Schools, churches, ethnic background, employment source, age level, transportation, and shopping accommodations contribute to the appeal of a neighborhood for renters.

Zoning is legally effective in establishing rental neighborhoods and single-family ownership neighborhoods. It would be unusual for a neighborhood of single family homes to have a high percentage of rental units.

Economic stability is related to job stability, and the sources of employment, either within or outside the neighborhood boundaries, will assist in establishing a criteria of economic soundness.

Before taking responsibility for the management of a property, a physical inspection of the property should be made. An inspection will disclose the condition of the property, the number of units in the building, and their composition. A survey of the neighborhood will reveal the most popular unit, the rent level, and the service which the tenant expects. The manager, by personal inspection, can elate the building to these factors and judge the ability of the building to meet these requirements. One of the most important decisions is whether the room composition of the units meets the greatest demand. The manager must know which composition of apartment is most popular. If the demand is for two-bedroom apartments, three or four-bedroom apartments will be surplus in the market and rent at a lower rental per room per month. An imbalance of units to market demand affects the ratio of income to expense, and lowers the net annual income.

The physical inspection reveals the condition of the building. The manager should report what repairs need immediate attention, what major replacements can be delayed, and other physical conditions of importance to the owner. Oftentimes owners are not aware of the necessity for a new roof, a boiler replacement, or the need for rehabilitation of kitchens and bathrooms. The manager protects himself against future requests for major expenditures when he alerts the owner in advance. The manager also shows his awareness and knowledge of building components and the necessity of keeping them in good condition. A leaking roof can cause falling plaster and a leaking faucet a high water bill. A complete report of the physical condition of the property should be rendered periodically.

A property either relates to a neighborhood or does not. The manager, by making a survey of the neighborhood, knows the needs of the people of the neighborhood. He has learned that the neighborhood has a predominance of families requiring one bedroom, two bedrooms, or some other composition. He has found that the rental bracket is $180 per month to $300 per month. He is aware of the change taking place in the income group and the demand for modern equipment. By his physical inspection of the property and relating it to other properties in the neighborhood, he becomes aware of the qualities in his building which may or may not meet the demands of prospective tenants. This is important in setting rents, estimating expenses, and makes him aware of the service he can render his tenants. Every property is in a competitive position, and the manager must prepare himself with knowledge of his competition and formulate a program to meet it. Service is often a nebulous word, but tenants in competitive buildings are aware of quality management and will recommend to their friends buildings which have a reputation for good management. Awareness of the quality of management in competitive buildings is a valuable tool to evaluate the quality of management of a particular building.

Budgeting

Budgeting is necessary. The setting of income and expense goals serves as guidelines for good performance. A knowledgeable manager knows the necessity of budgeting his income and expenses. In establishing the gross income of the property, the physical condition of the property, the composition of the units, and his competitive position will guide him to determine his maximum rent role. Although 100 percent occupancy is a desirable goal, it is not necessary to attain it. Managers must consider maximum occupancy and normal vacancy. Real estate appraisers, in valuing income property, consider vacancies as a normal condition and will allow a vacancy ratio of 2 percent to 10 percent of gross income. Loss of rent is an allowable deduction from gross income and may be considered a part of the vacancy ratio. In estimating gross rent, the manager will find his competitive buildings are producing a per room per month figure. A careful analysis of this method is necessary. As an example, a $30 per room per month apartment will not offer the same amenities as a $70 per room apartment, and yet each may contain 4 rooms. Again, an apartment of 6 rooms renting for $25 per room per month (or $150 per month), may be renting at this lower rental per room per month because of a lower demand for 6 rooms in the neighborhood, or because of the age of the building and its accommodations. The number of baths, the location of the unit in the building, per room expense, services, size of rooms, and method of room count must receive consideration in establishing per room rents by the competitive room rent method.

The Institute of Real Estate Management publishes an annual *Apartment Building Income and Expense Analysis* booklet that is invaluable to managers of apartment buildings. The analysis covers apartment buildings located throughout the country. The breakdown of income and expense is by age level, room count, and building types. The book may be ordered through the Institute at the office of the National Association of Boards of Realtors.

Determining the required rent to make a project profitable is often the assignment of the manager. In such assignments, the manager must know the price paid for or the cost to produce the property. The value of the property (land and building) is derived by establishing a net income—gross effective rent less expenses and taxes—which is capitalized at a rate of return which produces interest on the capital invested and a return of capital over a period of years representing its economic life. This process is the property residual technique of the capitalization approach to value. The rent necessary to make the project profitable may not be attainable and the proposal may, therefore, not be feasible. Great responsibility rests on the manager in setting rents and net income on proposed projects.

The value of an investment property lies in its ability to produce net income. In the process of preparing a budget, in addition to setting the effective gross rent, expenses and taxes must be estimated. Certain items of expenses cannot be controlled. Janitor wages, doorman wages, water bills, electric bills, garbage collections, and other labor or utility controlled expenses are examples of such items. Careful supervision of wasted water, electricity, and heating will reduce these expenses to a minimum. Painting and decorating, interior and exterior, are controllable, but should not be reduced to adversely effect either occupancy or deterioration of the building. Repairs, such as roof, porches, tuckpointing, minor plumbing and heating, screens, carpentry, electric, plaster, and sheet metal expenses should receive immediate attention to avoid later major expense. Determination of these expenses is difficult, but can be estimated by comparison with buildings of like construction and age. Use of the Institute of Real Estate Management Income and Expense book is invaluable as a guideline.

After inspection of the building, the manager can estimate the necessity for replacements. Shades, carpets, stoves, refrigerators, boilers, furnaces, and air conditioners have a physical and economic life. An estimate of their remaining life and cost to replace must be made to establish replacement reserve. These estimates are made by an estimate of physical life of each item against its cost to replace. An item with a 20-year life will have an annual replacement charge of 5 percent or $5 per year for each $100 of replacement cost.

Other budget expenses are collection charges, legal fees, and auditing fees. These are negotiable. Although management organizations and real estate boards in the past have had suggested management fees, they have never been strictly observed.

Taxes should receive the attention of the manager annually and also at quadrennial or established reassessment periods. The tax rate and the assessed value of the property establish the taxes. Errors occur in both the tax assessors' and clerk's office and the records should be checked. Although there are tax specialists who can handle the review of the value assessment and the tax rate, the manager should confirm the correctness of both, either by his personal handling or by others.

From a budget the owner can estimate the value of his investment and control his financial obligations. If a mortgage is on the property, he has an estimate of the net rent available to meet mortgage payments. The manager may be instructed to retain sufficient income to make mortgage payments and the owner receive the balance of net income.

Interest and amortization payments are not a management responsibility and should not be included in a budget unless requested by the owner.

Income property is bought for net return to the investor and cash flow is the primary concern of owners and managers. The manager must have knowledge of real estate investment analysis and must be acquainted with tax laws as they are changed periodically by local, state, and national governments.

The brokerage office

The management department of a brokerage office has an opportunity to service other departments. The management personnel has continuous contact with the tenants of the building which is managed and many personal services may be rendered. The tenant may require personal and household insurance on his property and may develop as a life insurance client as the result of the personal contact with rental personnel. The management personnel should be alert to inquiries and advise the insurance department of the names of renters and conversations held with them. This is especially true of tenants from other cities when a new lease is made. Rarely will the newcomer be referred by a former insurance agent to an agent in the new city. The rental agent should not pose as an insurance expert, but can properly refer the tenant to the insurance department and make contact for the insurance personnel. Insurance clients can become permanent clients, and the relationship continue as tenants move to other locations served by the insurance department.

The insurance department should work in close cooperation with the brokerage department. Every purchaser and seller is a prospect for insurance. Whether it be a home-owner's policy, or household furniture, automobile, accident, or life insurance policy, the rental manager has an opportunity to engage the tenant in a discussion of his insurance needs. The condominium owner is oftentimes not aware of the need for insurance on the property within the walls of his unit. Furniture and personal property of the condominium owner are not covered by the trustees or managers of the condominium common areas unless specific arrangements are made for this coverage. When this coverage is available, the manager's insurance agent may insure articles of special value, such as wall decorations and fixtures that may be the unit owner's personal property. At slight additional cost, these items can be covered by a special policy and thus avoid any question about responsibility in case of loss. In these cases, the rental agent has the opportunity to discuss these matters with the renter or condominium owner. The expertise of the insurance department may then be called upon and the proper policy written.

The close contact of management personnel with tenants gives the rental personnel the opportunity to ascertain the permanency of occupancy of the tenant. If his residence in the city is temporary, tenancy may be the desirable housing arrangement. If the tenant expects to be located permanently in the city, however, home ownership may be desirable, and a client for the sales department can be developed. Here again, the rental agent becomes familiar with the tenants' needs and a friendly introduction to the sales department can be effected. This cooperation between departments can prove to be profitable and raise the morale between the departments of the office. The broker should make cooperation rewarding to office personnel and foster it by split-commissions or listing fees. Rental agents are licensed as salesmen and therefore entitled to serve as sales people and enjoy the sharing of sales commissions.

Sales referrals between out of city or out of state brokers may be initiated with the rental agent who may be the first to learn of the removal of a tenant from the city. National referral organizations cooperate in referrals and some title companies have established departments for this purpose. Broker cooperation through the Brokers Institute of the National Association of Real Estate Boards is fostered by their directory.

As a large percentage of real estate sales require financing, the cooperation between departments may be illustrated by the reference of the sales department to the finance or mortgage department which may be the final link in the successful culmination of a profitable transaction for the brokers office.

The greatest source of property management business is from private real estate investors. Some large investors have formed their own companies and restrict their operations to their private holdings. Banks, insurance companies, corporations, trust companies, and estates require the services of property managers. With constantly changing ownership, the opportunity to obtain new business is ever present. The alert broker can find prospects within his own organization through the activity of the sales department. Changing ownership through sales gives the management department an opportunity to induce the new owner to change management. When a new owner is satisfied with the conduct of a purchase by the sales department, he will have confidence that the firm can service him with the same expertise in management.

State, local, and the national governments have managed their properties through management departments. During recent years, with the problems of management increasing in specific areas, the administrators of various agencies have been turning to the professional management organizations for assistance. Under government management, the training of employees, turnover of personnel, and the specific problems which are encountered in management of government properties, efficient management has suffered. A brokerage office with a department of well-trained personnel has an opportunity to serve the various governments engaged in residential real estate property management. As the housing programs change from time to time, it is suggested that the manager broker keep in contact with the agencies and be alert to the opportunities which governments present.

CHAPTER SEVENTEEN

Financial control

In addition to the furnishing of professional services, as a real estate broker, you must conduct your activities as a business enterprise, the basic purpose of which is to make a profit.

Effective financial control of operations is essential to success. You may have an excellent office location, the best office equipment and layout, an efficient office staff, and a top-quality sales force, but if your expenses exceed your income over any considerable period of time, you will go broke and your career in real estate brokerage will come to an end.

There are certain expenses that you must incur whether or not you have any income—whether or not your firm makes any sales or earns any fees for other services. These expenses are reoccurring—month after month—year after year. They may have little if any relation to sales activities. If they are extravagant or not carefully controlled, they can break you. These various items of expense will be enumerated and discussed briefly in this chapter.

There are other items of expense that are closely related to sales activities—that must be incurred in order to develop sales—to get listings, to find prospects, and to implement the sales process. These items of expense, also, must not be extravagant or uncontrolled if you expect to operate your business without having a serious deficit at the end of the year. They, too, will be enumerated and discussed in this chapter.

Your problem as the manager of your business is twofold: (1) to produce the largest possible gross income, and (2) to hold expenses to the absolute minimum consistent with effective operations. Insofar as expenses are concerned, this means that (1) you must budget your costs, with careful consideration of each item, however small, to make sure that it is not excessive, and (2) that you must be prepared from time to time to increase or curtail the amount of money allocated to an item if necessary. You cannot afford to let any item of cost get out of hand. Through frequent periodic reports, you must keep yourself informed on your detailed cost of operation and take prompt action to make whatever revisions may be necessary to keep expenditures under control.

You will be smart and use good judgment if you attach to your staff a qualified CPA who is also an experienced tax expert, or employ on a retainer basis such a man who is an independent practitioner in the accounting and tax service field. He can be invaluable in helping you develop your annual budget, in reviewing your financial status from time to time, in advising you how to handle deals that involve tax considerations, and in preparing income tax returns and other tax reports. He can save you money, keep you from making costly mistakes, and shield you from worry.

You should begin each year with a detailed itemized estimate of all income you are likely to realize and an itemized estimate of all expenses you have reason to believe you will incur.

In adopting a budget, consideration must be given to the type of office the broker is operating. If the office is the type known as a one-man office—the space, number of assistants required, and the general overhead will be considerably less than that of the larger office with many salesmen and various departments. Certain fixed expenses will, however, prevail but in relation to the number of producing personnel. One person is necessary for answering the telephone, answering inquiries in reference to advertisements, typing letters, and performing other routine matters. The bookkeeping is not as involved in the smaller office as in the larger office in which commissions, proportionate advertising costs, employee expense items, and records for tax purposes must be kept.

The large office with various departments must keep office records of the operation of each department. The managers of the various departments must keep production records. The salesmen in the insurance department, the sales department, and the rental managers in the management department have income and expense records which apply to their activities. To keep harmony between top management and the various personnel, these records must be available for the allocation of charges and for the proper payment of expenses, salaries, commissions, and bonuses. When proper records are kept, disputes as to earnings are kept to a minimum, and accurate reports for income tax purposes are available to employees.

Many brokerage offices form syndicates to buy and sell property with the profit motive as a basis for operation. The keeping of records of such operations is extremely important. The amount of investment of each investor, the contribution made to deficit operations, the reporting of income and expenses for the distribution of net earnings, depreciation computations for tax purposes—all require the most accurate accounting. The CPA attached to the office and the attorney familiar with syndicate operations must be kept available for advice and counsel on reports of syndicate operations. Upon closing a syndicate investment through either sale or other form of liquidation, the statements rendered to investors must be uniform and prepared in compliance with government regulations. The broker must protect himself against the possible misunderstanding of clients in their investments. An independent check by people knowledgeable in real estate investment trust matters is essential.

The broker is often confronted with what appears to be opportunities to invest in real estate on his own account and thus add to his profit. Such investments should be separated and not be made a part of his brokerage business. Brokers are more successful when they separate their private investments from their clients' investments. If the broker does not suggest that he is willing to take part of the investment, then the purchaser will not rely on the broker to help make his decision. The purchaser may or may not be influenced by the statement by the broker that he thinks highly enough of his recommendation to invest himself. The investor-broker relationship can become tarnished when the broker becomes part owner. There are many factors which enter into a broker-investor relationship which can cause friction. One is the question of commission at purchase and sale. The management of the property may come under scrutiny. The division of profits and losses for income tax purposes requires the maintenance of accounting practices which do not intermingle the broker's earnings from his brokerage business with that of his personal investments.

The capital required to operate a brokerage business depends on to what extent the broker engages in activities other than sales. If sales are the only activity, the daily, monthly, or annual expenses are the only cash requirements. Advertising, clerical salaries, rent, light, stationery and mailing, telephone, and transportation, in addition to the living expenses of the broker, are the only items which require his capital. However, if the business is expanded into departments of insurance, mortgage servicing, renting and management, appraising, and counseling, additional capital will be necessary. Bank credit may be relied upon to a degree, but the financing of mortgages and insurance premiums may require advances from the broker's own funds. Fees and charges are not always paid upon receipt of the bill, and expenses, if promptly paid, must be paid from the broker's capital funds. At times, commissions must be advanced to salesmen and drawing accounts allowed which require cash from capital funds.

A brokerage business may be operated as a corporation, partnership, or an individual business. In a corporation, stock may be held by one or more persons and the capital for operations raised according to the needs of the business. A partnership or individual ownership supplies the necessary funds according to the needs of the business and the division of ownership. Most partnerships have a limitation of liability. Where limited partnership exists, clients of the office should be aware of the limitation. If all the stockholders in the corporation are active in the business, the stockholders are aware of the activities of the office. Stockholders who are pure investors will require reports to keep them informed. This information must be available and given at regular intervals. If the officers of the corporation are active in the brokerage business, they must be licensed in most states as real estate brokers. As officers of the corporation they are responsible to the state authorities who supervise real estate activities.

Care must be exercised that the books of the business are always up to date and available for inspection by the examiners of the state department in charge of licensing. In many states, the funds of clients must be separated from that of the owners of the business or the corporation. Deposits on sales, rents, and other escrow funds must be available for disbursement and cannot be used by the broker for his expenses. At the time of closing of a sale or at such time as a commission is earned, the escrow deposits may be transferred to the broker's account. Salesmen cannot be reimbursed from deposits on a contract until the contract is closed.

All 50 states have brokers and salesmen laws which regulate the sale and renting of real estate. The financial condition of the business is subject to examination by the state. The finances of the business must be carefully managed not only for the success of the business but also for examination by public bodies who have authority to make inspections and examinations.

There are two distinct sources of income for a broker. One is constant, and a reasonably accurate estimate can be made from year to year. The source of this income is from the renting and management department and the insurance department. A broker who has a management department can estimate his income from the number of buildings or rental units which he manages. The fees for management are not legally fixed but are established by custom and recommendation of the local real estate board. These fees are accepted by owners of property as customary and fair. Commission rates may be obtained from the office of the real estate board. Rental commissions are obtained from two sources: (1) a gross commission for negotiating a lease, and (2) a commission commensurate with the monthly or annual rents collected and the services rendered. In the latter case, the management contract will state the specific duties to be performed by the managing broker and the fees established will be commensurate with the duties performed. The collection of rent and the leasing of units are not the only duties performed in the management function. The care of the building, tax assessment, employment of personnel, advice on care and maintenance over and above the routine chores of cleaning and decorating are responsibilities which must be considered in the fee charged. The manager of real estate may be the cause for an increase or decrease of the net income of a property and thus greatly control its value. Owners recognize competent management and are willing to pay for competent care of their properties.

The insurance department of a broker's office can be another source of constant income. The insurance of real estate is an integral part of a broker's business. When the sale of property is consummated, the insurance on the property must be transferred. The mortgagee must be protected by insurance and the mortgagor must be protected in the amount of his equity. These matters receive the attention of the broker at the time of listing the property for sale and at the time the contract is closed. Often the owner is unaware that his property is underinsured and that he does not carry certain desirable insurance coverage. The broker can bring this to his attention and suggest that he take out additional insurance. To properly present insurance requirements, the broker must be informed on all phases of insurance including fire, extended coverage, personal and public liability, and various forms of hazard insurance. The broker who places a mortgage may also have the opportunity to write insurance for the mortgagee. Although new business may be an irregular source of income, the renewal premiums can be estimated by the expiration dates of policies. A competent clerk can take care of renewals and prove to be a valuable aid to a broker and his staff.

The servicing of mortgages can be a constant and recurring income to a brokerage office that develops mortgage outlets and serves as a correspondent for mortgage lending institutions. Insurance companies, pension funds, banks, university endowment funds, private investors, and estates are sources of contact for the placing and servicing of real estate mortgages. As business expands, the increase of business requires little expansion of personnel although income to the firm may grow substantially.

A broker never knows when he will negotiate a sale. No pattern of income can be established from year to year. The broker, however, knows that there will be a certain number of owners who for reasons of their own will offer their property for sale. From such an estimate of probable sales, the broker can budget his income from sales. The weekly or monthly budget may prove to be inaccurate, but over the year the budget should be met. Real estate sales run in cycles, and to smooth out the curves is difficult. Sales often come with great rapidity and a drought may follow. The real estate broker must reckon with these conditions and allow for them in his budget and cash flow requirements.

Appraisal fees and consultation fees fall in the same category of uncertain estimation as brokerage fees. When called upon to make an appraisal, the client usually wants prompt attention, and the broker before taking an assignment should be careful not to overcommit himself. To make an appraisal requires careful consideration of many factors in regard to the property, and the report is time-consuming in its preparation. A broker never should take an assignment with which he is not familiar. A great responsibility rests upon a broker who makes an appraisal report. A consulting assignment may or may not be analogous to an appraisal report. A client who seeks consultation on real estate matters is usually one who is disturbed about general real estate conditions or the feasibility of making a real estate investment. A broker who offers himself for this type of counseling must be a mature, knowledgeable person who has had a great number of years of experience in the real estate business. His knowledge must be in every phase of the business, and his personal participation and experience is necessary to guide a client to a reasonable decision. Real estate counseling does not always involve the writing of a report but may be an "armchair" discussion of the problem. Many brokers are receiving assignments of this nature from real estate investors.

Expenses

In budgeting expenses, the broker is again faced with the problem of estimating the known and unknown expenses.

If a broker rents his quarters, the expenses of taxes, heating, and other operating expenses assumed by the owner are fixed. "Occupancy" expense is therefore a fixed monthly or annual item. If the lease agreement requires the occupant to decorate, clean, and maintain the premises, these items must be included in his rent expense. If, however, the broker owns his property, taxes, heating, decorating, electricity, janitorial service, painting and decorating, insurance, mortgage interest and payments, repairs, and ground maintenance are "costs of occupancy."

In addition to quarters, office equipment must be provided.

Chairs, tables, desks, carpets, bookcases, filing cabinets, typewriters, copying machines, stationery, business cards, and file folders are items which are used or depreciate daily during the operation of the business.

Automobile expenses, telephone, membership dues, conventions, and client entertainment are necessary expenses which should be budgeted.

A careful budgeting of advertising is necessary so that this item can be properly controlled. In a large office with many salesmen this item can get out of hand. Salesmen are inclined to want to advertise more than necessary on properties which are difficult to sell. Billboards, signs, and other fixed advertising items may be institutional advertising and can definitely be controlled.

The following list of expense items should be budgeted:

1. Rent
2. Real estate taxes and license fees
3. Fuel, water, gas, and electricity
4. Interior maintenance of office
    a. Janitor
    b. Painting and decorating
    c. Cleaning
5. Exterior maintenance of building and grounds
6. Furniture and equipment
    a. Desks, chairs, files, tables, typewriters
    b. Replacement, repairs and amortization
    c. Accounting machines
7. Insurance
    a. Building, and equipment—fire, extended coverage, and theft
    b. Automobile
    c. Health and accident
    d. Retirement income
    e. Social security
    f. Public liability
8. Mortgage principal and interest
9. Interest on invested capital and borrowed funds and recapture of capital investment
10. Public relations and advisory counseling
11. Salaries, drawing accounts, and bonuses

12. Telephone and telegraph
13. Attorney fees
14. Membership dues
    a. Real estate board
    b. State association
    c. National association
    d. Institutes
    e. Clubs
    f. Others
15. Conventions, entertainment, meetings, and travel expense
16. Business cards, stationery, maps, and postage
17. Advertising
    a. Classified—newspapers and trade publications
    b. Display
    c. Direct mail
    d. Brochures and photographs
    e. Billboards
    f. Signs
18. Automobile
    a. Depreciation
    b. Gas and oil
    c. Repair
    d. Insurance
19. Miscellaneous office supplies
    a. Carbon paper
    b. Stencils
    c. Photographic film
    d. Printed forms—leases, contracts, appraisals
    e. File folders

If your accountant-tax counselor has had or is having experience with financial control in other real estate brokerage firms, he will be able to keep your expenses at the same level as other firms.

A few years ago, the California Real Estate Association surveyed the operations of 39 real estate brokerage firms in that state. This survey revealed that the division of these brokers' expenses were as follows:

1. Occupancy, including property taxes, mortgage interest, rent utilities, janitor, etc.—7 to 10 percent of expenses

2. Telephone—5 to 9 percent of expenses
3. Sales manager's salary—7 to 20 percent of expenses
4. Salaries, including secretaries, receptionists, but not management—20 to 25 percent of expenses
5. Advertising, including newspapers, signs, brochures, etc.—15 to 27 percent of expenses
6. Return for the owner's listing and sales activities, administrative management, capital investment, training, future growth, good will, and income tax—24 to 41 percent of expenses

You see there was considerable variation in these percentages. You cannot adopt any of these percentages as a hard and fast rule in your own business, but they reflect the administrative results of 39 leading California real estate brokers, and they may suggest a tentative pattern for your operations, to be revised from time to time as you pilot your business into future years.

CHAPTER EIGHTEEN

Government aid and restrictions

Real estate is the largest and the most important form of accumulated wealth in our nation. Its ownership, its tenancy, and its utilization exert profound controlling influences upon the welfare of owners, tenants, the community in which the real estate is located, and the nation. These influences can contribute to the prosperity and happiness of individuals, or they can produce severe hardships and harm to individuals and to communities.

For these reasons, governments (local, state, and federal) have enacted a great variety of laws and adopted numerous regulations affecting ownership and tenancy. Some of these are designed to assist in acquisition of ownership and tenancy. Some impose penalties for actions that are detrimental to other owners, nonowners, and tenants. In addition, for the protection of the public, various limitations have been placed upon the activities of persons engaged in the real estate vocation—brokers, salesmen, appraisers, managers, mortgage men, developers, and builders.

Our economy and our society are both dynamic—are constantly undergoing changes. This results in new legislation, new regulations, and revisions, all of which add to the vast volume of laws and regulations of which the practicing real estate broker must have a working knowledge.

A detailed catalogue with comments on the significance of these laws and regulations would fill a volume, requiring far more space than can be devoted to them in this book. For this reason, and because they are in a constant state of change, we shall avoid a detailed discussion of them here.

As a real estate broker, you must be familiar with existing laws and government regulations that affect your business. This knowledge can help you create transactions helpful to sellers and buyers alike. This knowledge can help you avoid costly mistakes and avoid penalties for violations.

It is difficult for any one person to keep himself fully informed on these matters. If you have a competent staff, you can divide responsibilities with some of your associates. They can keep you posted on new developments. Just remember that you are responsible for any errors or misrepresentations made by your employees and associates. You can depend to a large extent, also, on your attorney and your tax expert. It is wise to consult both of them on each complex transaction.

You should have personal contact and be acquainted with each key government official who has administrative responsibilities for government regulations affecting real estate transactions and who has his office in your territory. It is a good policy to have periodic personal conferences with them.

You should develop and maintain reference files in which to keep information about local, state, and federal regulations affecting your business. Each of these files should be appropriately subdivided, and you should have a master cross-reference card file.

Although state and federal regulations affect the sale and occupancy of real estate, the local laws are close to the broker's operations and should be understood by him from both a theoretical and practical viewpoint. A brief discussion of the more important laws follows.

For many years, zoning laws were opposed as an interference in the property rights of an owner to use his property as he thought most profitable. The mixing of residential, commercial, and industrial land was prevalent and is noted in the pattern of our older cities. The first serious discussion of zoning in American cities was in 1911, and in 1916 the first zoning law was adopted by the city of New York. Use of property prior to the enactment of a zoning ordinance is not affected by the passage of an ordinance which may change the use of vacant or surrounding property. Upon the

Government aid and restrictions   217

abandonment of the nonconforming use, the owner must comply with the ordinance provisions. The broker or salesman must never misstate zoning to a prospective buyer. To do so is a violation of ethics and could be cause for legal action for misrepresentation. Villages, cities, and counties have published zoning ordinance books that are available at the clerk's office. As changes are made, an up-to-date copy should be obtained and be available to the office staff.

Building restrictions relate to the height, land coverage, building lines, side yards, and many other limitations on the placement of buildings on the land. These restrictions are incorporated into the zoning ordinance. Building codes refer to the type of construction, materials, number and size of rooms, and provision for light and air. Incorporated in building codes are sanitary provisions, electrical specifications, exit provisions, and safety requirements. Building codes are being changed frequently with improvements in design and the development of new materials. A building owner is subject to prosecution for violation of a building code and must keep his property within the provisions of the existing code. In the sale of property, many mortgage lending companies require a statement that there is no violation of the building code and a commitment for a loan is issued subject to an inspection report of the property by the inspection department of the building authority. In offering a building to a prospective purchaser, the broker should advise the purchaser of the existence of the building code and its provisions. Older structures are susceptible to violations, and an inspection report should be obtained. Physical conditions are a matter of fact and can be observed. Ethical conduct requires the broker to reveal to a prospective purchaser all the facts which he may know about the physical condition of a building. In some states a clause in the sales contract provides for certification by the seller that there are no building code violations.

Some owners of rental property attempt to restrict the occupancy of their property to certain uses or persons. The use of property is a matter of zoning and private restriction by the owner. Under recent federal legislation and Supreme Court rulings,[1] an owner cannot restrict the use or occupancy of a property because of race, creed, or color. Local city, village, and state laws supplement the federal laws. Rent control was prevalent during

1/ 1866–Title 42 Sec. 1982.

war times and is still in effect in certain cities. A broker should be cognizant of these laws.

State, local, and federal governments are frequently passing new laws which restrict the use of real estate or grant assistance in the construction of housing by financial aid or abatement of taxes.[2] Public housing provides housing for low-income citizens. Financial assistance for remodeling or renewal of residential structures gives housing assistance to the lower- and middle-income renter. Subsidy of rents and fixed low-interest mortgages are granted by local housing authorities and federal agencies as assistance to senior citizens for rental and to families for purchase of homes.[3]

The Federal Housing Administration and Veterans Administration provide mortgage funds by mortgage insurance to qualified buyers of homes. The broker should be aware of the rules and regulations of the Veterans Administration for veterans and the Federal Housing Administration for qualified buyers and use them in making sales. Offices of these agencies are in every large city, and approved mortgagees are located in every village or city which has a commercial bank, savings and loan association, or mortgage financing institution. Rates and terms are changed with the change in economic conditions. The broker should be acquainted with the administrators of these agencies and have close contact with mortgage outlets who can keep the broker up to date on agency rules and regulations and the availability of funds.

City planning is becoming a prominent activity by city government. The building of federal highways, clearance of slums under the aegis of urban renewal projects, provision for open space, and public parking have an impact on the real estate business. Brokers who are knowledgeable on zoning changes are called upon to advise with city planners on the best location for parks, playgrounds, and street patterns. The real estate broker is well-equipped through his knowledge of neighborhoods to advise on these matters. A close liaison should be kept by the broker with officials in charge of these programs. As a part of the urban renewal program and the eradication of slums, the law requires the housing of displaced persons. Firms engaged in the rental of dwellings can supply this need. When property is purchased, the original owner is a

---

2/ 1968 Housing Act.
3/ 1968 Housing Act, Sec. 235-237-202-312.

prospect for other accommodations. This activity is becoming more pressing as the plight of the displaced owner of property in the inner core of cities is recognized and government increases its activity in urban renewal or rehabilitation.

The broker should take note of the opportunities brought about by city planning and the creation of model cities. As the population grows and urban centers continue to absorb the immigration of young people from nonurban areas, the role of government in real estate activities will continue. As modes of living change, social and economic problems will become more acute, and it will fall to the government to provide the pattern of residential, commercial, and industrial real estate and to relate them to transportation and recreational areas. The right of eminent domain gives the government the right to purchase real estate for the public benefit. The social and economic needs of the people will more and more require the regulation of the use of land. To this end, the government has a mandate to provide the pattern which best serves the needs of the citizen. The real estate broker can be a vital force in directing the officials of government to the practical aspect of development of the peripheral areas of our cities and to the rebuilding of the inner core. Brokers can gain great satisfaction in playing an important role as advisers to city, state, and federal governments as they progress in the task of reshaping the American city and countryside.

As cities and villages grow and land on the periphery is required for expansion of the urban pattern, the real estate broker becomes an important person in land development. The land developer and the builder, whether residential, commercial, or industrial, will seek his advice on the potential of an area for the development proposed. To properly advise a client, the broker must have knowledge of adequacy of public utilities and the rules and requirements of governmental bodies to expand or use present facilities. The adequacy of water and sewerage treatment plants is of great concern to city fathers, and engineering requirements must be met before development can proceed. The broker should be acquainted with the village engineer, the superintendent of public works, the village manager, the local zoning commission, and the board of trustees of the villages and cities in which he is operating. The policies of villages and cities vary with the citizens who serve on the village boards. These policies should be known to the real estate broker. Much time and effort can be saved when the broker knows that certain projects will be looked upon with favor or disfavor.

The National Highway Program has vitally affected the transportation business in America and thus affected the location of industrial, commercial, and residential projects. The location of highways in relation to airports and existing road and street patterns vitally affects land use. The broker with knowledge of future plans and policies of highway departments can foster projects with confidence. The broker who serves on village and city plan commissions—planning boards which may control county, state, and federal projects—has advance knowledge as well as an opportunity to perform a public service.

The real estate broker is licensed in all 50 states. Each state has a broker's and salesmen law which defines the business of real estate, who may engage in the business, the rules for granting a license, and the conditions under which a broker may have his license revoked. There are no two broker's and salesmen license laws alike, but the method of granting a license and the control by boards, commissions, or license authorities are very much alike. The National Real Estate organization and the National Association of Real Estate License Law Officials—which is the national organization of enforcing officials—has tried to bring about a national policy of educational requirements and uniform examinations. To this end, a pattern license law was adopted in 1961 and revised during 1968. The definition of the real estate business adopted by the National Association of Real Estate Boards is as follows:

An individual or legal entity is engaged in the real estate business who, for another and with intent to receive any valuable consideration performs one or more of the following acts with respect to real property: lists for sale, sells, purchases, leases, manages, exchanges, appraises or offers to perform, or negotiates for the performance of, or counsels respecting, any of the foregoing.

It will be noted that this definition is specific in its relation to real estate brokerage and management activities. Although financing and insurance of real estate are important for ownership, they are considered a part of the agency relationship in the conduct of the sale and handling of a real estate investment. The securities and insurance laws of the states govern the conduct of persons engaged in the finance and insurance business.

In most states, a person must meet minimum age, education, and experience requirements before he is eligible for examination. A high school education is the minimum in many states, and in lieu of experience as a salesman for one or more years, a college degree is necessary. The objective of a uniform license law is to grant reciprocity between states. This can be accomplished by uniform educational requirements and equal quality of examinations. The professionalism of the business is being accomplished by and through stricter license law requirements.

A broker should be well versed in the violations of the License Law Act of his state. The loss of his license is a loss of his business. The protection of the public is basic in government policy, and the importance of property ownership and its protection against unscrupulous operators is a public trust.

Many states require a separate escrow account for clients' funds or require a bond for the protection of clients against the possible misuse of moneys deposited by clients. The Institute of Real Estate Management, which is an affiliate of the National Association of Real Estate Boards, has a special designation for members of the institute who comply with the rules and regulations that protect the funds of clients. The organization thus disciplines its own membership.

The following regulation on suspension and revocation of a license is from the State of Illinois law:

Sec. 8 (Refusal, suspension or revocation of certificate—Grounds) The Department may refuse to issue or to renew or may suspend or revoke any certificate of registration for any one or any combination of the following causes:

a) Where the applicant or registrant has by false or fraudulent representation obtained or sought to obtain a certificate of registration;

b) Where the registrant has been convicted of any crime, an essential element of which is dishonesty or fraud or of a felony, larceny, embezzlement, obtaining money, property or credit by false pretenses or by means of a confidence game;

c) Where the registrant is mentally ill, mentally deficient or in need of mental treatment as provided in the Mental Health Code;

d) Where the applicant or registrant has sold or intends to sell real estate in a retail sales establishment, from an office, desk or space that is not separated from the main retail business by a separate and distinct area within such establishment;

e) Where the registrant in performing or attempting to perform or pretending to perform any act as a real estate broker or salesman, or where such registrant, in handling his own property, whether held by deed, option, or otherwise, is deemed guilty of;

1. Making any substantial misrepresentation, or untruthful advertising, or

2. Making any false promises of a character likely to influence, persuade, or induce, or

3. Pursuing a continued and flagrant course of misrepresentation or the making of false promises through agents or salesmen or advertising or otherwise, or

4. Any misleading or untruthful advertising, or using any trade name or insignia of membership in any real estate organization of which the registrant is not a member, or

5. Acting for more than one party in a transaction without the knowledge of all parties for whom he acts, or

6. Representing or attempting to represent a real estate broker other than the employer, or

7. Failure to account for or to remit for any moneys or documents coming into his possession which belong to others, or

8. Failure to maintain and deposit in a special account, separate and apart from his personal or other business accounts, all moneys belonging to others entrusted to him while acting as a real estate broker, or as escrow agent, or the temporary custodian of the funds of others, until the transaction involved is consummated or terminated, or

9. Failure to furnish copies upon request of all documents relating to a real estate transaction to all parties executing the same, or

10. Paying a commission or valuable consideration to any person for acts or services performed in violation of this Act, or

11. Having demonstrated unworthiness or incompetency to act as a real estate broker or salesman in such manner as to safeguard the interests of the public, or

12. Commingling the money or other property of his principal with his own, or

13. Employing any person as a salesman on a purely temporary or single deal basis as a means of evading the law regarding payment of commissions to nonregistrants on some contemplated transactions, or

14. Any other conduct, whether of the same or a different character from that hereinbefore specified which constitutes dishonest dealing, or

15. Of displaying a "for rent" or "for sale" sign on any property without

the written consent of an owner or his duly authorized agent, or advertising that any property is for sale or for rent in a newspaper or other publication without the consent of the owner or his authorized agent, or

16. Failing, within a reasonable time, to provide information requested by the Department as the result of a formal or informal complaint to the Department, which would indicate a violation of this Act, or

17. Disregarding or violating any provision of this Act, or the published rules or regulations promulgated by the Department to enforce this Act. As amended by act approved Aug. 31, 1967. L.1967, p-H.B. No. 311.

To foster the professionalism of the real estate business, members of the vocation have organized associations, institutes, and societies. These organizations have rigid requirements for admission. They present to the public an image of honesty, integrity, and ability. With the opportunity to affiliate with these professional organizations, specialists in appraising, management, and brokerage have become segments of the business. The appraisers have several organizations which have rigid qualifications and examinations for membership. These organizations are the American Institute of Real Estate Appraisers, the Society of Real Estate Appraisers, the American Society of Appraisers, and the Society of Farm Brokers and Appraisers. The qualifications of Real Estate Appraisers have been raised by these organizations, and public confidence has increased in the quality of reports rendered by members of these organizations.

Appraising has direct effect on the public welfare. Appraising for assessment purposes, estate taxes, depreciation allowances for income tax purposes, valuation for mortgage purposes, and valuation for insurance of mortgages by the Federal Housing Administration and the Veterans Administration are a small part of the involvement of government in real estate valuation. The vast program of national highways, public recreation centers, and the involvement of the federal government in the New Community Development and Model Cities Program under the 1968 Housing Act requires the skill of knowledgeable real estate brokers and appraisers. In some states appraisers are included in the Brokers and Salesmen act. Bills have been introduced in some states for the certification or licensing of real estate appraisers. A real estate brokerage firm which has an appraisal department should have a member of the department as a member of one of the recognized appraisal organizations. Prestige is added to the firm when a member of the firm carries a professional designation.

Federal and state governments have for some time been interested in the control of land sales. Several states have laws which control the sale of lots in subdivisions by land developers who draw their purchasers from other states. In the 1968 Housing Act, provision is made for the registration of sellers of more than 50 unimproved lots and the delivery of a prospectus to a prospective purchaser 48 hours before entering into a binding contract.

The real estate management firm has great opportunity to take over the management of government housing. The administration of public housing is now acting under a pilot program which will extend greater responsibility to the broker. Brokers who contemplate undertaking management activities should study the provisions of the various sections of the 1968 Act, such as 221 (*d*) 3, 235, 236 and the Civil Rights Act. The sale and rental of real estate is strictly controlled as to race, creed, and color by the Civil Rights Act of 1968 and the recent decisions of the Supreme Court upholding the Act of 1866 in *Jones* v. *Mayer*.

The Department of Housing and Urban Development is administered by a secretary who is a member of the President's Cabinet. Under his administration is an assistant secretary of the Federal Housing Administration and assistant secretaries for Renewal and Housing Assistance, Metropolitan Development, Demonstrations and Intergovernmental Relations, and Administration. Each of these departments has a function relating to finance, urban renewal, and development and coordination of city and rural affairs. These departments have liaisons with state and city government and coordinate programs initiated at both the local and federal levels. Real estate brokers should acquaint themselves with these programs and keep up to date.[4]

There are many other departments of the government which have administrative control over real estate. The total land area of the United States and its possessions is 2,271,000,000 acres, and 765,000,000[5] acres are under the direct supervision of the government. The following list of federal agencies is a partial list of

4/ Appendix Chart.
5/ Statistical Abstract of U.S.–1967.

agencies involved in the administration of the lands in government ownership:

Department of Agriculture
Army Corps of Engineers
Department of Commerce
Bureau of the Census
Bureau of Indian Affairs
Bureau of Land Management
Bureau of Outdoor Recreation
Bureau of Public Roads
Bureau of Reclamation
Farmers Home Administration
Federal Aviation Administration
Federal Home Loan Bank
Federal Housing Administration
Fish and Wildlife Service
Forest Service
General Services Administration
Department of Housing and Urban Development
Internal Revenue Service
Justice Department
National Park Service
Navy Department
Department of the Army
Post Office Department
Small Business Administration
Veterans Administration

In addition, there are innumerable state and local government agencies with which the real estate broker should be acquainted. The Library of Congress and state and local libraries can furnish this information.

Government agencies can supply much statistical information which is pertinent to the operation of a real estate office. The gross national product; private investment; personal consumption; the percentage of income used for housing expense, industrial relocation and employee relocation; interest rates and government fiscal and monetary policies can be obtained and prove to be invaluable to the real estate broker.

As the population of the country grows and interstate highways are completed, distance in time will shrink, causing more complex problems in urban and rural living. Governments will take a more active part in real estate matters, and the real estate broker must be aware of his opportunities to foster his business and the public welfare.

Bibliography

Chapter one

California Real Estate Association. *Successful Real Estate Office Administration Practice.* Los Angeles, Calif., 1966. See pp. 97-124.

Case, Frederick E. *Real Estate Brokerage.* Englewood Cliffs, N.J.: Prentice-Hall, 1965.

Hebard, Edna L. and Meisel, Gerald S. *Principles of Real Estate Law.* New York, N.Y.: Simmons-Boardman Publishing Corp., 1964. See pp. 361-426.

Kratoril, Robert. *Real Estate Law.* 4th ed. Englewood Cliffs, N.J.: Prentice-Hall, 1964. See pp. 86-107.

Lusk, Harold F. *Law of the Real Estate Business.* Rev. ed. Homewood, Ill.: Richard D. Irwin, 1965. See pp. 4-27.

McMichael, Stanley L. *How to Operate a Real Estate Business.* Rev. ed. Englewood Cliffs, N.J.: Prentice-Hall, 1967. See pp. 338-42.

National Institute of Real Estate Brokers. *The Brokers Institute Digest.* Chicago, Ill., 1962. See pp. 123-55.

Ring, Alfred A. and North, Nelson L. *Real Estate, Principles and Practices.* 6th ed. Englewood Cliffs, N.J.: Prentice-Hall, 1967. See pp. 247-59.

Unger, Maurice A. *Real Estate, Principles and Practices.* 3d ed. Cincinnati, Ohio: South-Western Publishing Co., 1964. See pp. 397-579.

Chapter two

Di Paola, Eugene F. *How to Multiply Your Real Estate Sales.* Englewood Cliffs, N.J.: Prentice-Hall, 1963. See pp. 1-35.

National Institute of Real Estate Brokers. *Keeping in Touch.* Chicago, Ill., 1965.

———. *New Spheres of Influence.* Chicago, Ill., 1964.

———. *Real Estate Salesman's Handbook.* 4th ed. Chicago, Ill., 1965. See pp. 17-21, 112-26.

Chapter three

Barlowe, Raleigh. *Land Resource Economics, the Political Economy of*

Rural and Urban Land Resource Use. Englewood Cliffs, N.J.: Prentice-Hall, 1958.

Brown, Robert Kevin. *Real Estate Economics; An Introduction to Urban Land Use.* Boston, Mass.: Houghton Mifflin Co., 1965.

Ely, Richard T. and Wehrwein, George S. *Land Economics.* New York, N.Y.: Macmillan Co., 1940.

Essays in Urban Land Economics. Los Angeles, Calif., University of California Real Estate Research Program, 1966.

Hoyt, Homer. *According to Hoyt; 50 Years of Homer Hoyt: Articles on Law, Real Estate Cycle, Economic Base Sector Theory, Shopping Centers, Urban Growth, 1916 to 1966.* Washington, D.C., 1966.

Ratcliff, Richard U. *Urban Land Economics.* New York, N.Y.: McGraw-Hill Book Co., 1949.

Renne, Roland R. *Land Economics: Principles, Problems, and Policies in Utilizing Land Resources.* Rev. ed. New York, N.Y.: Harper and Brothers, 1958.

Weimer, Arthur M. and Hoyt, Homer. *Real Estate.* 5th ed. New York, N.Y.: Ronald Press, 1966.

Chapter four

Hanford, Lloyd D., Sr. *Development and Management of Investment Property.* 2d ed. Chicago, Ill.: Institute of Real Estate Management, 1968. See pp. 17-23.

———. *Investing in Real Estate.* Chicago, Ill.: Institute of Real Estate Management, 1966. See pp. 3-7.

Husband, William H. and Anderson, Frank Ray. *Real Estate.* 3d ed. Homewood, Ill.: Richard D. Irwin, 1960. See pp. 179-239.

Ring, Alfred A. and North, Nelson L. *Real Estate, Principles and Practices.* 6th ed. Englewood Cliffs, N.J.: Prentice-Hall, 1967. See pp. 32-45.

Weimer, Arthur M. and Hoyt, Homer. *Real Estate.* 5th ed. New York, N.Y.: Ronald Press, 1966. See pp. 255-84.

Chapter five

American Institute of Real Estate Appraisers. *The Appraisal of Real Estate.* 5th ed. Chicago, Ill., 1967.

———. *Appraisal Terminology and Handbook.* 5th ed. Chicago, Ill., 1967.

———. *Condemnation Appraisal Practice.* Chicago, Ill., 1961.

Babcock, Henry A. *Appraisal Principles and Procedures.* Homewood, Ill.: Dow Jones-Irwin, Inc., 1968.

Friedman, E. J., ed. *Encyclopedia of Real Estate Appraising.* Rev. and enl. ed. Englewood Cliffs, N.J.: Prentice-Hall, 1968.

Knowles, Jerome, Jr. *Single Family Residential Appraisal Manual.* Chicago, Ill.: American Institute of Real Estate Appraisers, 1967.

May, Arthur A. *The Valuation of Residential Real Estate.* 2d ed. Englewood Cliffs, N.J.: Prentice-Hall, 1953.

Schmutz, George L. *The Appraisal Process.* 3d ed. Manhattan Beach, Calif., 1959.

Schmutz, George L. and Rams, Edwin M. *Condemnation Appraisal Handbook.* Englewood Cliffs, N.J.: Prentice-Hall, 1963.

Wendt, Paul F. *Real Estate Appraisal: A Critical Analysis of Theory and Practice.* New York, N.Y.: Henry Holt and Co., 1956.

Winstead, Robert W. *Real Estate Appraisal Desk Book.* Englewood Cliffs, N.J.: Prentice-Hall, 1968.

Chapter six

California Real Estate Association. *Real Estate Office Administration.* Los Angeles, Calif., 1963. See pp. 18-21 for discussion of forms of organization.

Case, Frederick E. *Real Estate Brokerage.* Englewood Cliffs, N.J.: Prentice-Hall, 1965. See pp. 244-68.

Friedman, E. J., ed. *Real Estate Encyclopedia.* Englewood Cliffs, N.J.: Prentice-Hall, 1960. See pp. 3-21, 45-76, 1367-79, 1380-1403.

National Institute of Real Estate Brokers. *Increase Efficiency, Cut Costs.* Chicago, Ill., 1963.

———. *Practical Answers to Your Brokerage Questions.* Chicago, Ill., 1960. See pp. 7-28.

———. *Real Estate as a Career.* Chicago, Ill., 1966.

———. *Real Estate Salesman's Handbook.* 4th ed. Chicago, Ill., 1965. See pp. 1-16.

———. *Real Estate Specializations.* Chicago, Ill., 1962.

Weimer, Arthur M. and Hoyt, Homer. *Real Estate.* 5th ed. New York, N.Y.: Ronald Press, 1966.

Chapter seven

California Real Estate Association. *Successful Real Estate Office Policies and Procedures.* Los Angeles, Calif., 1959.

Fortney, Ned. *The Successful Practice of Real Estate.* Englewood Cliffs, N.J.: Prentice-Hall, 1967. See pp. 167-77, 197-219.

Friedman, E. J., ed. *Real Estate Encyclopedia.* Englewood Cliffs, N.J.: Prentice-Hall, 1960. See pp. 22-44.

McMichael, Stanley L. *How to Operate a Real Estate Business.* Rev. ed. Englewood Cliffs, N.J.: Prentice-Hall, 1967. See pp. 35-55, 280-91.

National Institute of Real Estate Brokers. *The Brokers Institute Digest.* Chicago, Ill., 1962. See pp. 28-29.

———. *The Modern Real Estate Office.* Chicago, Ill., 1967.

———. *Office Planning and Design.* Chicago, Ill., 1960.

———. *Office Policies and Procedures.* Chicago, Ill., 1959.

———. *Visual and Mechanical Sales Aids.* Chicago, Ill., 1964.

Smith, Ray. *Real Estate Broker's Operating Handbook.* Dayton, Ohio: Mastercraft, 1958. See pp. 8-15, 194-288.

Unger, Maurice A. *Real Estate Principles and Practices.* 3d ed. Cincinnati, Ohio: South-Western Publishing Co., 1964. See pp. 423-52.

Vogel, Lois T. *How To Help Your Real Estate Salesmen Produce More Business.* Englewood Cliffs, N.J.: Prentice-Hall, 1957. See pp. 231-36.

Chapter eight

California Real Estate Association. *The Modern Concept of Real Estate Administration.* Los Angeles, Calif., 1958. See pp. 25-32.

———. *Real Estate Office Administration.* Los Angeles, Calif., 1963. See pp. 30-33.

Doris, Lillian. *The Real Estate Office Secretary's Handbook.* Rev. ed. Englewood Cliffs, N.J.: Prentice-Hall, 1966.

Chapter nine

California Real Estate Association. *Selecting, Training and Reducing Turnover of Real Estate Sales Personnel.* Los Angeles, Calif., 1957.

Case, Frederick E. *Real Estate Brokerage.* Englewood Cliffs, N.J.: Prentice-Hall, 1965. See pp. 103-32.

Fortney, Ned. *The Successful Practice of Real Estate.* Englewood Cliffs, N.J.: Prentice-Hall, 1967. See pp. 15-29.

McMichael, Stanley L. *How To Operate a Real Estate Business.* Rev. ed. Englewood Cliffs, N.J.: Prentice-Hall, 1967. See pp. 317-24.

Smith, Ray. *Real Estate Broker's Operating Handbook.* Dayton, Ohio: Mastercraft, 1958. See pp. 40-46, 55-69.

Women's Council of the National Association of Real Estate Boards. *Real Estate Salesmen: Training, Counseling, Development.* Chicago, Ill., 1965.

Chapter ten

California Real Estate Association. *Increase Real Estate Office Profits through Effective Administration.* Los Angeles, Calif., 1965. See pp. 105-128.

———. *Real Estate Office Administration.* Los Angeles, Calif., 1963. See pp. 131-80.

———. *Selecting, Training and Reducing Turnover of Real Estate Sales Personnel.* Los Angeles, Calif., 1957.

———. *Successful Real Estate Office Administration Practice.* Los Angeles, Calif., 1966. See pp. 21-39.

Case, Frederick E. *Real Estate Brokerage.* Englewood Cliffs, N.J.: Prentice-Hall, 1965. See pp. 103-64.

Fortney, Ned. *The Successful Practice of Real Estate.* Englewood Cliffs, N.J.: Prentice-Hall, 1967. See pp. 53-108.

Smith, Ray. *Real Estate Salesman's Training Manual.* 4th ed. Dayton, Ohio: Mastercraft, 1961.

Stone, David. *Training Manual for Real Estate Salesmen.* Englewood Cliffs, N.J.: Prentice-Hall, 1965.

Vogel, Lois T. *How To Help Your Real Estate Salesmen Produce More Business.* Englewood Cliffs, N.J.: Prentice-Hall, 1957.

Women's Council of the National Association of Real Estate Boards. *Real Estate Salesmen: Training, Counseling, Development.* Chicago, Ill., 1965.

Chapter eleven

California Real Estate Association. *Real Estate Office Administration.* Los Angeles, Calif., 1963. See pp. 53-86.

Case, Frederick E. *Real Estate Brokerage.* Englewood Cliffs, N.J.: Prentice-Hall, 1965. See pp. 34, 40-42, 158-61, 176-80.

McMichael, Stanley L. *How To Operate a Real Estate Business.* Rev. ed. Englewood Cliffs, N.J.: Prentice-Hall, 1967. See pp. 331-37.

Smith, Ray. *Real Estate Broker's Operating Handbook.* Dayton, Ohio: Mastercraft, 1958. See pp. 194-224.

Chapter twelve

Bohon, Davis T. *How To Get Salable Real Estate Listings.* Englewood Cliffs, N.J.: Prentice-Hall, 1961.

California Real Estate Association. *Listing Real Estate.* Los Angeles, Calif., 1969.

Davidson, Leo. *Using the Magic of Word Power to Multiply Real Estate Sales.* Englewood Cliffs, N.J.: Executive Reports Corp., 1972. See chaps. 1-3.

Gale, Jack L. *Listing Real Estate Successfully.* Englewood Cliffs, N.J.: Executive Reports Corp., 1972.

Krueger, Cliff W. *Successful Real Estate Selling.* New York, N.Y.: McGraw-Hill Book Co., 1960.

National Institute of Real Estate Brokers. *Real Estate Salesman's Handbook.* 4th ed. Chicago, Ill., 1965. See pp. 52-57.

Stone, David. *Training Manual for Real Estate Salesmen.* Englewood Cliffs, N.J.: Prentice-Hall, 1965. See pp. 20-84.

Teckemeyer, Earl B. *Teckemeyer on Selling Real Estate.* Englewood Cliffs, N.J.: Prentice-Hall, 1962. See pp. 10-17.

Chapter thirteen

Associated Home Builders of the Greater Eastbay. *The Condominium Development and Conversion Handbook.* Berkeley, Calif., 1973.

Berman, Daniel S. *How to Organize and Sell a Profitable Condominium.* Englewood Cliffs, N.J.: Prentice-Hall, 1966.

California Real Estate Association. *Condominium Workbook.* Los Angeles, Calif., 1971.

Clurman, David and Hebard, Edna L. *Condominiums and Cooperatives.* New York, N.Y.: Wiley-Interscience, 1970.

Friedman, E. J., ed. *Encyclopedia of Real Estate Appraising.* Rev. ed. Englewood Cliffs, N.J.: Prentice-Hall, 1968. See pp. 238-63, "Appraisal of Condominiums," by Percy E. Wagner.

Pierce, Leroy W. "F.H.A. and Condominiums," *National Capital Area Realtor,* December 1962.

Ramsey, Charles E. "Condominium: The New Look in Co-ops. Practical and Legal Problems." Chicago, Ill.: Chicago Title and Trust Company.

Reskin, Melvin A. and Sakai, Hiroshi. *Modern Condominium Forms.* Boston, Mass.: Warren, Gorham & Lamont. (looseleaf)

Rohan, Patrick J. and Reskin, Melvin A. *Condominium Law and Practice; Forms.* 2 vol. Albany, N.Y.: Matthew Bender and Co. (looseleaf)

Vogel, Harold N. and Pollack, Jonathan V. *Condominium—The Third Dimension in Apartment House Ownership.* Jackson Heights, N.Y.: Cities U.S.A. Research Co.

Wagner, Percy E. "Condominium—How It Works." Park Forest South, Ill.: Park Forest South Investments, Inc.

Chapter fourteen

California Real Estate Association. *Increase Real Estate Office Profits through Effective Administration.* Los Angeles, Calif., 1965. See pp. 67-82.

Di Paolo, Eugene F. *How To Multiply Your Real Estate Sales.* Englewood Cliffs, N.J.: Prentice-Hall, 1963. See pp. 49-78.

Friedman, E. J., ed. *Real Estate Encyclopedia.* Englewood Cliffs, N.J.: Prentice-Hall, 1960. See pp. 115-27.

Kirk, Tim H. *How To Avoid Beginner's Mistakes in Selling Real Estate.* Englewood Cliffs, N.J.: Prentice-Hall, 1963. See pp. 114-56.

Krueger, Cliff W. *Successful Real Estate Selling.* New York, N.Y.: McGraw-Hill Book Co., 1960. See pp. 18-56.

McMichael, Stanley L. *How To Operate a Real Estate Business.* Rev. ed. Englewood Cliffs, N.J.: Prentice-Hall, 1967. See pp. 56-76.

National Institute of Real Estate Brokers. *Marketing Real Estate Successfully.* Chicago, Ill., 1964. See pp. 3-36.

Chapter fifteen

Krueger, Cliff W. *Selling Real Estate Successfully.* New York, N.Y.: McGraw-Hill Book Co., 1960. See pp. 143-55.

Moser, Leslie E. *How To Find, Qualify and Induce Real Estate Prospects To Buy.* Englewood Cliffs, N.J.: Prentice-Hall, 1965.

National Institute of Real Estate Brokers. *Real Estate Salesman's Handbook.* 4th ed. Chicago, Ill., 1965. See pp. 86-95.

Stone, David. *Training Manual for Real Estate Salesmen.* Englewood Cliffs, N.J.: Prentice-Hall, 1965. See pp. 85-132.

Teckemeyer, Earl B. *Teckemeyer on Selling Real Estate.* Englewood Cliffs, N.J.: Prentice-Hall, 1962. See pp. 59-71.

Chapter sixteen

Downs, James C. *Principles of Real Estate Management.* 10th ed. Chicago, Ill.: Institute of Real Estate Management, 1970.

Hanford, Lloyd D., Sr. *Property Management Process.* Chicago, Ill.: Institute of Real Estate Management, 1972.

Institute of Real Estate Management. *Property Manager's Guide to Forms & Letters.* Chicago, Ill., 1971. See Vol. 1, *Renting the Residential Unit.*

———. *Resident Manager; On-Site Management Handbook for Apartments and Condominiums.* Chicago, Ill., 1973.

Journal of Property Management. Published bi-monthly by Institute of Real Estate Management.

National Apartment Association. *Professional Apartment Management; Incorporating Apartment Management Proven Procedures.* Houston, Texas, 1969.

Chapter seventeen

California Real Estate Association. *Increase Real Estate Office Profits through Effective Administration.* Los Angeles, Calif., 1965. See pp. 1-42.

———. *Real Estate Office Administration.* Los Angeles, Calif., 1963. See pp. 33-37.

Case, Frederick E. *Real Estate Brokerage.* Englewood Cliffs, N.J.: Prentice-Hall, 1965. See pp. 200-215.

Encyclopedia of Accounting Systems. Englewood Cliffs, N.J.: Prentice-Hall, 1957. 5 vols. See vol. 5, pp. 1594-1609.

Hefti, Wilma C. *Real Estate Office Bookkeeping Simplified.* Englewood Cliffs, N.J.: Prentice-Hall, 1958.

Institute of Real Estate Management. *A Cost Accounting System for the Real Estate Office.* Chicago, Ill., 1958.

Chapter eighteen

Chapin, F. Stuart, Jr. *Urban Land Use Planning.* 2d ed. Urbana, Ill., University of Illinois Press, 1965.

Haar, Charles M. *Land-Use Planning: A Casebook on the Use, Misuse, and Re-Use of Urban Land.* Boston, Mass.: Little, Brown and Co., 1959.

Nelson, Richard L. and Aschman, Frederick T. *Real Estate and City Planning.* Englewood Cliffs, N.J.: Prentice-Hall, 1957.

Ring, Alfred A. and North, Nelson L. *Real Estate, Principles and Practices.* 6th ed. Englewood Cliffs, N.J.: Prentice-Hall, 1967. See pp. 405-35.

Webster, Donald H. *Urban Planning and Municipal Public Policy.* New York, N.Y.: Harper and Brothers, 1958.

Weimer, Arthur M. and Hoyt, Homer. *Real Estate.* 5th ed. New York, N.Y.: Ronald Press, 1966. See pp. 85-109.

appendix A

Code of ethics of the National Association of Real Estate Boards

Preamble

Under all is the land. Upon its wise utilization and widely allocated ownership depend the survival and growth of free institutions and of our civilization. The Realtor is the instrumentality through which the land resource of the nation reaches its highest use and through which land ownership attains its widest distribution. He is a creator of homes, a builder of cities, a developer of industries and productive farms.

Such functions impose obligations beyond those of ordinary commerce. They impose grave social responsibility and a patriotic duty to which the Realtor should dedicate himself, and for which he should be diligent in preparing himself. The Realtor, therefore, is zealous to maintain and improve the standards of his calling and shares with his fellow-Realtors a common responsibility for its integrity and honor.

In the interpretation of his obligations, he can take no safer guide than that which has been handed down through twenty centuries, embodied in the Golden Rule:

"Whatsoever ye would that men should do to you, do ye even so to them."

Accepting this standard as his own, every Realtor pledges himself to observe its spirit in all his activities and to conduct his business in accordance with the following Code of Ethics:

Part I.—Relations to the public

ARTICLE 1.—The Realtor should keep himself informed as to movements affecting real estate in his community, state, and the nation, so that he may be able to contribute to public thinking on matters of taxation, legislation, land use, city planning, and other questions affecting property interests.

ARTICLE 2.—It is the duty of the Realtor to be well informed on current market conditions in order to be in a position to advise his clients as to the fair market price.

ARTICLE 3.—It is the duty of the Realtor to protect the public against fraud, misrepresentation or unethical practices in the real estate field.

He should endeavor to eliminate in his community any practices which could be damaging to the public or to the dignity and integrity of the real estate profession. The Realtor should assist the board or commission charged with regulating the practices of brokers and salesmen in his state.

ARTICLE 4.—The Realtor should ascertain all pertinent facts concerning every property for which he accepts the agency, so that he may fulfill his obligation to avoid error, exaggeration, misrepresentation, or concealment of pertinent facts.

ARTICLE 5.—The Realtor should not be instrumental in introducing into a neighborhood a character of property or use which will clearly be detrimental to property values in that neighborhood.

ARTICLE 6.—The Realtor should not be a party to the naming of a false consideration in any document, unless it be the naming of an obviously nominal consideration.

ARTICLE 7.—The Realtor should not engage in activities that constitute the practice of law and should recommend that title be examined and legal counsel be obtained when the interest of either party requires it.

ARTICLE 8.—The Realtor should keep in a special bank account, separated from his own funds, monies coming into his possession in trust for other persons, such as escrows, trust funds, client's monies and other like items.

ARTICLE 9.—The Realtor in his advertising should be especially careful to present a true picture and should neither advertise without disclosing his name, nor permit his salesmen to use individual names or telephone numbers, unless the salesman's connection with the Realtor is obvious in the advertisement.

ARTICLE 10.—The Realtor, for the protection of all parties with whom he deals, should see that financial obligations and commitments regarding real estate transactions are in writing, expressing the exact agreement of the parties; and that copies of such agreements, at the time they are executed, are placed in the hands of all parties involved.

Part II.—Relations to the client

ARTICLE 11.—In accepting employment as an agent, the Realtor pledges himself to protect and promote the interests of the client. This obligation of absolute fidelity to the client's interest is primary, but it does not relieve the Realtor from the obligation of dealing fairly with all parties to the transaction.

ARTICLE 12.—In justice to those who place their interests in his care, the Realtor should endeavor always to be informed regarding laws, proposed legislation, governmental orders, and other essential information and public policies which affect those interests.

ARTICLE 13.—Since the Realtor is representing one or another party to a transaction, he should not accept compensation from more than one party without the full knowledge of all parties to the transaction.

ARTICLE 14.—The Realtor should not acquire an interest in or buy for himself, any member of his immediate family, his firm or any member thereof, or any entity in which he has a substantial ownership interest, property listed with him, or his firm, without making the true position known to the listing owner, and in selling property owned by him, or in which he has such interest, the facts should be revealed to the purchaser.

ARTICLE 15.—The exclusive listing of property should be urged and practiced by the Realtor as a means of preventing dissension and misunderstanding and of assuring better service to the owner.

ARTICLE 16.—When acting as agent in the management of property, the Realtor should not accept any commission, rebate or profit on expenditures made for an owner, without the owner's knowledge and consent.

ARTICLE 17.—The Realtor should not undertake to make an appraisal that is outside the field of his experience unless he obtains the assistance of an authority on such types of property, or unless the facts are fully disclosed to the client. In such circumstances the authority so engaged should be so identified and his contribution to the assignment should be clearly set forth.

ARTICLE 18.—When asked to make a formal appraisal of real property, the Realtor should not render an opinion without careful and thorough analysis and interpretation of all factors affecting the value of the property. His counsel constitutes a professional service.

The Realtor should not undertake to make an appraisal or render an opinion of value on any property where he has a present or contemplated interest unless such interest is specifically disclosed in the appraisal report. Under no circumstances should he undertake to make a formal appraisal when his employment or fee is contingent upon the amount of his appraisal.

ARTICLE 19.—The Realtor should not submit or advertise property without authority and in any offering, the price quoted should not be other than that agreed upon with the owners as the offering price.

ARTICLE 20.—In the event that more than one formal written offer on a specific property is made before the owner has accepted an offer, any other formal written offer presented to the Realtor, whether by a prospective purchaser or another broker, should be transmitted to the owner for his decision.

Part III.—Relations to his fellow-Realtor

ARTICLE 21.—The Realtor should seek no unfair advantage over his fellow-Realtors and should willingly share with them the lessons of his experience and study.

ARTICLE 22.—The Realtor should so conduct his business as to avoid controversies with his fellow-Realtors. In the event of a controversy between Realtors who are members of the same local board, such controversy should be arbitrated in accordance with regulations of their board rather than litigated.

ARTICLE 23.—Controversies between Realtors who are not members of the same local board should be submitted to an arbitration board consisting of one arbitrator chosen by each Realtor from the real estate board to which he belongs or chosen in accordance with the regulations of the respective boards. One other member, or a sufficent number of members to make an odd number, should be selected by the arbitrators thus chosen.

ARTICLE 24.—When the Realtor is charged with unethical practice, he should place all pertinent facts before the proper tribunal of the member board of which he is a member, for investigation and judgment.

ARTICLE 25.—The Realtor should not voluntarily disparage the business practice of a competitor, nor volunteer an opinion of a competitor's transaction. If his opinion is sought it should be rendered with strict professional integrity and courtesy.

ARTICLE 26.—The agency of a Realtor who holds an exclusive listing should be respected. A Realtor cooperating with a listing broker should not invite the cooperation of a third broker without the consent of the listing broker.

ARTICLE 27.—The Realtor should cooperate with other brokers on property listed by him exclusively whenever it is in the interest of the client, sharing commissions on a previously agreed basis. Negotiations concerning property listed exclusively with one broker should be carried on with the listing broker, not with the owner, except with the consent of the listing broker.

ARTICLE 28.—The Realtor should not solicit the services of an employee or salesman in the organization of a fellow-Realtor without the knowledge of the employer.

ARTICLE 29.—Signs giving notice of property for sale, rent, lease or exchange should not be placed on any property by more than one Realtor, and then only if authorized by the owner, except as the property is listed with and authorization given to more than one Realtor.

240   *Modern real estate practice*

ARTICLE 30.—In the best interest of society, of his associates and of his own business, the Realtor should be loyal to the real estate board of his community and active in its work.

Conclusion

The term Realtor has come to connote competence, fair dealing and high integrity resulting from adherence to a lofty ideal of moral conduct in business relations. No inducement of profit and no instructions from clients ever can justify departure from this ideal, or from the injunctions of this Code.

The Code of Ethics was adopted in 1913. Amended at the Annual Convention in 1924, 1928, 1950, 1951, 1952, 1955, 1956, 1961, and 1962.

Addenda

I.—Suggestions to the public

(The following suggestions are made, not as a part of this Code of Ethics, but to indicate to the public how they can co-operate with Realtors so as to secure the best service.)

(1) Your relationship with a real estate broker should be considered confidential; it is unfair to a broker for you to quote to others the terms and properties which he has offered you in confidence.

(2) Competent counsel in connection with real estate transactions is valuable and proceeds from years of training and study; it should not be expected gratis.

(3) By retaining the services of a single broker and placing your confidence in him, you enable him to render you more intelligent and satisfactory service.

(4) Do not injure your property nor your broker's chances of serving you by quoting one price to the broker and another to a prospective purchaser.

(5) Do not list your property unless you are willing and ready to sell it.

(6) When you ask a Realtor for an opinion, you should expect

it to be rendered in accordance with his best judgment, unbiased by your personal preferences.

II

The term **client** is used in this Code to denote one who retains a Realtor to represent his interests in real estate matters.

The term **customer** is used to denote one who transacts business with a Realtor but does not retain his services.

III

The By-Laws of the National Association of Real Estate Boards contain the following provisions.

Article IV.

"Section 1. Each Member Board shall adopt the Code of Ethics of the National Association as a part of its rules and regulations for violation of which disciplinary action may be taken.

"Section 2. Any Member Board which shall neglect or refuse to maintain and enforce the Code of Ethics with respect to the business activities of its members, may, after due notice and opportunity for hearing, be expelled by the Board of Directors from membership in the National Association."

appendix **B**

Code of ethics of the American Institute of Real Estate Appraisers

Land is the basic source of all wealth. Real estate wisely used and widely allocated in private ownership is essential to our national well-being. Upon its intelligent and proper evaluation depend the investments and lifetime savings of our people and their confidence in the economy which sustains our free institutions.

The functions of the real estate appraiser are strictly professional in character; he is charged with solemn business, civic, and social responsibilities.

Recognizing these obligations, we mutually pledge to each other our knowledge, our experience, and our sacred honor. Each Member of the American Institute of Real Estate Appraisers agrees that he will:

1. Conduct his professional activities in a manner that will reflect credit upon himself, other real estate appraisers, and the American Institute of Real Estate Appraisers.
2. Protect the professional reputation and prospects of other real estate appraisers who subscribe to and abide by this Code of Ethics.

3. Acknowledge the contribution of others who participate professionally with him in an appraisal.
4. Secure appraisal assignments by referral and through recognition of his professional competence without unprofessional solicitation or advertisement, without payment or acceptance of commission, without unprofessional fee bidding, and without contingencies dependent upon findings, conclusions, or value reported.
5. Accept only those appraisal assignments relating to which he has no current or prospective unrevealed personal interest or bias and which he is qualified to undertake and complete without his professional standing or integrity being placed in jeopardy.
6. Preserve a professional confidential relationship with his client, revealing or reporting only to his client his conclusions and valuation.
7. Render properly and adequately developed valuations without advocacy for accommodation of any particular interests, being factual, objective, unbiased, and honest in presenting his oral or written analyses, conclusions, and opinions.
8. Cooperate with the Institute and its officers in all matters, including investigation, censure, discipline, or dismissal of members who, by their conduct, prejudice their professional status or the reputation of the Institute.
9. Conform in all respects to this Code of Ethics and to the Standards of Professional Conduct adopted by the American Institute of Real Estate Appraisers as the same may be amended from time to time.

Adopted by the Governing Council of the American Institute of Real Estate Appraisers, November 10, 1958.

appendix **C**

Real estate license law, and supplementary rules and regulations

This pattern license law is a model prepared by the National Association of Real Estate Boards through its License Law Committee.

An Act

To Define and to Provide for the Licensing of Real Estate Brokers and Real Estate Salesmen; to Provide for the ―――――――― Real Estate Commission, to Define its Powers and Duties; and Providing Penalties for Violation of this Act.[1]

Be it enacted by the People of the State of ―――――――― represented in the ――――――――――――――――――――[2]

Short title; license required

Section 1: This Act shall be known and may be cited as the Real Estate License Act of 19――; and from and after the effective

---

[1] State constitutions generally require that the subject of an act be expressed in its title; and when an act contains penal provisions this, too, must be expressed in the title.

It is suggested that there be a preface to the act, which states at the outset: "The intent of the Legislature in enacting this statute is to elevate the standards and improve the competency of persons engaged in the real estate business, and for the protection of the public."

[2] The "enacting clause" may vary from state to state. The form here used is required in Illinois.

date of this Act it shall be unlawful for any person to engage in or conduct, directly or indirectly, or to advertise or hold himself out as engaging in or conducting the business, or acting in the capacity, of a real estate broker or a real estate salesman within this State without first obtaining a license as such broker or salesman, as provided in this Act.[3]

Definitions

Section 2: As used in this Act, the following terms shall have the following meanings except where the context clearly indicates that another meaning is intended:

"Real estate"

(a) The term "real estate" shall mean leaseholds, as well as any other interest or estate in land, whether corporeal, incorporeal, freehold or nonfreehold, and whether the real estate is situate in this State or elsewhere.

"Broker"

(b) The term "broker" shall mean any person who for a fee, commission or other valuable consideration, or with the intent or expectation of receiving the same, negotiates or attempts to negotiate the listing, sale, purchase, exchange or lease of any real estate or of the improvements thereon, or collects rents or attempts to collect rents, or who advertises or holds himself out as engaged in any of the foregoing activities.[4] The term "broker" also includes any person employed by or on behalf of the owner or owners of real estate to conduct the sale, leasing, or other disposition thereof

---

[3] License laws are penal in character, and for that reason they are strictly construed. The act, therefore, begins by reciting that it shall be unlawful to operate as a real estate broker or salesman without first obtaining a license.

[4] This Pattern Law lists the *basic* activities of a broker—those that may be considered as the *minimum.* Controversial activities, such as negotiating a loan, auctioneering, appraising, and others, are not included. Business opportunity brokers, cemetery lot operators, and oil and gas lease operators are also not included, although they are regulated in some states under the real estate act and in others—i.e., California—by separate statute. This also does not include persons selling their own lands—i.e., subdivisions, owners of large tracts of land. To include this category, suggested language might be: "Is engaged wholly or in part in the business of selling real estate, whether or not such real estate is owned by such person."

at a salary or for a fee, commission or any other consideration; it also includes any person who engages in the business of charging an advance fee or contracting for collection of a fee in connection with any contract whereby he undertakes primarily to promote the sale of real estate through its listing in a publication issued primarily for such purpose, or for referral of information concerning such real estate to brokers, or both.[5]

"Salesman"

(c) The term "salesman" shall mean any person employed or engaged under contract by or on behalf of a licensed broker to participate in any activity included in Section 2 (b) of this Act for compensation or otherwise.[6]

"Person"

(d) The term "person" shall mean and include individuals, corporations, partnerships or associations, foreign and domestic.

Exempted classes

Section 3: The provisions of this Act shall not apply to an owner[7] of real estate or to his regular employees with respect to

---

5/ A provision regulating firms that charge an advance fee for so-called advertising services is contained in the amended license laws of a number of states—i.e., California, Maine, Montana, and Nevada. A similar provision in the Connecticut amended law of 1953 was held unconstitutional in the case of *United Interchange, Inc., et al*, v. *Spellacy, Insurance Commissioner.* (October Term, 1957.) Several firms were investigated by the Federal Trade Commission and ordered to desist in their advance fee practices, and also the advance fee service companies were the subject matter of Congressional hearings.

6/ If it is desirable to create a lesser license for a salesman, then the definition should be limited to those activities a salesman will be authorized to perform. The definition of duties for a salesman, if exactly the same as a broker, might give rise to the question whether there is a need for separate licenses for a salesman and a broker. The Florida Real Estate Commission adopted a regulation that it would be in violation for any broker to employ a part-time salesman. The Florida Supreme Court later held the regulation invalid in the case of *Lee* v. *Delman,* 66 So. (2d) 252 (1953), stating that there was no connection between the public interest and the time a salesman may devote to the occupation of a real estate salesman.

7/ This section would exempt all owners of real estate or their employes and would need to be eliminated if it was intended that owners engaged in certain phases of the business were required to hold a license. This section also would blanket attorneys into the real estate business without a license when acting as an attorney (but not otherwise) and also other individuals when acting under a power of attorney from an owner.

property owned or leased by him, or to an attorney in fact under a duly executed power of attorney authorizing the consummation of a real estate transaction, or to an attorney at law in the performance of his duties as an attorney, or to a public official in the conduct of his official duties, or to a person acting as receiver, trustee, administrator, executor or guardian, or while acting under court order or under the authority of a will or of a trust instrument.[8]

Single act

Section 4. Any person who, for another, with the intention or upon the promise of receiving a fee, does, offers, attempts or agrees to do, directly or indirectly, any single act defined in Section 2(b) of this Act, whether as a part of a transaction, or as the entire transaction, shall constitute such person a broker or salesman within the meaning of this Act.[9]

Real Estate Commission; powers and duties

Section 5. (a) There is hereby created the _____ Real Estate Commission,[10] hereinafter referred to as "Commission,"[11] to consist of three persons,[12] each of whom shall have been a citizen of this State and shall have been engaged in business as a broker in this State for at least ten years prior to the date of his appointment. The members of the Commission shall be appointed by the Governor within sixty days after the effective date of this

---

8/ This section covers all transactions not specifically exempted under the provisions of Section 3.

9/ Exceptions contemplate bona fide isolated transactions. Any exemptions, if provided, should be clearly stated in the law in order to avoid enforcement problems resulting from attempts to evade.

10/ Most licensing acts (45) provide for administration by commission or by a state department counseled by an advisory board. The appointment of veteran real estate men to serve on a real estate commission is truly a democratic administration by the governed. In a composite commission of three or five members, the possibility of a miscarriage of justice is lessened because a decision is subjected to the cautious interpretation of several minds. Six states still have a single commissioner: Connecticut, Michigan, Minnesota, Montana, New Hampshire, and New York.

11/ It is preferable to use the term Real Estate Commission in place of Board in order to avoid confusion with real estate boards in the industry.

12/ Nineteen states have 3 commissioners, 1 has 4 members, 16 states have 5 commissioners, 3 have 6 members, 5 have 7 members, and Indiana has 13 commissioners.

Act,[13] one member shall be appointed for a term of two years; one member for a term of four years; one member for a term of six years; and thereafter the term of the members of the Commission shall be for six years and until their successors are appointed and qualify. Each appointee, before entering upon the duties of his office, shall take and subscribe the constitutional oath of office, which shall be filed with the Secretary of State. Members appointed to fill vacancies shall be appointed for the remainder of the unexpired term. Upon the qualification of the members appointed, the Commission shall organize by selecting from its members a chairman, and may do all things necessary and proper for carrying out the provisions of this Act, and may from time to time promulgate and amend necessary rules and regulations for such purposes.

Commission secretary; employees

(b) The Commission shall employ a secretary and such other employees as it shall deem necessary to assist in the discharge of the duties imposed upon it by this Act, and shall prescribe the duties and fix the compensation of its employees, subject to the general laws of the State.[14]

Compensation and expenses of Commission members

(c) Each member of the Commission shall receive as compensation for each day actually spent on his official duties the sum of $_____ and his actual and necessary expenses incurred in the performance of his official duties.[15]

13/ In many states, the appointment of commissioners is made by the governor with the consent of the senate. Suggested language would then be added as follows: "... by and with the advice and consent of the Senate."

14/ If the particular state has a civil service system, it is advisable to extend it to personnel employed by the commission. It is clear that the effectiveness of any license law depends largely on the manner in which it is enforced. Thought may be given also to whether it is advisable to have the secretary or director a member of the commission, appointed by the governor, rather than an appointee of the commission.

15/ If the compensation the commissioners are to receive is not adequate, there is a danger that the office may take on the color of being more a position of honor than a responsibility. Nine states pay commissioners no per diem salary, merely expenses. Most states pay $10 or $15 per diem with expenses. Illinois pays $5, Alabama, $20, and North Carolina $25. Several states have a limit on the aggregate amount to be paid to a commissioner in any one year.

Seal

(d) The Commission shall adopt a seal of such design as it shall prescribe. Copies of all records and papers in the office of the Commission, duly certified and authenticated by the seal of the Commission, shall be received in evidence in all courts with like effect as the original. All records of the Commission shall be open to public inspection under such reasonable rules and regulations as it shall prescribe.

Real Estate Commission fund created

(e) All fees collected under this Act shall be paid by the Secretary of the Commission at least monthly, accompanied by a detailed statement of the source thereof, into the Treasury of the State to the credit of a fund to be known as "The Real Estate Commission Fund" which is hereby created.[16] Disbursements from the fund shall not in any year exceed the moneys credited to it. _____ percent of all license fees paid into the fund may be used by the Commission for educational purposes for the benefit of licensees.

Applicants for license

Section 6: (a) Licenses shall be granted only to persons who are deemed by the Commission to be of good repute and competent to transact the business of a broker or salesman in such manner as to safeguard the interests of the public.[17]

Qualifications for broker applicants

(b) Each applicant for a broker's license shall be a citizen of the United States at least 21 years of age.[18] The Commission shall

---

16/ In states that have a comprehensive act relating to state finances, it will be necessary, also, to amend that act so as to add "The Real Estate Commission Fund" to the special funds in the state treasury. Modifications may also be necessary to accommodate state constitutional provisions regarding the disbursement of moneys in the state treasury.

The great bane of enforcement is inadequate appropriation of funds for that purpose. Too many legislators do not realize that fees paid by licensees should be used for require such information as it may deem necessary from every applicant to determine his honesty, trustworthiness, and competency.[19] Each applicant for a broker's license shall have been actively engaged for two years as a licensed salesman in this State, or shall furnish to the Commission proof of experience equivalent thereto, or a certificate that he has passed a course of study in real estate at an accredited university or college.[20] Every officer of a corporation acting as a broker and every member of an association

---

administration, that license laws are regulatory, not revenue-producing, measures. Revenue derived from the license fees should be used up to at least 90 percent by the commission for expenses, adequate enforcement, and such worthy purposes as education. California, Colorado, Nevada, and Oklahoma are states that have fairly full control in the expenditure of license fee receipts. See also Note 51.

17/ License laws represent exercise of the police power of the state, so that the right to engage in the real estate business is restricted to those who possess certain educational and character qualifications. In *Roman* v. *Lobe,* 243 N.Y., S1, Judge Cardozo points up the peril of incompetency over and above the danger of untrustworthiness.

Basic qualifications for licensure for a broker should include evidence of good reputation, minimum age of 21 years, citizenship, experience, and proof of competency. Good repute and competency are the prime requisites. Most states require at least two citizen or propertyowner recommenders, certifying to the broker applicant's good reputation. Arkansas requires 5 citizen propertyowners; Idaho, 10 freeholders of the county; Vermont, 5 propertyowners. Florida requires residence of a broker applicant for 1 year; Nevada, for 6 months; Texas, for 60 days.

18/ Every state licensing act should require a broker to be at least 21 years of age, since in most states he cannot be held legally liable on a contract if he is a minor. Citizenship should certainly be a prerequisite.

19/ Although it would appear that the commission has implied power to require any pertinent information relative to the applicant in order to establish trustworthiness, a suggested provision is as follows: "The commission may require such other proof, through the application or otherwise, as it shall deem desirable with due regard to the paramount interests of the public, as to the honesty, truthfulness, integrity, and competency of the applicant."

The commission should not be limited to the application in obtaining the information it wants relative to the qualifications of an applicant. Hence, the commission may require proof, either through the application or otherwise (e.g., credit report). The commission is expressly vested with the power and authority to make and enforce any and all such reasonable rules and regulations connected with the application for any license as shall be deemed necessary to administer and enforce the provisions of the act. See also No. 1 of Pattern Rules.

Many states require an applicant to submit two photographs with the application. This is highly desirable, to identify the applicant both at the examination and after he obtains a license. See also No. 2 of Pattern Rules.

20/ The purpose of apprenticeship is clearly to indoctrinate the neophyte into the proper real estate practices and ethics. Courses in accredited higher institutions of learning may be accepted in lieu of this two-year experience requirement, since the student receives competent instruction and study for the achievement of the same ends. Several states require an applicant for broker's license to have experience as a salesman prior to receiving the broker's license. Also, several states—i.e., Illinois, New Jersey, and others— require varying degrees of education prior to obtaining a broker's license.

or partnership acting as a broker, who engages in the real estate business, shall obtain a broker's license.

Qualifications for salesmen applicants

(c) Each applicant for a salesman's license shall be at least 18 years of age. His application shall be accompanied by the recommendation of the licensed broker by whom the applicant will be employed or engaged under contract, certifying that the applicant is of good repute and that the broker will actively supervise and train the applicant during the period the requested license remains in effect.

Issuance of license

(d) The Commission shall issue to each broker and to each salesman licensee a license and a pocket card in such form and size as the Commission shall prescribe.

Written examination; contents, time, and place; exemptions

Section 7: (a)[21] In addition to proof of honesty, trustworthiness and good reputation, each applicant shall pass a written examination[22] prepared by or under the supervision of the Commission. The examination shall be given at such times and at such places within the State as the Commission shall prescribe. The examination for a broker's license shall include business ethics, composition, arithmetic, elementary principles of land economics and appraisal, a general knowledge of the statutes of this State relating to deeds, mortgages, contracts of sale, agency and brokerage, and the provisions of this Act. The examination for a broker's license shall be of a more exacting nature and scope and more stringent than the examination for a salesman's license. An appli-

---

21/ See also No. 6 of Pattern Rules.
22/ States generally, with a possible single exception, require an applicant for a broker's license to pass an examination. There is a lack of uniformity in examination standards, content, and grading, but improvement generally is rated. An analysis of examination results for 1956 shows that percentages for broker applicants successfully passing the examination varied from 33 percent to 100 percent; for salesmen applicants, from 51 percent to 98 percent. The nationwide average was 60 percent of brokers passing and 75 percent of salesmen.

cant who has failed twice in succession to pass the examination shall be ineligible for a further examination until six months have passed.

NOTE: The remainder of this paragraph should be omitted if the Act now is in effect and the above provisions or a portion thereof are being offered as an amendment.

Provided, however, that any person who has acted as a broker in this State prior to the effective date of this Act, upon complying with the other requirements for a broker's license may obtain a broker's license without examination if application therefor is made within 90 days after the effective date of this Act; and provided further that any person who has acted as a salesman for at least one year prior to the passage of this Act, upon complying with the other requirements for a salesman's license may obtain a salesman's license without an examination if application is made within 90 days after the effective date of this Act.

Cannot operate until license has been issued

(b) No applicant shall engage in the real estate business either as a broker or salesman until he has satisfactorily passed the examination, complied with the other requirements of this Act, and until a license has been issued to him.

Optional provision re bonding[2][3]

States desiring to provide for bonding of licensees may add the following as paragraph (c) of this Section:

(c) Compliance with the other requirements of this Act notwithstanding, the Commission shall not issue any broker's license or salesman's license, or any renewal thereof, until the applicant

---

23/ A bond provision has long been controversial. The present trend appears to be in favor of a bond requirement. Ohio has increased its bond from $1,000 to $5,000.

The optional bond provision in the Pattern Law is taken from the Oklahoma law. This is sometimes termed open-end bond. It is contended that a single claim will not exhaust the bond. It is contended that any number of claims can be made, but ceiling liability on any single claim is $1,000. This contention is not, however, accepted by all bond companies, on the theory that the bonding company cannot estimate its potential liability. The question is in litigation in Alabama. Care must be taken that bonding provisions will be exacting and will not mislead the public.

has filed with the Commission a cash bond or a surety bond in the sum of $_____, and if the latter, it shall be executed by a surety company authorized to do business in this State. The bond shall be conditioned that the principal named therein shall conduct his business in accordance with the provisions of this Act, and will not do any of the acts penalized by the suspension or revocation of his license under the provisions thereof. The bond shall provide that the obligor therein will pay, to the extent of $_____, any judgment which may be recovered against such licensee for loss or damage arising from his violation of the provisions of this Act.

Fees

Section 8: The following fees shall be charged by the Commission and paid into the Real Estate Commission Fund.[24]

(1) For each examination a fee of $_____.
(2) For each original broker's license issued, a fee of $_____ and for each annual renewal thereof, a fee of $_____.
(3) For each original salesman's license issued, a fee of $_____, and for each annual renewal thereof, a fee of $_____.
(4) For each additional office or place of business, an annual fee of $_____.
(5) For each change of place of business or change of employer or contractual associate, a fee of $_____.
(6) For each duplicate license, where the original license is lost or destroyed and affidavit is made thereof, a fee of $_____.
(7) For each duplicate pocket card, where the original pocket card is lost or destroyed and affidavit is made thereof, a fee of $_____.

24/ For purposes of convenience, all fees and charges prescribed by the act should be listed in one section. The amount of any particular fee necessarily varies among the states. In determining what the fees should be, due consideration should be given to the cost of operating the licensing system. The sum total of all moneys collected under the act should bear some reasonable relation to the total cost of operation. It should be borne in mind that the licensing statute is never intended as a revenue measure, and the funds realized should be appropriated for administering and enforcing the act. (See Section 5(e).) The purpose of fees being to provide a fund for defraying the cost of regulation, the validity of license fees is generally held to be conditioned on their having reasonable relation to the amount needed for regulation and administration. Whether a state can also require a license fee for revenue purposes, in addition to the license law fee, is questionable (*West Virginia* v. *Jackson,* 120 W. Va.531).

Section 9: (a) Each resident licensed broker shall maintain a fixed office within this State[25] which shall be so located as to conform with zoning laws and ordinances! The original license as broker and the original license of each salesman in the employ of or under contract to such broker shall be prominently displayed in the office. The address of the office shall be designated in the broker's license,[26] and no license issued under this Act shall authorize the licensee to transact real estate business at any other address, except a licensed branch office.

Change of business address; notice

In case of removal from the designated address,[27] the licensee shall make application to the Commission before such removal or within ten days thereafter, designating the new location of his office, and paying the required fee, whereupon the Commission shall issue a license for the new location for the unexpired period, if the new location complies with the terms of this Act. Each licensed broker shall maintain a sign on the outside of his office of such size and content as the Commission shall prescribe. In making application for a license, or for a change of address, the licensee shall verify that his office conforms with zoning laws and ordinances.

Licensing of branch offices

(b) If the applicant for a real estate broker's license maintains more than one place of business within the state, he shall apply for and obtain an additional license for each branch office so maintained by him. Every such application shall state the location of the place of business for which such branch office license is desired, and the name of the person in charge of it. Each branch

---

25/ See also Nos. 3 and 4 of Pattern Rules.
26/ It is important that the licensing tribunal know at all times the current address of the place of business of the broker. Many licensees are lax in notifying the commission of a change and thereby jeopardize their right to enforce collection of commissions when their licenses are not in conformance with the law.
27/ See also No. 5 of Pattern Rules.

office shall be under the direction and supervision of a licensed broker.

Change of employer or contractual association by salesman; notice; termination of employment or contractual association

(c) A salesman shall not be employed by or under contract to any other broker than is designated upon the license issued to the salesman. Whenever a licensed salesman desires to change his employment or contractual relationship from one licensed broker to another, he shall notify the Commission promptly in writing of the facts attendant thereon,[28] pay the required fee, and return his license and pocket card. The Commission shall forthwith issue a new license and pocket card. No salesman shall, directly or indirectly, work for or with a broker until he has been issued a license to work for or with that broker. Upon termination of a salesman's employment or contractual relationship he shall surrender his license and pocket card to his broker, who shall return them to the Commission for cancellation.

Only one license to a salesman

(d) No more than one license shall be issued to any salesman to be in effect at one time.

Transactions with non-resident brokers

Section 10: (a) It is unlawful for any licensed broker to employ or compensate any person who is not a licensed broker or a licensed salesman for performing any of the acts regulated by this Act; provided, however, that a licensed broker may pay a commission to a licensed broker of another state if such non-resident broker does not conduct in this State any of the negotiations for which a commission is paid.[29]

28/ It is vitally important for a salesman to notify the commission when changing employment, and to receive its approval and reissuance of the license to the new employer or contractual associate.

29/ The subjects of non-resident brokers and reciprocity are so closely intertwined that it is virtually impossible to separate them. Attitudes pro and con on reciprocity are equally strong, depending on the specific state concerned. However, regardless of

Optional provision re licensing of non-resident brokers[30]

States desiring to provide for licensing of non-resident brokers from other states on a reciprocal basis may add the following paragraphs as (b) and (c) of this Section:

(b) A non-resident of this State who is a licensed broker in another state may obtain a license as a broker in this State by complying with all provisions of this Act, provided that the non-resident broker is regularly engaged in the real estate business and maintains a place of business in the other state, and provided that state offers the same privileges to the licensed brokers of this State. Such non-resident licensee need not maintain a place of business within this State. The Commission may license such non-resident broker without examination if (1) he has qualified for a broker's license in the state in which he resides by written examination, and (2) his state of residence permits licenses to be issued without written examination to brokers resident in and licensed by this State. The Commission may, in its discretion, refuse to issue a broker's license to an applicant who is not a resident of this State.

(c) Every non-resident applicant shall file an irrevocable consent that legal actions may be commenced against him in the proper court of any county of this State in which a cause of action may arise, in which the plaintiff may reside, by service of process or pleading authorized by the laws of this State, or by any member of the Commission or the Secretary thereof, the consent stipu-

---

whether or not a state law has a reciprocity provision, the minimum provision it should contain is one like that shown here, permitting co-brokerage with out-of-state brokers.

30/ Some state acts are susceptible of the construction that proof of a license issued by another state, in and of itself, entitles the applicant to a license within the state, although it is not clear that such was the intention of the legislature. The New York law expressly authorizes reciprocity, "provided that the laws of the state of which he is a resident require that applicants for licenses as real estate brokers and salesmen shall establish their competency by written examinations but permit licenses to be issued to residents of the state of New York, duly licensed under this article, without examination." The Pennsylvania law permits reciprocity "in the case of an application from a non-resident broker of those states having similar requirements under the laws of which similar recognition and courtesies are extended to licensed real estate brokers and real estate salesmen of this State."

It should always be remembered that each state is sovereign in its own jurisdiction so that reciprocity is a matter of indulgence and not of *right*. Where a licensed broker in New York is engaged to sell real estate in New Jersey, and the broker finds an acceptable purchaser in New York, the broker is entitled to his commission although he is not licensed in New Jersey, since all of the services were performed in New York State.

lating that the service of process or pleading shall be taken in all courts to be valid and binding as if personal service had been made upon the non-resident broker in this State. The consent shall be duly acknowledged, and if made by a corporation, shall be authenticated by its seal. Any service of process or pleading shall be by duplicate copies, one of which shall be filed in the office of the Commission and the other forwarded by registered mail to the last known principal address of the non-resident broker against whom said process or pleading is directed, and no default in any such action shall be taken except upon affidavit certification of the Commission or of its Secretary, that a copy of said process or pleading was mailed to the defendant as herein provided, and no default judgment shall be taken in any such action or proceeding until twenty days after the day of mailing of process or pleading to the defendant.

Grounds for refusal, suspension or revocation of license

Section 11: The Commission may upon its own motion, and shall, upon the verified complaint in writing of any person setting forth a cause of action under this section, ascertain the facts and, if warranted, hold a hearing for the suspension or revocation of a license. The Commission shall have power to refuse a license for cause or to suspend or revoke a license[31] where it has been obtained by false representation, or where the licensee, in performing

---

[31] The need for strong disciplinary grounds is ever present, as it pointed up by the lucid and decisive language of the eminent jurist, Justice Cardozo, in the case of *Roman v. Lobe*, 152 N.E. 461 (1926) as follows:

> The legislature has a wide discretion in determining whether a business or occupation should be barred to the dishonest or incompetent [citing cases]. Callings, it is said, there are, so inveterate and basic, so elementary and innocent, that they must be left open to all alike, whether virtuous or vicious. If this be assumed, that of broker is not one of them. The intrinsic nature of the business combines with practice and tradition to attest the need of regulation. The real estate broker is brought by his calling into a relation of trust and confidence. Constant are the opportunities by concealment and collusion to extract illicit gains. We know from our judicial records that the opportunities have not been lost. With temptation so aggressive, the dishonest or untrustworthy may not reasonably complain if they are told to stand aside. Less obtrusive, but not negligible, are the perils of incompetence.... The broker should know his duty. To that end, he should have a 'general and fair understanding of the obligations between principal and agent.' ... Disloyalty may have its origin in ignorance as well as fraud. He should know, as the Legislature has said ... what is meant by a deed or a lease or a mortgage.

or attempting to perform any of the acts mentioned herein, is found guilty of:[32]

(1) Making any substantial misrepresentation,[33] or
(2) Making any false promises of a character likely to influence, persuade, or induce,[34] or
(3) Pursuing a continued and flagrant course of misrepresentation, or making false promises through agents or salesmen or any medium of advertising, or otherwise,[35] or
(4) Any misleading or untruthful advertising,[36] including use of the term "Realtor" by a person not authorized to do so, or using any other trade name or insignia of membership in any real estate organization of which the licensee is not a member,[33] or
(5) Failing within a reasonable time to account for or remit any moneys coming into his possession which belong to others, co-mingling funds of others with his own, or failing to keep such funds of others in an escrow or trustee account,[37] or
(6) Being convicted in a court of competent jurisdiction of this or any other state of forgery, embezzlement, obtaining money under false pretenses, extortion, conspiracy to defraud, or any similar offense or offenses, or pleading guilty or nolo contendere to any such offense or offenses, or
(7) Violating any reasonable rule or regulation promulgated by the Commission in the interests of the public and in conformance with the provisions of this Act, or

32/ The grounds for refusal, suspension, or revocation of license constitute the teeth of the act. License laws are penal statutes and therefore strictly construed. The stated grounds vary from 4 in New York to 21 in Alabama. The Pattern Law enumerates 15 grounds, which are found commonly in most license laws.

33/ Material misrepresentation constitutes a very frequent ground for complaint, along with misleading advertising. California, the District of Columbia, Illinois, Kentucky, Nevada, Oregon, Texas, and Washington provide that misuse of the term Realtor is sufficient grounds for suspension or revocation of license. The National Association of Real Estate Boards has established its exclusive right to this designation by court decisions—e.g., *NAREB* v. *Peninsula Real Estate Association,* U.S. Dist. Ct., No. Dist. of Calif., So. Div., 1957. See also No. 15 of Pattern Rules.

34/ See also No. 13 of Pattern Rules.
35/ See also No. 11 of Pattern Rules.
36/ See also No. 12 of Pattern Rules.

37/ The NAREB License Law Committee recommends that the broker's responsibility for handling of deposit moneys be covered in principle in the body of a license law, as shown in this provision, but that the details and mechanical procedures be spelled out as a supplemental rule of the Real Estate Commission. See No. 8 of the Pattern Rules.

(8) Failing to furnish a copy of any written instrument to any party executing the same at the time thereof,[38] or

(9) Any conduct in a real estate transaction which demonstrates bad faith, dishonesty, untrustworthiness or incompetency.[39]

(10) [See note 37] Failing, if a broker, to place, as soon after receipt as is practicably possible, any deposit money or other money received by him in the course of a real estate transaction,[40] in a custodial, trust, or escrow account maintained by him in a banking institution or title company authorized to do business in this State, wherein the funds shall be kept until the transaction is consummated or otherwise terminated, at which time a full accounting thereof shall be made by the broker. Records relative to the deposit, maintenance, and withdrawal of such funds shall contain such information as may be prescribed by the Rules and Regulations of the Commission relative thereto.

(11) [See note 37] Failing, if a salesman, to place, as soon after receipt as is practicably possible, in the custody of the broker with whom he is licensed, any deposit money or other money entrusted to him by any person dealing with him as the representative of the broker with whom he is licensed.

(12) Failing to furnish the seller with a completely filled out and executed copy of any exclusive contract of employment at the time of the execution thereof, and failing to state a definite expiration date in such contract, which shall not require an owner to notify a broker of his intention to terminate.[41]

(13) Failing to disclose to an owner his intention or true position

---

38/ The NAREB License Law Committee recommends that the requirement that copies of any written instruments in a transaction be furnished voluntarily to the parties involved be covered in the body of a license law, as shown in this provision, but that the details and mechanical procedures be spelled out as a supplemental rule of the Real Estate Commission. See also No. 9 of Pattern Rules.

39/ This is a catchall clause, under which a licensee can be charged with any misconduct or unscrupulous dealing that might not fall within the language of the other disciplinary provisions. See also Nos. 13 and 15 of Pattern Rules.

40/ The handling of deposit money constitutes one of the main subjects of complaint to real estate commissions. Several states deal with the broker's responsibility by rules and regulations. Some states have adopted regulatory measures with regard to handling of deposit moneys. Since complaints are frequent, the Pattern Law deals with the subject by requiring the broker to keep all deposit money inviolate until the transaction is consummated or otherwise terminated.

41/ See also No. 9 in Pattern Rules.

where he directly or indirectly purchases for himself, or acquires or intends to acquire any interest in, or options to purchase property which he or his associates has been employed to sell.[42]

(14) Failing to make known for which party he is acting, or receiving compensation from more than one party, except with the full knowledge of all parties.[43]

(15) Dividing a commission or any other valuable consideration with any person who is not authorized to engage in the real estate business.

Hearings; procedures

Section 12: (a) Before any license is suspended or revoked, or before a licensee is otherwise disciplined, the licensee shall be entitled to a public hearing.[44] The hearing shall be held after due notice to the licensee of the filing of a complaint, together with a copy thereof, sent by registered mail to the last known address of the licensee. The licensee shall file an answer to the complaint,[45] in triplicate, within twenty days after notice has been mailed by the Commission. The Commission shall thereupon notify the parties to the dispute of the time and place of hearing, which shall be held in accordance with rules promulgated by the Commission in conformity with the laws of this State.

Subpoenas

(b) The Commission is authorized and empowered to issue subpoenas for the attendance of witnesses and the production of

---

[42] See also No. 11 in Pattern Rules.

[43] Under the law of agency, an agent cannot have two masters. His employment by one is incompatible with his employment by the other, as the interests of buyer and seller are incompatible. The law is well established that when a broker attempts to represent these conflicting interests he cannot recover from either party, unless he can establish that his dual employment is known to both parties and accepted by them.

[44] The procedure of a court is covered in the administrative code of each state. Several state real estate commissions include in their rules and regulations provisions on filing complaints, holding hearings, filing decisions, appealing to the courts, and so on, but considering the many technical and legal ramifications this subject has not been covered in the Pattern Rules and Regulations.

[45] On filing of a complaint, the licensee should be required to file an answer so that an issue can be framed and the hearing proceed. All parties are entitled to a prompt disposition of the complaint.

records or documents. The process issued by the Commission may extend to all parts of the State, and the process may be served by any person designated by the Commission. The person serving such process shall receive such compensation as may be allowed by the Commission, not to exceed the fee prescribed by law for similar services. All witnesses subpoenaed who shall appear in any proceedings before the Commission shall receive the same fees and mileage allowances as allowed by law, and all such fees and allowances shall be taxed as part of the cost of the proceedings.

(c) Where, in any proceeding before the Commission, any witness shall fail or refuse to attend upon subpoena issued by the Commission, or shall refuse to testify, or shall refuse to produce any records or documents the production of which is called for by the subpoena, the attendance of the witness and the giving of his testimony and the production of the documents and records shall be enforced by any court of competent jurisdiction of this state in the same manner as are enforced the attendance, testimony of witnesses and production of records in civil cases in the courts of this State.

Appeal to court; supersedeas; bond

Section 13:[46] (a) Any person aggrieved shall have the right of appeal from any adverse ruling, order, or decision of the Commission to a court of competent jurisdiction in the county where the hearing was held within thirty days from the service of notice of the action of the Commission upon the parties thereto.

(b) Notice of appeal shall be filed in the office of the Clerk of the Court, which shall issue a writ of certiorari directed to the Commission, commanding it, within ten days after service thereof, to certify to the court its entire record in the matter in which the appeal has been taken. The appeal shall be heard, in due course, by

---

46/ In states that have adopted the Uniform Administrative Review Act, the following may be substituted as Section 12:

The provisions of the Administrative Review Act and all amendments and modifications thereof and the rules adopted pursuant thereto shall apply to and govern all proceedings instituted hereafter for the judicial review of final administrative decisions of the Commission rendered pursuant to the powers conferred on it by this Act or as otherwise conferred. The term "administrative decision" is defined as in Section 1 of the Administrative Review Act.

the court, which shall review the record and, after hearing thereon, make its determination of the cause.

(c) Any order, rule or decision of the Commission shall not become final until after the time for appeal shall have expired. In the event an appeal is taken by a licensee or applicant, the appeal shall not act as a supersedeas unless the court so directs, and the court shall dispose of the appeal and enter its decision promptly.

(d) Any person taking an appeal shall post a bond in the amount of $_____ for the payment of any costs which may be taxed against him.

Penalties for violation (misdemeanor)[47]

Section 14: (a) Any person acting as a broker or salesman without first obtaining a license shall be guilty of a misdemeanor[48] and upon conviction thereof, shall be punishable by a fine of not less than $100.00 nor more than $500.00,[49] or by imprisonment in the county jail for a term not to exceed ninety days, or both. Upon conviction of a subsequent violation, the person shall be punishable by a fine of not less than $500.00 nor more than $1,000, or by imprisonment in the county jail for a term not to exceed one year, or both; and if a corporation, be punishable by a fine of not less than $2,000.00 nor more than $5,000.00

Civil recovery; punitive damages authorized

(b) In case any person shall have received any money, or the

47/ Complaints frequently are based on the broker's misappropriation of funds entrusted to him. In states that do not afford a complainant redress through a bond provision in the act, it is suggested that a provision be included to make the reinstatement of a broker's license contingent on his making restitution. Such a provision could be added as paragraph (e) of Section 12:

(e) After the revocation of any license, no new license shall be issued to the same licensee within a period of one year from and after the date of such revocation, nor at any time thereafter except in the sole discretion of the Commission, and before any license is issued, restitution of funds, if any, must be made and the costs of the proceedings must be paid by the licensee.

48/ Some states provide by law that offenses punishable by fine or by imprisonment for over one year are felonies and not misdemeanors. This provision should be modified if necessary so that the offense remains a misdemeanor.

49/ Penalties for operating without a license range in various states from $25 to $500 for the first offense to a fine not to exceed $5,000 or imprisonment of not less than 10 days, nor more than 6 months, or both.

equivalent thereof as a fee, commission, compensation, or profit by, or in consequence of, a violation of any provision of this Act, he shall, in addition, be liable to a penalty of not less than the amount of the sum of money so received and not more than three times the sum so received,[50] as may be determined by the court, which penalty may be recovered in any court of competent jurisdiction by any person aggrieved.

Absence of license bar to commission

Section 15: No person shall maintain an action in any court of this State for the recovery of a commission, fee, or compensation for any act done the doing of which is prohibited under this Act to other than licensed brokers, unless such person was licensed hereunder as a broker at the time of the doing of the act.

Real estate meetings and clinics open to all licensees

Section 16: (a) The Commission is authorized to conduct, hold, or assist in conducting or holding real estate clinics, meetings, courses or institutes and to incur the necessary expenses in connection therewith.[51]

(b) The Commission is authorized to assist libraries and educa-

---

50/ In the Pattern Law, a penalty up to three times the amount of commission collected is added to the monetary fine as a deterrent. Otherwise, an unlicensed person with the prospect of receiving a substantial commission might not hesitate to risk paying a nominal fine if prosecuted for violation of the law.

51/ Any educational program that will improve competency of licensees and further protect the public should be sponsored and encouraged by the commission, and license fees should be used in this connection.

Where states experience difficulty in obtaining an adequate appropriation to effectuate these worthy purposes, it is suggested that the license law specifically earmark a portion or percentage of each license fee paid for educational purposes, as in the California and Oregon laws, respectively. An appropriate section would read: "The Commission may expend an amount not to exceed $3.00 of each license fee collected under this Act for the purpose of distributing printed matter of an educational nature and conducting real estate educational meetings, institutes, and clinics for the benefit of licensed real estate brokers and salesmen."

It should be noted, however, that in some states, the creation of such a fund can create problems. A large accumulation established as a special fund or frozen into the law can attract pressure groups and may have undue political implications.

Broad, all-inclusive, educational programs that overlap and/or conflict with the existing programs of the state real estate association should be carefully considered before being put into effect.

tional institutions in sponsoring studies and programs for the purpose of raising the standards of the real estate business and the competency of licensees.

Publication of directory

Section 17: The Commission may annually publish a directory of licensees, including a list of licenses suspended and revoked, which shall contain such other data as the Commission may determine to be in the interest of real estate licensees and the public.

Unconstitutionality; severability

Section 18: If any provision of this Act is held invalid, that provision shall be deemed to be excised from this Act and the invalidity thereof shall not affect any of the other provisions of this Act. If the application of any provision of this Act to any person or circumstance is held invalid it shall not affect the application of such provision to such persons or circumstances other than those to which it is held invalid.

Effective date

Section 19:[52] This Act shall become effective on the _____ day of _____, 19____ A.D.

Rules and regulations

As authorized under Section 5(a) of Public Act_____ of 19___, the following Rules and Regulations have been adopted by the _____ Real Estate Commission:[53]

---

[52] In some instances, a delayed effective date is preferred by the legislature to enable persons affected by an act to comply with its terms. Normally, state constitutions provide that legislative acts shall become effective on their approval by the governor or, if not vetoed, on a fixed date (e.g., July 1 in Illinois).

[53] These Suggested Rules and Regulations are designed to be supplemental to the Pattern Real Estate License Law. They are not intended to be all-inclusive, but to indicate the type of rules that may be adopted by a commission to provide administrative and enforcement procedures in greater detail than is possible in the legislative act itself.

1. *Credit Report.* The Commission shall require each applicant for a real estate license to furnish a current credit report.[54]

2. *Photograph.* Each applicant for a broker's or salesman's license shall furnish the Commission, for identification purposes, two unmounted recent photographs of himself, bareheaded and in street clothes, and endorsed and dated by the applicant. A passport size and type photograph is acceptable.

3. *Office Requirements.* A broker's office shall be in a room used only for the transaction of the real estate brokerage business, or allied business, such as real estate management, appraising, building, mortgage financing, land developing, or insurance.

4. *Sign on Office.* A broker's business sign of sufficient size to identify it shall be displayed outside his real estate office. If a broker is authorized to use the term "Realtor," that term may be substituted for the words "Licensed Real Estate Broker."

5. *Change of Address.* A broker who changes the location of his office shall promptly return to the Commission his license and card, inform the Commission in writing of the location of his new and old offices, and pay the prescribed fee for the issuance of the new license.

6. *Examination.* (a) Broker's and salesman's license examinations shall be given periodically as designated by the Commission. The Commission will notify all applicants of the time and place of the examination in all instances where their applications have been filed at least 20 days prior to the date of the examination.[55]

(b) All completed examination papers shall remain the property of the Commission.

7. *Reinstatement of Veteran's License.* Licensees entering the armed services may have their licenses reinstated within one year after discharge without examination upon application therefor

---

54/ It is doubtful whether a commission can fix requirements of age, citizenship, apprenticeship, education, or residence in a state by edict. This would constitute a usurpation of the legislative authority. For that reason, the only suggested area for regulation by the commission is a credit report. Since the law requires an applicant to be a person of good repute, it would appear that the commission would have the authority to investigate such good repute through a credit report.

It may be desirable for the commission to order the credit report to be paid from the license fee or separately by the applicant, rather than to allow an applicant to furnish a credit report that may be of unknown origin.

55/ Provision may be made in this rule to allow the applicant to waive the notice of examination.

accompanied by a photostatic copy of discharge or separation papers for reasons other than dishonorable.

8. *Handling of Funds.* (a) All moneys received by a broker as agent for his principal in a real estate transaction shall be deposited on or before the next banking day in a separate custodial or real estate trust account and remain there until consummation or termination of the transaction, when the broker shall make a full accounting thereof to his principal.[5][6]

(b) All moneys received by a salesman in connection with a real estate transaction in which he is engaged on behalf of his broker, shall be by him immediately delivered to his broker.

(c) A broker shall not comingle money or any other property of his principal with his own money or property.

(d) A broker shall maintain in his office a complete record of all moneys received or escrowed on real estate transactions, including the sources of the money, the date of receipt, depository, and date of deposit: and when a transaction has been completed, the final disposition of the moneys.

(e) A broker charged with closing a sale, shall prepare and deliver to the buyer and seller on completion of a transaction, a detailed closing statement of all their respective accounts, showing receipts and disbursements.

9. *Copies of Written Instruments.* A broker shall immediately (at the time of signing) deliver a duplicate original of any instruments to any party or parties executing the same, where such instrument has been prepared by such broker or under his supervision and where such instrument relates to the employment of the broker or to any matter pertaining to the consummation of a lease, or the purchase, sale or exchange of real property or any other type of real estate transaction in which he may participate as a broker.

10. *Listing Contract; Expiration Date.* Every written listing contract shall provide for its existence for a definite period of time and for termination without prior notice at the expiration of that period. It shall not require an owner to notify a broker of his intention to terminate the listing.

56/ It may be desirable to specify by rule the type of minimum bookkeeping system a broker must maintain with respect to his real estate trust account.

11. *Blind Ads.* A broker shall not advertise the sale, purchase, exchange or lease of real property other than the sale, exchange or lease of his own in a manner indicating the offer to sell, purchase, exchange or lease is being made by a principal. Every such advertisement shall clearly indicate that it is an advertisement of a broker and shall not be confined to publication of only a post office box number, telephone number, or street address.

12. *Advertising by Salesman.* A salesman shall not advertise the sale, purchase, exchange or lease of real property, for another or others without including in the advertisement the name of the broker with whom he is associated.[57]

13. *Enticements or Inducements.* A broker shall not solicit, sell, or offer to sell real property by offering prizes, free lots, or conducting lotteries or similar inducements for the purpose of influencing a purchaser or prospective purchaser of real property.

14. *Unauthorized Placement of Signs.* A broker shall not display a "For Sale" or "For Rent" sign on any real property without the consent of the owner or his authorized agent.

15. *Disclosure of Limited Activity.* A broker or salesman not regularly engaged in the real estate business shall not list real property for sale without disclosing the true facts as to his limited activity as a broker or salesman.[58]

---

[57] It may be desirable to place the responsibility for advertising on the broker by providing that the broker shall not permit his salesman to advertise, etc., without his consent and without including the name of the broker in said advertisement.

[58] It may be desirable to require that notification of limited activity be included in the listing contract signed by the seller.

Index

A

Adding machines, 84
Addition of capital, 34-35
American Institute of Real Estate Appraisers, 223
American Society of Appraisers, 223
Anticipation, principle of, 32-33
Appraisal, 153
  defined, 52
  function of, 223
  principles and methods, 51-62
    bracketing, 53
    correlation of, 62
    cost as evidence of value, 53-54; *see also* Cost approach
    income approach, 53, 57-59
    knowledge of, importance of, 51-53
    market data approach, 53, 60-61
Assessments, 149
Association, 148
Association membership, 72-73, 223

B

Balance, principle of, 38-39
Basic policies
  community program participation, 73
  contacts with others of value to career, 72-73
  employment; *see* Personnel of broker's office
  geographic area, study of, 64-65

Basic policies—*Cont.*
  legal counsel, 65-66
  legal practice, 65
  location of office, 69-72
  membership in associations and other organizations, 72-73
  office manual, 87, 97-98
  population in area, 64
  reference library facilities, 70-71, 85-86
  specialization, 65
  tax counsel, 66-67
  territory of broker, 64-65
  training and supervision of salesmen, 111-12
  type of organization for operation, 67-69
Bibliography, 227-234
Blue Cross insurance, 99
Blue Shield insurance, 99
Bond requirements, 221
Books of account, requirements for, 208-9
Bracketing, 53
Broker; *see* Real estate broker
Brokerage; *see* Real estate brokerage
Brokerage office
  cooperation, 201
  financing, 203
  insurance, 202
  sales, 203
Budget preparation, 206
  items for, 212-13
Building codes, 21, 217

Building restrictions, 217
Business, real estate brokerage as, 2-3, 127
Buyers, need for broker, 7-8; see also Prospects

C

Cameras, 84
Capital requirements, 208
Capitalization rate, 59
Carnegie, Dale, 119
Change, principle of, 28-29
Checklists
  expense items for budget, 212-13
  federal agencies, 224-25
  listings
    comprehensive form, single-family dwellings, 170-75
    summary data in useable form, 175-76
  of sources of prospects, 186-90
City planning, 218-19
Civil Rights Act, 224
Classification of prospects, 118-19, 182
Closing room, 78
Code of ethics, 2, 15
Coffee breaks, 96
Community
  need for broker, 8-9
  services of broker, 12-14
"Community builder," real estate broker, as, 9
Comparison approach, 60
Compensation
  of real estate broker, 3
  methods of payment, 7-8
  of salesmen
    advances against future commissions, 129
    basis for, 130
    bonus at end of year, 131
    commission on prospects, 133-35
    conditions for earning of commissions, 135
    drawing accounts, 129
    50-50 percentage basis with raise in commission rate, 131
    50-50 split, 130
    listing commissions, 132-33
    payment of, 135
    percentage of commission, 131-32
    policy and method variations, 128
    requirements of broker, 128
    salary basis, 129
Comptometers, 84
Condominium
  analysis, 152
  appraisal, 153

Condominium—*Cont.*
  architecture, 152
  checklist for developing, 165
  concept, 147
  construction lending procedure, 161
  equity, 154-63
  freedom, 151
  location, 152
  management, 150
  mortgage
    application, 154
    liens, 155
    participation, 149-56
    payout precautions, 155-63
  sponsorship, 160
Condominium law
  conversions, 150
  cooperative, 149
  eligible property
    apartment size, 148
    industrial, 148
    offices, 148
  federal housing, 148
  first enacted, 147
  procedure, 149
Conference room, 78
Contribution, principle of, 34-35
  defined, 35
Control
  financial, 205-14
  of listings, 169-79
  of prospects, 181-92
Corporate operation, 67-69, 208
Cost approach, 53-54
  depreciation, 56-57
  reproduction cost methods, 55
  site valuation, 54
  steps in, 54
Cubic foot method, 55

D

Declaration
  association, 148
  recording, 148
Deed, condominium, 149
Definitions
  appraisal of real property, 52
  listing, 137
  listing contract, 137
  market, 44
  net listing, 177
  principle of contribution, 35
  profession, 2
  prospect, 183
  real estate market, 44

Department of Housing and Urban Development, 224
Depreciation, estimation of, 56-57
Deterioration, 56
Dictating machines, 83
Diminishing returns, point of, 36
Duplicating equipment, 83

E

Economic obsolescence, 56-57
Economics
　factors influencing real estate, 19-20
　land utilization, 25-41
Employee policies; *see* Personnel of broker's office
Employee records, 94-95
Employment policies; *see* Personnel of broker's office
Engineering, function of, 29
Equipment of broker's office; *see* Office organization and equipment
Esprit de corps, 90, 100, 125
Ethical conduct, 14-16
Exclusive listing contract, 138-40
Exclusive right-to-sell contract, 138, 140
Executive control of listings, 169-79
Executive control of prospects, 181-92
Expenses of broker, 211-14
　control of, 205
Experienced salesmen
　new men observing sales by, 120
　training of, 120-22

F

Federal agencies, list of, 224-25
Federal Housing Administration regulations, 218
Federal regulations, 22-23; *see also* Regulations *or other specific topics*
Files
　"dead," 176-77, 185
　employee records, 94-95
　listings data, 175-76
　prospects, 191-92
　space and equipment for, 79-81
Financial control of operations, 205-14
　books of account, 208-9
　budget preparation, 206
　　items for, 212-13
　capital requirements, 208
　expenses, 205, 211-14
　investments separated from real estate brokerage operation, 207-8
　organizational form as element in, 208
　overhead expenditures, 206

Financial control of operations–*Cont.*
　problems in connection with, 206
　record requirements, 206-7
　sources of income for broker, 209-11
　state law regulations, 209
　tax counsel, employment of, 206
"For Rent" signs, 85
"For Sale" signs, 80, 84-85
　listings source, 143-44
　placement on listed property, 178
Forms, supply and types of, 86-87
Functional obsolescence, 56-57

G

Geographic area, 64-65
Government aid and restrictions; *see* Regulations
Government housing, 224
Governmental regulations; *see* Regulations
Gross income, estimation of, 58-59
Group insurance, 99

H

Health and hospital insurance, 99
Health regulations, 21
Highest and best use, principle of, 31-32
Hours for opening and closing office, 95
Housing Act of 1968, 223
How to Make Friends and Influence People, 119

I

Illness, periods of, 96-97
Incentives
　health and hospital insurance, 99
　life insurance, 99
　retirement insurance, 99-100
　salaries, 98-99
Income approach, 53, 57-59
Income sources for broker
　appraisal fees, 211
　commissions on sales, 210-11
　consultation fees, 211
　insurance department, 209-10
　management of properties, 209-10
　mortgage servicing, 210
　rental commissions, 209-10
Increasing and decreasing returns, principle of, 35-36
Insurance
　condominium units, 159-63
　losses, 158
　health and hospital, 99
　life, 99
　retirement, 99-100

272 Modern real estate practice

Integrity, 14–16
Inventory of prospects, 183–84
Investment in property, tests for sufficiency of, 34
Investments of real estate broker, separation from brokerage operation, 207–8

J-K

Jones v. *Mayer*, 224
Kiplinger service, 50

L

Land utilization principles, 25–41
  addition of capital, 34–35
  anticipation, 32–33
  balance, 38–39
  change, 28–29
  contribution, 34–35
  highest and best use, 31–32
  increasing and decreasing returns, 35–36
  priority of claim upon gross income of improved real estate, 41
  productive factors, 40–41
  proportionality, 39–40
  scarcity, 29–31
  substitution, 36–38
Landscaping of office, 72
Layout of office, 76
Legal counsel, 65–66
Legal practice, 65
Library facilities, 73–74, 85–86
Licensing laws, 14–15, 220–23
Life insurance, 99
Listing contract; *see also* Listings
  defined, 137
  essential elements of, 137–38
  exclusive, 138–40
  exclusive right to sell, 138, 140
  inspection of property prior to, 170
  multiple, 138, 140–41
  open listing, 138–39
  standard forms of, 138
  types of, 138–41
Listings; *see also* Listing contract
  advertisements as source, 143–44
  canvass of owners in territory as source, 142
  card files kept on, 175–77
  checklist of items on
    comprehensive, 170–75
    summary data in useable form, 175–76
  competitors', 178
  contact with owners who submitted, 177–78
  defined, 137

Listings–*Cont.*
  direct-mail solicitation as source, 143
  executive control of, 169–79
  filing system for, 175–77
  "For Sale" signs on, 178
  net, 177
  news columns of local papers as source, 144–45
  pictorial display of, 179
  reasons for making, 141
  reports required of, 178–79
  salability of, 169–70
  sources of, 141–45
  telephone canvass as source, 142–43
  training of salesmen in getting, 116–117
  unsolicited individuals' contacts as source, 145
  volume to be handled by individual salesmen, determination of, 177
Location of office, 69
  architectural design, 72
  district of city to consider, 69–70
  downtown areas versus outlying or suburban areas, 70–71
  ground floor level versus upper floor level, 70
  landscaping, 72
  parking facilities, 72
  renting versus owning of space, 71–72
  retail store property, 72
  temporary, 71
"Lone wolf" operations, 67–68, 208
Lunch hours, 96

M

Management
  amenities, 194
  income increase
    enhancement, 194
    expenses, control of, 194, 200
    investment, 200
    net return, 201
    reasonable, 194
    value, 194–200
  owners' interest, 193
  prestige, 194
  science, 193
Management sources
  fees, 201
  government, 204
  mortgage, 201
  private, 203
  public, 203
  replacements, 200
  zoning, 197

Manager
 budget, 199-200
 contract, 196
 CPM income and expense analysis, 199
 demand, 198
 duties, 196
 inspection, 198-200
 leases, 196
 markets, 198-99
 neighborhood analysis, 197
 programs, 196
 status symbol, 194, 197
 taxes, 201
Manual; *see* Office manual
Maps, supply of, 80, 81-82, 113-14
Market, defined, 44
Market data approach, 53, 60-61
Marketability factors, 18
Markets for real estate; *see* Real estate markets
Mimeograph machines, 83
Model cities, creation of, 219
Morale-building devices, 100
Multiple listing contract, 138, 140-41

N

National Association of Real Estate Boards
 code of ethics of, 2, 15
 educational material available from, 113
 insurance procured through, 99
 library facilities, 85
 membership in, 72
 seminars conducted by, 74
National Highway Program, 220
Net listing, 177
New Community Development and Model Cities Program, 223
New employees in office; *see* Personnel of broker's office

O

Obsolescence, 56-57
Occupancy maps, 81-82
Office location; *see* Location of office
Office manual
 basic policy to develop and adopt, 87
 form and contents of, 97-98
 salesmen's reading of, 112
Office organization and equipment, 75-87
 adding machines, 84
 cameras, 84
 closing room, 78
 comptometers, 84
 conference room, 78

Office organization and equipment—*Cont.*
 duplicating equipment, 83
 efficiency of operations as goal, 76
 files, space and equipment for, 79-81
 forms supply, 80-81, 86-87
 layout, principles controlling, 76
 library facilities, 85-86
 manual, 87
 maps, supply of, 80, 81-82
 photographs, 84
 private offices, 78-79
 reception area, 77-78
 recording machines, 83
 signs, 80-81, 84-85
 size, principles controlling, 75-76
 typewriters, 83-84
Office personnel; *see* Personnel of broker's office
Office rules
 coffee breaks, 96
 hours for opening and closing, 95
 illness, periods of, 96-97
 lunch hours, 96
 manuals for instruction and guidance, 97-98
 overtime records, 96
 salesmen's familiarity with, 112
 vacations, 97
On-the-job training of salesmen, 121
Open listing contract, 138-39
Organization membership, 72-73, 223
Organization of office; *see* Office organization and equipment
Organizational form of operation, 67-68
Outline maps, 81, 114, 116
Overtime records, 96
Owners of real property; *see also* Listings
 broker's services, need for, 4-7
 reasons for changes by, 4-6
Ownership maps, 81-82

P

Partnership operation, 68, 208
Personal conferences with salesmen, 124
Personnel of broker's office, 89-100
 application form, requirement and style of, 92-93
 dependence upon, 89-90
 employment agencies as source, 91
 help wanted newspaper ads as source, 90-91
 importance of, 89-90
 incentives, 98-100
 insurance
  health and hospital, 99

Personnel of broker's office—*Cont.*
  insurance—*Cont.*
    life, 99
    retirement, 99–100
  morale-building devices, 100
  need for, 89
  orientation of, 93–94
  personal interview as prerequisite, 93
  recommendations as source, 90
  records to be kept of, 94–95
  rules for office operation, 95–98
  salaries, 98–99
  selection of new employees, 92–93
  sources of new employees, 90–92
  supervision of, 93–94
  training of, 93–94
  upward movement of, 90
Photographs, 84
  display of listings, 179
Physical approach, 53
Physical deterioration, 56
Policies of real estate brokerage; *see* Basic policies
Political regulations; *see* Regulations
Population
  factor for consideration by broker, 63–64
  real estate broker's knowledge of trends in, 16–17, 30–31
Potential prospects; *see* Prospects
Principles of land utilization; *see* Land utilization principles
Priority of claim upon gross income of improved real estate, principle of, 41
Private offices, 78–79
Private property system, 3–4
Productive factors, 40–41
Professions
  defined, 2
  real estate brokerage as, 2–3, 12, 127
  source of new real estate salesmen, 104
Profit opportunities, condominium
  conversions, 158
  success, 159
Proportionality, principle of, 39–40
Prospects
  analysis of, 190–92
  classification of, 118–19, 182
  commissions of salesmen on, 133–34
  control of, 181–92
  "dead" files, 185
  defined, 183
  disposition of records upon completion of dealings with, 185
  essential features of executive control of, 183–85
  executive control of, 181–92

Prospects—*Cont.*
  file data, 191–92
  importance of, 181
  inventory of, 183–84
  need for, 181
  recording preliminary data concerning, 184
  report of salesmen regarding, 185
  review of files of, 185
  salesmen assigned to, 184
  screening of, 184
  sources of; *see* Sources of prospects
  training of salesmen to get, 117–20
  types of, 118–19, 182
Public housing, 218, 224
Purchases of real property, reasons for, 7–8

Q

Qualifications of real estate broker, 11–23
Quantity survey method, 55

R

Real estate; *see* Real property
Real estate broker; *see also* Real estate brokerage *and other specific topics*
  attributes required of, 1–2
  buyer's need for, 7–8
  community services of, 12–14
  community's need for, 8–9
  compensation of, 3
    methods of payment, 7–8
  economic trends, knowledge of, 19–20
  ethical conduct, 14–16
  functions of, 4, 7, 8–9, 11, 19
  integrity of, 14–16
  knowledge of, 16
  obligations of, 7
  personal services of, 12–13
  population trends, knowledge of, 16–17, 30–31
  qualifications of, 11–23
  regulations governing real estate, knowledge of, 20–23
  seller's need for, 4–7
  sincerity of purpose, 12–14
  social factors of significance to, 16–19
  social trends, 16–19
  state license laws, 14–15, 220–23
  unethical conduct of, 15
Real estate brokerage; *see also* Real estate broker *and other specific topics*
  basic policies, 63–64
  business status of, 2–3, 127
  competitive nature of field, 63
  dual character of, 2

Real estate brokerage—*Cont.*
  factors to be considered for career in, 63-64
  functions of, 1
  legal matters involved in, 66
  motivations for entering field of, 12
  national significance of, 3
  office organization and equipment, 75-87
  organizational form for operation of, 67-69
  professional status, 2-3, 12, 127
  purposes of, 1
  service vocation, 11
  success in, attainment of, 63
  tax problems involved in, 66-67
  vacancies in office of, personnel for; *see* Personnel of broker's office
Real estate fundamentals, training of salesmen in, 112-13
Real estate markets
  buyers', 45
  clues to condition of, 46-47
  condition of, determination of, 46-47
  defined, 44
  demand for properties, 47-49
  economic conditions, influence of, 49
  essential features of all, 44
  knowledge essential, 43
  property embraced in, 44-45
  sellers', 45
  special types, 44
  supply of properties, 45-47
  territorial considerations, 45
  trends in, determination of, 45-50
Real Estate Research Corporation letter service from Chicago, 50
Real property
  changes in ownership of, reasons for, 4-6
  forces affecting value of, 16
  governmental agencies for problems of, 3
  importance of, 3
  market types and classes of, 44-45
  purchase of, reasons for, 7-8
  regulations governing, 20-23
  sale of, reasons for, 4-6
  university chairs of, 3
  value of, 3
  volume of transactions involving, 4
"Realtor," creation of term, 15
Reception area, 77-78
Recording machines, 83
Records
  employees, 94-95
  financial control of operations, 206-7
  overtime, 96

Reference library facilities, 73-74, 85-86
Regulations
  building codes, 21, 217
  building restrictions, 217
  city planning, 218-19
  constant changes in, 215-16
  federal, 22-23
  federal government programs, 224
  health safeguards, 21
  knowledge of, requirements of, 216
  miscellaneous, 22
  public housing, 218, 224
  reasons for, 20
  reference files to be kept on, 216
  rent control, 217-18
  tax laws, 22
  use and occupancy restrictions, 217
  zoning laws, 21, 216-17
Rent control, 217-18
Reports
  of listings, 178-79
  of salesmen, 123
Reproduction cost, methods of estimating, 55
Retirement insurance, 99-100
Rules for office operation; *see* Office rules
Rural property, shift to urban property from, 26

S

Salaries of employees, 98-99
Sales approach, 60
Sales of real property, reasons for, 4-6
Sales quotas, 124-25
Salesmen; *see also* Compensation of salesmen; Selection of salesmen; Supervision of salesmen; *and* Training of salesmen
  apprenticeship period, 130
  experienced, training of, 120-22
  listings volume to be handled by, determination of, 177
  major functions of, 117-18
  observing work of, by new salesmen, 120
  responsibility of, 134
  selection of
    ability to command confidence and respect, 109
    ability to talk freely, 110
    advertisement responses as source, 102
    applications and supplementary letters as prerequisite, 104-6
    attitude toward study and self-improvement, 108-9
    confidential credit report, 110

Modern real estate practice

Salesmen—*Cont.*
  selection of—*Cont.*
    decision as to source of supply, 104
    employment changes, record of, 108
    experience requirements, 107
    firm's rules and regulations, importance of, 109
    foreign language, knowledge of, 108
    hobbies, significance of, 108
    home visit, 110
    importance of, 101–2
    knowledge prerequisites, 108
    personal interviews, 106–7
    process of, 104–10
    professional persons as source, 104
    recommendations as source, 102–3
    retired executives as source, 103–4
    sources of new salesmen, 102–4
    universities and colleges as source, 103
    unsolicited applications as source, 102
Scarcity, principle of, 29–31
Selection of new employees, 92–93
Sellers; *see* Listings
Signs, supply of, 80–81, 84–85
Sincerity of purpose, 12–14
Site valuation, 54
Size of office, 75–76
Social factors, 16–19
Society of Farm Brokers and Appraisers, 223
Society of Real Estate Appraisers, 223
Soil maps, 81
"Sold" signs, 81, 85
Sources of income for broker; *see* Income sources for broker
Sources of listings, 141–45
Sources of new employees, 90–92
Sources of new salesmen, 102–4
Sources of prospects, 118, 185–86
  apartment dwellers, 188
  arrivals and moves in the city, 187
  directories and rosters, 187–88
  former customers or clients, 188
  friends and acquaintances, 186
  high income taxpayers, lists of, 188
  investors, 189
  local newspaper columns, 187
  man next door, 186
  miscellaneous, 189–90
  other real estate brokers, 189
  owners of large properties, lists of, 188–89
  persons who have listed properties for sale, 186–87
  persons who have recently sold property, 187
Specialization, 65
Square foot method, 55
State laws, 2; *see also* Regulations
  legal practice, 65
  licensing of real estate brokers and salesmen, 14–15, 220–23
  sale and renting of real estate, 209
Street maps, 81–82
Strip maps, 81–82
Substitution, principle of, 36–38
Summation approach, 53
Supervision of employees, 93–94
Supervision of salesmen
  functions of, 122–23
  personal conferences, 124
  purpose of, 125
  reports required, 123
  sales quotas, 124–25
  technique of, 123–25

T

Tax counsel, 66–67, 206
Tax laws, 22
Taxes, condominium, 150
Tenants
  incomes, 197
  interests, 195
  organization, 195
  peace, 195
  rents, 196–98
  rights, 195
  safety, 195
  security, 195
Territorial considerations, 64–65
  real estate market, 45
  training of salesmen, 114–15
Training of employees, 93–94
Training of salesmen
  basic policies, 111–12
  block-by-block survey of territory, 114–15
  class meetings in broker's office, 113
  experienced salesmen, 120–22
  interviews for familiarity with territory, 114–15
  kibitzing actual sales, 120
  listings, production of, 116–17
  maps covering territory, 113–14
  meetings, attendance at, 121–22
  office procedures, 112
  on-the-job, 121
  prospects, finding of, 117–20
  real estate fundamentals, instruction in, 112–13
  territorial analysis, 113–16
  textbooks available for, 113
Typewriters, 83–84

U

Unit-costs-in-place method, 55
Units, condominium
  additional, 148
  common areas, 149
  expansion, 148
  marketability, 151
  space percentages, 150
Urban centers, growth of, 219
Urban community, needs of, 27–28
Urban property
  building in advance of demand, 33
  failure to use properly, 26
  value of, 26
Use and occupancy restrictions, 217

V

"Vacancy" signs, 85
Vacations, 97
Value
  cost as evidence of, 53–54
  estimate of, 52; *see also* Appraisal principles and methods
  urban property, 26
Veterans Administration regulations, 218

W-Z

Wenzlick letters from St. Louis, Missouri, 50
Zoning laws, 21, 216–17
Zoning maps, 81–82